DREAMTIME
&
INNER SPACE

DREAMTIME & INNER SPACE

The World of the Shaman

Holger Kalweit

Translated from the German by Werner Wünsche

FOREWORD BY ELISABETH KÜBLER-ROSS

SHAMBHALA
Boston & London
1988

For Julia and Amelie

Shambhala Publications, Inc.
Horticultural Hall
300 Massachusetts Avenue
Boston, Massachusetts 02115

9   8   7   6
Printed in the United States of America on acid-free paper ⊗
Distributed in the United States by Random House, Inc.,
and in Canada by Random House of Canada Ltd

Library of Congress Cataloging-in-Publication Data
Kalweit, Holger.
    Dreamtime and inner space.
    Translation of: Traumzeit und innerer Raum.
    Bibliography: p.
    Includes index.
    1. Shamanism.   2. Shaman.   3. Psychical research.
I. Title.
BL2370.S5K3513   1986   291.6′2   87-28842
ISBN 0-87773-406-2 (pbk.)

CONTENTS

CONTENTS

FOREWORD

This book gives an astonishingly comprehensive account of the practices and experiences of many different types of tribal healers and shamans from the most diverse regions of the world, ranging from so-called primitive African tribes, to Eskimos, Australian aborigines, North American Indians, and many others.

Their narratives are, at first sight, rather difficult to comprehend, because in their descriptions of initiatory experiences shamans frequently make use of extremely unfamiliar and symbolic language. Perhaps one would have to be a shaman oneself to appreciate them in their full depth. After all, these are reports about extraordinary experiences in a "fourth dimension" penetrated by these men and women, who went through enormous inner struggles and great sufferings in their search for paranormal powers, for an ability to heal and/or foresee the future.

On the other hand, I am grateful and happy that a book such as this should remind me that always and all over the world people have known about an existence after death and endeavored to prepare themselves by preempting it—an existence in which we no longer have need of a physical body and can communicate by a kind of telepathy rather than words. This mode of "being" enables us to travel through other realms, and on our passage to these other planes of reality we have to overcome many an obstacle. Here, in fact, we reap what we have sown—a person who has led a good and compassionate life is able to cross the river of death without difficulty, whereas others, according to the degree of self-perfection and goodness they have attained in the course of their lives, have to struggle for either a short or apparently endless period of time before reaching the other shore.

Only a few of us who live in modern Western civilization understand that benevolent "helping spirits" and "imaginary friends" are by no means projections of an imagination gone riot. The critically ill children in my care refer to these spirits as their "playmates." They are very real companions to them—guides and helpers at a time of isolation, loneliness, and suffering. Such companions are known by children everywhere. Only when children grow up in an unbelieving world, that tends to laugh at such follies, do they as a rule lose their ability to recognize these helpers.

It is extremely important that our modern Western culture subject its values and opinions to a critical examination—particularly its views about sickness and suffering. In order to promote such a reexamination I have founded a worldwide organization called Shanti Nilaya, that has taken the following statement for its basic motto: "If we were to protect all ravines against all storms and avalanches we would never be able to admire the beauty of their scarred surfaces." People who have gone through great trials and tribulations in their early life—like the shamans, whose experiences are recorded in this book—often are particularly gifted, believing that they are guided, that there is a life after death, and that the whole of life is a school for spiritual growth.

If we can, at least occasionally, sever the chains that bind us to our material world and turn inward, we are rewarded by an expansion of our consciousness and a corresponding insight into the realities beyond this three-dimensional world. We will then become aware of our true spiritual potential, of what has been called the "divine spark" that dwells in every one of us.

Those who have experienced revelations of this kind will be aware of the remarkable similarities between them and the shamanic experiences dealt with here. They will thus find confirmation of what they already know: namely, that the basic experiences of humanity all over the world are the same and that we all have a common source, to which we shall return when we have learned our lessons and overcome our trials. For we all are children of the same God.

ELISABETH KÜBLER-ROSS

DREAMTIME
&
INNER SPACE

INTRODUCTION

Snake Does Not Bite Man;
Snake Bites What Man Thinks[1]

We are like prisoners in a cave, staring grimly at its walls, upon which we perceive moving shadows. They are the shadows of objects, which—invisible to us—are passing behind our back and are lit by a great fire outside our field of vision. We do not turn around to explore the source of these shadows, and because of that we are convinced that the shadow images before us are the real world of sensory perceptions. Yet, if one of the prisoners were able to muster the strength and courage to leave the cave, he would discover the actual objects, the cause of those vague shadows. If he left the cave altogether, he would—after rubbing his smarting eyes—behold the sun. Were he to return to the cave after such an overpowering insight into the illusory nature of his world of shadows, no one there would believe his fantastic tales. He would forthwith experience an intense aloneness and consider it his task to cure his fellow beings of their blindness and demonstrate to them the shadow nature of their world. However, the question is whether such an insight can only be gained by someone who has himself ventured out of the cave.

This famous parable relates to the theory of cognition and comes from Plato's *Republic*. It contains a much quoted but rarely heeded directive for the world of science. The principles of the theory of cognition contained in Plato's Parable of the Cave also apply to the basis of shamanic training and we shall follow them in our analysis of the latter.

Who is this man that stands up, turns around, and leaves the cave in order to confront these shadow creatures? Could he be the shaman summoning his spirits? The medicine man, looking "through" others with his spiritual sight? Or the magician flying through the air and leaving his half-dead body behind?

The shaman's view of the world leaps across our conventional ideas about time and causality, contracts space telepathically, and subscribes to communicating with all that is. It considers the individual as being harnessed to a universal energy field of magic, in which even the most fleeting thought causes the whole universe to tremble, the spoken word kills your neighbor, and common sense is annihilated by ecstatic communion with the environment. Many people feel that a world view according to which man is able to influence the earthly realm of the corporeal by the use of entities from the Beyond is too far removed from everyday twentieth-century thinking and reasoning to merit serious consideration. In an age characterized by an unshakable faith in science it has become the task of anthropology to provide a rational explanation for such wayward and illogical notions and concepts.

The "perverse" upside-down physics of the shamanic universe—in which time is stretchable, space is solid, matter is transparent, and conventional manifestations of energy are replaced by invisible subtle forces—cannot be grasped by our customary mode of perception. Nevertheless, all tribal societies as well as our ancestors—and cultures of both the Old World and our present world—did at one time subscribe to the idea of such a universe. Our modern Western culture forms the only exception to this general rule. Its determined scientific exploration and experimentation has confined itself to what is observable within three-dimensional space. In other words, it has concentrated itself exclusively on a reality accessible to a system of logic based on purely sensory perceptions.

The experiences of the shaman, on the other hand, are genuinely transpsychic. Nevertheless, they can be repeated by anyone capable of summoning up sufficient courage and self-discipline to overcome our limited intellect and our perceptually restricted normal awareness, because beyond this "standardized" awareness there exists a whole spectrum of expanded modes of perception. The ascendant scale of experience, revealing new forms of being at every level, has always been a metaphor of growing insight.

Two special factors have strongly influenced Western civilization: the first of these is the idea—also shared by Nietzsche—that we are alone in a hostile universe; the other is the notion that in the last resort life is meaningless. The shaman, on the other hand, speaks of the vitality of all that exists and of a global relatedness to all beings and phenomena at every level. To him the universe is pervaded by a creative essence which not only transcends normal existence but lends to it an inner cohesion.

The shaman is part of the age-old tradition of the Perennial Philosophy—the mystical teaching of the unity of all things and all beings. In the realm of magic everything is interrelated; nothing exists in isolation.

Here rules the principle of *pars pro toto*. This level of consciousness, like a gigantic telephone exchange, affords access to all other levels of awareness. All mystical paths are agreed that such a way of experiencing requires a suspension of normal awareness and of rational thought by means of special techniques of mind training. An empty mind allows an alternative way of being and affords access to the existential level of transpersonal experience.

Since the dawn of the so-called Age of Enlightenment and the subsequent industrial revolution there has been growing opposition to the idea that psychic experiences can make a genuine contribution to explaining what human life is about. A widespread aversion to theological thought, to the notion of an inner world based on Christian principles, and to divine revelation, has steered our culture toward a one-sided view of what life itself is and what it is about. Objective observation of the factual and material has continued to gain ground, and as a result, the psyche has come to be forgotten. Our materialist attitude has thus caused us to "pour out the baby with the bath water." We have expelled Psyche from our earthly paradise.

Let us not forget that psychology, in its early days, found it extremely difficult to establish itself as a recognized field of knowledge capable of presenting, or at least postulating, an inner world subject to recognizable mental structures and mechanisms. Today, psychology finds itself confronted by what it has rejected—either in an attempt to defend its territory or out of fear that it might be considered unscientific—namely the need to recognize altered and heightened states of consciousness.

Western thought finds itself in a crisis situation and is trying to shake off its self-imposed manacles by finding its way back to the primordial. In this process the shaman and the metarational sphere of the religious, with their expanded structure of consciousness, have an important role to play. For that reason our growing interest in primitive religions is no longer confined to those areas which hitherto were held to be academically and anthropologically "acceptable."

Of course, there have always been social groups, cults, and philosophical fashions that have adopted for themselves the ideas of exotic cultures, or what one might call an alien lifestyle. However, all too often such attitudes went hand in hand with a naive hedonism, covert ethnocentrism, and abstruse cultural syncretism. Our modern interpretation and understanding of religious ideas is by no means free from remnants of traditional dogmatism and social pathologies. Nevertheless, the urge toward a pure inner experience, or what is thought of as true spirituality, presents us with an opportunity to at least partially free ourselves from religious collectivism, superstition, and sanctimoniousness.

Although religion is a living experience, which ultimately cannot be written about, this book is an attempt to write about spiritual awareness, because science and religion are increasingly approaching each other and may even shake hands in the foreseeable future. When this happens Albert Einstein's statement that "Science without religion is lame and religion without science is blind" will no longer be topical. Science and religion can be united by the realization that life is an adventure in consciousness. Einstein considered all scientific theories to be free inventions of the human spirit. Conversely, to someone experiencing the world spiritually, all states of consciousness are free creations, limited only insofar as they represent aspects of cosmic unity.

Within the imperialist framework of Western civilization tribal societies are subjected to discrimination and isolation. We accord them marginal status and our attitude toward them is often somewhat condescending. Their unique characteristics are frequently described in psychopathological terminology. By simply ignoring them we reduce their status to one of quasi-nonexistence. Frequently they are the victims of genocidal policies. Their members are labeled as primitives. Biologists tend to look upon them as evolutionary relics. Sociologists see them as cultural abnormalities. To the psychologist they may be a prerational species, to the economist an underdeveloped society. As far as military strategists are concerned they are nonexistent, and well-fed tourists see them as romantic and exotic travel book images. Yet despite all this, their healers and medicine men exercise an enormous fascination for the people of the so-called civilized world.

The shaman, too, tends to be seen as a kind of trick artist, a psychologically disturbed person, characterized by all the irrational excesses of a predominantly non-Aristotelian view of the world. As such, he has always been the strongest possible challenge to the interpretative addiction of Western academics interested in the Theory of Culture. This is because the shaman is seen as an intolerable bogey by any ideology limited to such basic tenets as "normal" awareness, three-dimensional logic, and strength of ego.

The history of the exploration of shamanism is the story of a conspiracy against nonrational, nonobjective, and non-Cartesian thought. To the "enlightened" mind, the medicine man, the trance medium, the visionary, and the sorcerer have always been the archenemies of common sense. The learned scientists, in their conceit, look upon the shaman as a monstrous product of human superstition. In short: Any intellectual movement dealing with this "orphan" of science runs the risk of wielding the double-edged sword of scientific ruin, if it refuses to treat the subject from the point of view of behaviorist sociology or other naively materialistic concepts, which are academically recognized and acceptable.

Fortunately, research into shamanism has ceased to be a peripheral discipline confined to exalted academics. The basic values of Western thought are becoming somewhat shaky and threadbare. As a result of this new ideas about the nature of consciousness are rapidly gaining ground, and the shaman has become a focal point of their attention. It is almost as if a king who had been banished for his folly were reclaiming his realm. Shamanic experiences bring us once again closer to the sacred dimension of nature, and profane science, sacred inspiration, and genuine wisdom are beginning to unite, giving birth to a new kind of metarational science. In other words, the gaping wound of duality is beginning to heal.

This book deals with the experiences of supernormal or paranormal people who, through their voluntary exposure to tremendous hardships and great dangers, have catapulted themselves into the world of the superconscious. This can provide us with a more comprehensive view of human existence once we have overcome the limitations of our mundane ego.

Shamans always hold a prominent status within their tribal communities. In fact, they are the central constellation of their society, the focal point of the religious, political, and social community. This book is an attempt to present a positive and constructive explanation of the shaman's view of the world—an explanation from which not only every psychiatrist but in fact anyone in search of self-completion and ego transcendence can learn a great deal. The theoretical repertoire for this investigation comes, in the main, from a new scientific orientation, one that has lost its specifically Western character, because it gives full recognition to the psychologies and philosophies of other cultures and strives to bring these into harmony with our modern knowledge. This new scientific orientation is known as Transpersonal Science.

For those who consider it beneath their intelligence to concern themselves with anything but realistic problems, the study of exotic people, particularly of "primitive" magicians, will of course not merit the attention of our present civilization, dominated as it is by the idea of progress. Nevertheless, we are witnessing today a growing interest in magic, the occult, and the extrasensory. The very reason these things are being given more and more attention is that the latest findings of orthodox science appear to be not unrelated to these hitherto neglected fields of study.

Shamanism and similar mysterious areas of research have gained in significance because they postulate new ideas about mind and spirit. They speak of things like vastly expanding the realm of consciousness. They do so at a time when Western thought finds itself in a general crisis and traditional models of thinking are being questioned.

The traditional premises of the natural sciences and our ethical and moral codes of value seem to be no longer adequate; their restrictive apparel is coming apart at the seams, and through the gaps we can perceive aspects of the shaman's world. If modern science wishes to avoid an increasing alienation from these new insights and realities it cannot afford to ignore them. We have begun to explore the darkest corners of the human mind, and many ideas belonging to the primitive and primordial are coming to be looked upon as progressive and as extremely significant for the future of mankind. The saints, shamans, and yogins are exposing the shortcomings of our Western mentality, and many notions that up to now were considered primitive and naive have turned into challenges that will have to be faced for the sake of our further cultural development. If we do not succeed in integrating that which we have suppressed or crowded out for so long, the dark shadow hovering over our mechanistic and materialistic lifestyle will become ever more ominous.

In fact, our culture needs a great deal more than a changed lifestyle. In the Western mind, thought-structures and the relationship between consciousness and matter are badly out of balance, so that our world has become wholly pervaded by a materialism that is threatening to squash us to death. We are in a state of materialistic hypertrophy, and our eventual self-destruction would in fact be no more than the logical consequence of our attitudes.

Here is what the Indian shaman Lame Deer says on this subject:

> Only human beings have come to a point where they no longer know why they exist. They don't use their brains and they have forgotten the secret knowledge of their bodies, their senses, or their dreams. They don't use the knowledge the spirit has put into every one of them; they are not even aware of this, and so they stumble along blindly on the road to nowhere—a paved highway which they themselves bulldoze and make smooth so that they can get faster to the big, empty hole which they'll find at the end, waiting to swallow them up. It's a quick comfortable superhighway, but I know where it leads to. I've seen it. I've been there in my vision and it makes me shudder to think about it.[2]

PART ONE

The Religion of the Twice-Born

A medicine man once died. Before he died, he commanded peo-
ple to burn him after his death. They did. He came to life again.
At his second death, they hung his body on a drying rack as he
had commanded. He came alive again. At the third death, they
tied him in a kayak, towed him out to sea and set him adrift. He
came back. At the fourth death, they cut him up and cooked him
in five pots, then scattered the pieces around anywhere, all this
at his command. He returned to life. When he died the fifth time,
he was reborn as a baby.   [Lantis 1946, p. 308]

1

A Geography of Death

To Plato death meant *lysis* (loosening) and *chorismos* (separation). Philosophy he defined literally as *phaedros melete thanatou* (practice and preparation for death). Such knowledge, he felt, made death less awesome for the philosopher than for ordinary people. When one of Plato's friends came to his deathbed and asked him to state his philosophy in one simple sentence, Plato is said to have replied: "Practice to die."

The intimate relationship of the shaman to dying, death, and life after death, as well as the mental and spiritual techniques by which he projects himself to the very boundary between life and death, make him an excellent proponent of Plato's philosophy.

Modern research into death is no longer all that far removed from the quintessence of Plato's philosophy, although this modern research concerns itself, in the main, with trying to discover what happens to someone who has been extremely close to death and then recovers consciousness. The investigations of Osis and Haraldsson, who compared Indian and Western cases, show that the near-death experience (NDE) does not vary, irrespective of cultural differences.[1] So far, the sequence of events of journeys to the Beyond in tribal cultures has not been the subject of a systematic study in the light of modern knowledge. Perhaps at some point in the near future, when ethnologists acquire detailed data on the psychology of death, thereby emancipating themselves from the state of a mere listener to that of a genuine partner in experience, they will no longer misinterpret shamanic experiences as symbolic and cultural artifacts. If that happens, we can look forward to a rapid expansion of thanatology.

Let us look at some typical observations made by thanatologists about the postmortal condition. Such an exercise will better enable us to compare these observations to the experiences of shamans during their journeys to the Beyond.[2]

Before the consciousness of a dying person separates from the body, that person often hears a curious noise, described as a cracking, clicking, or rushing sound, but sometimes also as wonderfully harmonious. A twenty-eight-year-old man, who attempted suicide in prison, reported that almost immediately he heard curious sounds: "(I) heard all this ringing, this loud, loud ringing, and then a black hole and all these luminous things around and beautiful music, the most beautiful music I had ever heard. The ringing came from a low to a peak, which faded into choral music which was all around me. It was the most beautiful experience I think I've ever had, just totally encompassed in sound, the most beautiful voices I'd ever heard."[3]

Dying persons, after various acoustic sensations, suddenly find themselves in a strange situation: They are able to see their bodies from the outside, as it were; they feel themselves separate from their bodies, weightless, perhaps even floating just under the ceiling, gliding along and sometimes even passing through solid objects. They hear and see everything that happens around their bodies, but remain unimpressed by the words of the "living," such as, for instance, the doctor operating on them or even pronouncing them dead. They try to communicate but nobody reacts. With lightning speed they move from one place to another and feel themselves transposed into a state in which time and space no longer have any meaning. Soon after that they become aware that they still own a body but that this body is not solid; rather, it manifests as something misty, cloudlike, foglike, gaseous, or as an energy field. In this out-of-body state, many people have telepathic contact with others and transcend the frontiers of the material world.

After the clicking sounds (or heavenly music) and the subsequent separation from the body, people feel themselves drawn into a dark tunnel or space like a cave or hole. A twenty-five-year-old man, who was revived after a suicide attempt, said that he suddenly lost the feeling that he had a body. He felt like energy in the universe. There was total darkness and he was rushing along at enormous speed toward something pitch black. He was being sucked toward it, or drawn toward it.[4]

The theme of a frontier or obstacle is frequently encountered in myths and transpersonal experiences. Perhaps the best known image of a dividing line between this world and the Beyond is that of a river; other examples are fog or mist, expanses of water, fences, and doors. These borders have to be crossed or overcome by the disembodied consciousness.

After passing through the tunnel or darkness, a brilliant light is perceived. Bathed in this light, the traveler experiences a feeling of love and appreciation and all feelings of guilt in relation to his life disappear. The bright light assumes an almost personal quality. It is one of the most characteristic features of an NDE and leads to a profound spiritual transformation. In this brightness the dying person perceives other creatures of light, friends and acquaintances that passed away before him. Sometimes protective beings or spiritual helpers are encountered. Voices emerging from the light are not perceived acoustically, but in the very center of one's consciousness. The appearance of the beings encountered may be amorphous or they may look like humans, or like what we commonly think of as a ghost. In one such case, the dying person perceived the form to be his dead grandfather: "It was white silk-type gowns, just sort of flowing things, no real substance to them, but there was substance to them. It was sort of another state, very, very light, delicate and sturdy. They were singing. . . ."[5]

Some dying persons encounter humans or other beings, who are in a pitiful state. They have died, yet are still caught by the longings, desires, and material functions of their former earthly existences. Charles Garfield and other researchers have collected and classified such visions of hell, while yet others make no mention of such states.[6]

Frequently—and sometimes without any of the usual features of the Beyond being mentioned or present—there is a review of one's life. This happens regularly when there is an encounter with other beings. The dying person is granted a view of his whole life, during which he perceives all stages of development simultaneously or in a lightning-quick sequence. Many dying persons experience this life review as a sort of judgment, because the light-beings keep stressing the importance of love and of the acquisition of wisdom, as well as the effects of our own actions upon others. As a result of this, a dying person realizes instantly where he acted rightly or wrongly in his life. Plato speaks of "signs" which are attached to souls after their judgment and upon which their actions are recorded. In a somewhat similar way, the Tibetan Book of the Dead refers to a "mirror of karma."

Now the dying person enters a world of radiant colors and golden light. He finds himself in a landscape filled with beautiful flowers. Those that have returned from this world say that present, past, and future exist simultaneously there, and that to enter this world is tantamount to enlightenment. Many people felt that in some inexplicable way they had gained total knowledge. For this reason, the majority of dying people did not want to return to our ordinary world. One person who returned said: "It seemed that all of a sudden, all knowledge—of all that had started from the very beginning, that would go on without end—that for a second I knew all the secrets of the ages, all the meaning of the universe, the stars, the moon—of everything."[7]

Another theme we meet again and again is the curious manner of return into the body. The spirit guides of the dying person take him at first to another, somehow superior, Being which orders his return, because his time span has not yet elapsed. After that, he is taken back by the spirit guides, and the next thing he is aware of is that he has woken up in bed or in a hospital. Many people that have been revived are angry at the doctor's successful intervention and are extremely reluctant to return to our world.

The aftereffects of an NDE are often marked by a radical change in the lifestyle of the person in question. Such people become interested in philosophical ideas, occupy themselves with religious matters, and pursue humanistic values and aims. Their sense of being in the here and now is strengthened—in short, one might say that their existence has been intensified. According to Kenneth Ring, 60 percent of all "returners" questioned by him stated that their life had changed, 40 percent said that this had been the most important experience of their life, and 89 percent would gladly have repeated it.[8] It would seem, then, that NDEs are connected with a sort of psychic rebirth and an affirmation of human existence. Through their survival of clinical death, most people develop a new understanding about dying; they lose their fear of death and gain a more positive attitude toward life.

The shaman's near-death experience is also a transformation. He returns from the Beyond with wise counsel, revelations, and messages from the dead. For many shamans, the ascent to heaven or the descent to the underworld are central initiatory experiences. They emerge from them as changed persons upon whom the beings of the Beyond have bestowed special powers.

The criticism of near-death phenomenology is two-pronged. One group of critics fears a revival of spiritualism in scientific garb and for that reason tries to play down such phenomena by arguing that they can be ascribed to physiological or biological factors. The second school of critics continues to make use of the outdated concept of hallucinations.

Ronald Siegel maintains that NDEs mirror the inner structure of the brain, and that the tunnel effect and the life review are generated by the brain itself. According to him, blocked memories are frequently liberated by psychoactive drugs, traumatic experiences, or electrical excitation/ stimulation of the brain. The panoramic review of life may be explained in this way. As for hearing sounds and music, Siegel points out that sensory information continues to reach the brain of patients under anesthesia. The light-experiences he considers to be due to an excitation of the central nervous system imitating a light effect.[9] Yet other critics see these light-experiences as a result of the diminished supply of oxygen to the posterior lobe of the brain, where the visual cortex is situated.

Against this, Moody points out that tunnel experiences and noises occur not only in patients under narcosis, but in all ordinary situations of dying. The critics have compared the sound phenomenon to the auditory hallucinations announcing a mild attack in people suffering from temporal lobe epilepsy. Such people also frequently experience a panoramic memory. However, these NDE phenomena occur not only in schizophrenics, but also in completely normal people who have an accident or are seriously ill.

In any case, we need not concern ourselves with whether such NDE phenomena are the result of toxic psychosis, lack of oxygen, epilepsy, or anesthesia, or whether they are pure psychic experiences of great spiritual energy and transformative power. When we come to consider the physiological means by which shamans intentionally bring themselves close to death, we shall see that these two interpretations are not necessarily mutually exclusive. The interruption of the supply of blood and/or oxygen to the brain, narcosis-like conditions, and trancelike states not unlike an epileptic attack are all part of the shaman's psychomethodological repertoire, as are the generation of fear, stress, shock, and actual near-death situations. We therefore will have to redefine how changes of consciousness occur during epileptic attacks, in psychotic states, or under narcosis, because these states would appear to contain transpersonal reserves of consciousness that have not yet been explored.

In view of the positive aftereffects on a person's attitude to life and death it would seem, at least for the moment, irrelevant whether such psychic phenomena are neurophysiological in nature, hallucinatory experiences, transpersonal, or spiritual. The neurophysiological explanation is blinkered against psychic reality. To describe such phenomena as hallucinations implies a denial of their reality and classifies them as pathological. The transpersonal approach, on the other hand, would seem to be more fruitful, both from a heuristic as well as a practical point of view, because it sides with the experiencer, helps him to integrate his experiences, and is based on the idea of a latent, and as yet largely untapped, potential of consciousness into which the NDE affords us a first glimpse.

2

Life Beyond Birth and Death

The world is not only that [which] we can see. It is enormous and also has room for people when they die and no more walk about down here on earth.

Mankind does not end its existence because sickness or some other accident kills its animal spirit down here on earth. We live on, and there are those who say that it is what we call the soul that prevents us from dying.

This is not simply what the shamans tell us, those who understand the hidden things; ordinary people who know how to dream have many times seen that the dead appeared to them, just as they were in life. Therefore we believe that life does not end here on earth. —Nalungiaq, *a Netsilik Eskimo*[1]

For a seventy-five-year-old man it does not come amiss to reflect now and then upon death. The thought of death does not in the least disturb me, because I am firmly convinced that our spirit is altogether indestructible and thus continues from eternity to eternity. It is like the sun, which to our eyes seems to disappear beyond the horizon, while in actual fact it goes on shining continuously. —Letter from Goethe to Eckermann,

2 May 1824

The simplest and most drastic way to change someone's state of consciousness is to kill him or bring him close to death. In the world of the shaman, out-of-body experiences (OBES) and journeys to the Beyond are considered high points of altered consciousness, because they offer the shaman optimal conditions for gaining supersensory knowledge. In this context a report by the famous Polar explorer Knud Rasmussen about the Caribou Eskimo shamaness Kinalik may serve as an example. Rasmussen describes her as being about thirty years of age, very intelligent, neat, trusting, and communicative. She became a shamaness as a result of a vision of death; more precisely, she "died" from being shot.

She was chosen for shamanic training because she had dreamt that a man of her tribe would become ill. This was taken as a sign of her shamanic talent—the spirits had imparted news to her in a dream. She was taught by her brother-in-law Igjugarjuk, whom Kinalik's mother begged to "shoot" her. Kinalik had previously spent five whole days out in the open, tied to tent poles, so that Hila, the mystical force, might notice her. During those five days the spirits protected Kinalik against the bitter cold and icy snowstorms. When Igjugarjuk shot her—not with a lead bullet but with a small pebble—the other members of the tribe were present and watched. As soon as Kinalik fell to the ground they all began to chant. Kinalik lay dead throughout the night.

When Igjugarjuk went to revive her the next morning she regained consciousness of her own accord. She had been shot in the heart. Later the pebble was extracted and is now preserved by her mother. After this initiation Kinalik said that her dead brother was now her main Protecting Spirit. He had often come to visit her by gliding through the air with his legs and head down. But as soon as he landed on the ground he was able to walk like an ordinary man. Kinalik mentioned that the polar bear was another of her helping spirits. Igjugarjuk did not carry her training further as he thought it a pity to let her suffer more. The more pain and suffering a shaman takes upon himself during his training the greater his shamanic powers.

Igjugarjuk had another pupil, a man called Aggiartoq. In his case another form of dying was chosen, namely death by drowning. Aggiartoq was tied fast to a long tent pole and carried down to a big lake. A hole was hewn through the ice and Aggiartoq was lowered, fully dressed, to the bottom of the lake and left there for five whole days. When they pulled him up he was as dry as if he had never been touched by water. Thereafter his dead mother and an unnamed human skeleton became his Helpers.[2]

The belief, the knowledge, and even the experience that our physical world of the senses is a mere illusion, a world of shadows, and that the three-dimensional tool we call our body serves only as a container or dwelling place for Something infinitely greater and more comprehensive than that body and which constitutes the matrix of the real life—this surely is the most powerful idea man has ever conceived. It has been the main theme of all his actions, and has not been surpassed by any thought, speculation, or theory in any epoch.

In the languages of different peoples and nations, the soul has been called many things: shadow, breath, pneuma, entelechy, spirit, and double, to mention just a few. The idea of a soul reduces our visible world of form and characteristics to that of a derived or secondary world. The shadow becomes the source, and matter the child or offspring of a higher, uniform, and super-dimensional reality. Are we then living in a universe of projected images and predetermined actions? An antipodean world, in which the soul stages a puppet game with our body? A game in which our psyche represents the strings by which our body is turned and manipulated? Is this world of ours a topsy-turvy world, in which reality has dwindled to a mere illusion? Have all the cultures of all the epochs, civilizations, and continents merely dreamt this dream of physical existence from the beginning of time to the present day? Is our existence no more than a dream of the soul, which, like a film projector, presents us with a lot of busy comings and goings, and which ultimately has no more substance than the images on a cinema screen? Is the soul the source of energy, the breath of life, that which makes it possible for us to switch on our senses, to activate the receptive mechanisms of our skin and eyes and to crank up our thinking centers and keep them running?

Prominent thinkers of all ages have said that the soul is a prerequisite for intelligence, normal life functions, and even the moving of a finger. Not only is the theory of the soul the oldest, most enduring, and most widespread philosophical solipsism; it is also the most original and most firmly-based idea about human existence. If we feel that our experience of the world is no more than the bursting foam upon a mountainous wave, that we are no more than a short-lived monad fettered to or dependent upon a greater ground of being, then we shall inevitably end up with an idealistic philosophy, because such a world view reduces our material existence to something of secondary significance, to a mere happening.

The notion of the existence of a life principle beyond the body is central to all tribal cultures. They, in turn, form the first link in a long chain of cultures, all of which subscribe to that one idea. True, each society has added its own specific adornments and intellectual colorings and has adapted the philosophy of the soul to the mythology and lifestyle of its culture, but the idea of the existence of an animatory principle behind our corporeal world has been preserved throughout history, nourished again and again by Man's spontaneous experiences.

There is hardly any need to produce specific examples for the existence of this leading theme in the history of mankind. The fact that the primary and most universal factor of human existence is the idea of a life-giving energy that is independent of the body and directs or guides each individual speaks for itself. Our material existence is only a reflection of our immaterial soul, just as a shadow has no existence of its own but is dependent on the presence of a solid body. The existence of a soul and its postmortal connection with our lives is the ground of all traditional spiritual philosophy. For that reason the soul is also the first theme of our investigation. Using it as a starting base, we shall penetrate the occult experiences and esoteric knowledge of the shamans, who are the technicians of the Sacred, the specialists of the Beyond.

The shaman is the classic investigator of the realm of death; he explores the routes of travel to and in the Beyond and thereby produces a map of the postmortem terrain. As a scientist of the transpersonal dimension and the nonterrestrial domain of consciousness, his culture or tribe respects him as a great authority, as one who not only is conversant with the ordinary psyche but also knows the spirit that manifests independently of the body. During his period of initiation the shaman learns to control psychic and physiological functions, to regulate his body chemistry and to master such mental techniques as concentration and contemplation.

In the case of many shamans their abilities may be confined to such psychophysical techniques of self-control. For many others, however, they are just the starting point for the ascent or descent to the realm of the dead. Supported by protectors and helpers, these shamans contact people who have died, and encounter demons and spiritual beings who give them advice related to coping with life on earth. The shaman undergoes several years of hard training, which finally enable him to intentionally induce in himself a state of death, during which his soul leaves his body. He then carefully feels his way toward the dangers and trials awaiting him and learns how to deal with them. Depending on his strength and ability, his soul can penetrate the most distant and remote realms of the spirit.

But not all shamans are equally skilled, so that they make longer or shorter journeys to the Land of the Dead, all according to their powers:

> In all likelihood many features of conventional funeral rites, as well as several themes of the mythology of death, could be traced back to the ecstatic experiences of shamans. The places they visit and the people or beings they meet on their journeys to the Beyond are described by them as precisely as possible both during their trance as well as after

their return. In this way, the unknown and frightening world of the dead is given a form and becomes ordered in accordance with consistent examples. Finally this world reveals its own structure, which, with the passing of time, becomes better known and ultimately familiar. The supernatural denizens of the death realm become visible and reveal their personality, perhaps even a sort of biography, so that the world of the dead becomes more and more recognizable as time passes. A thorough study of the reports about the ecstatic journeys of shamans helps us to "spiritualize" the death realm and at the same time enrich it with wondrous forms and figures.[3]

As a Chosen One, as someone who, during his own lifetime, succeeds in penetrating the frontiers of transcendence, the shaman moves as a messenger between two worlds—the world of living humanity and the world of the dead or of nonmaterial existence. He is a hero who overcomes supernatural dangers and, as such, is celebrated in the tradition of the people, immortalized in their myths and epic poems. The shaman transcends the profane order of existence, leaves the world of the banal and travels to an etheric subtle sphere, accessible to ordinary people only in death or as a result of serious illness, accident, shock, violent emotions, and in dreams. This conscious and controlled penetration into such a closed realm must be counted among the greatest achievements of Man. This is the reason why shamans are respected and honored wherever they practice their art.

In advanced cultures shamanic journeys into the underworld are found only as a theme of ancient myths and epic tales. In tribal cultures, however, such a journey to the Beyond continues to be an experienceable daily reality, which all members of the tribe, present at a shamanic ritual or ceremony, can share as they hear the spirits speak and comment on the future, the present, and things closely related to life. In this way the members of tribal cultures have a closer relationship with death and the death realm than people of later civilizations. Philosophically and existentially speaking it could even be said that tribal members are standing on the threshold to the Beyond. Their shaman affords them contact to the land of shadows and a dialogue with the dead. Moreover, they themselves have the possibility of becoming shamans and of exploring this other world. The Christian priest and his abstract ministrations grant us, at best, a mere glimpse of the Beyond, so that the sphere of the supernatural no longer forms part of our existence or of our view of life. The Beyond comes to be seen as an abstruse concept of the primitive mind. However, what we think of as our higher cultural development is in fact no more than the result of an increasing alienation from the beings of the postmortal and transpersonal realm and thus also from our primordial energy and powers, through which, by means of psychic training and appropriate techniques of ecstasy, we could unlock the door to higher domains of consciousness.

The shaman should therefore not be branded as some sort of archaic hero or as a relic of the past, who, although historically redundant, somehow continues to vegetate on the fringe of our technological civilization. In the light of the revolutionary findings of recent researches into the nature of dying and death, the shaman should be considered as a most up-to-date and knowledgeable psychologist. Modern thanatology has reawakened the shaman from the sleep into which our science had cast him, and we are coming to realize that our ideas about him were only a reflection of our own scientific limitations and empirical narrowmindedness.

But thanatological research is only the first step in freeing the shaman from the thorny hedges with which generations of explorers, missionaries, adventurers, and anthropologists, by their profuse writing and learned conclusions, have surrounded him. Academics from many different disciplines have now begun to exhume the shaman from this tangle of rationalist theories and romantic ideas, so that our modern research into shamanism could, in fact, be seen as a sort of archeology of the western mind and spirit. An exhumation is normally followed by an autopsy, but in this case there will be no need for that, because the face of the shaman will shine forth in all its dignity once the mass of ideological and historical ravings has been removed. I firmly believe that modern consciousness research has begun to demythologize the rationalistic myths of anthropological researchers.

Our society suppresses any thoughts or mention of death and dying; it is no longer willing to concern itself with values genuinely and intimately related to life. It seeks instead to find and define its reality in technological artifacts and trifling pastimes. The disappearance of the death cult goes hand in hand with our inability or unwillingness to reflect upon the thought that life is impermanent. In consequence, the death cult has been replaced by an extremely materialistic compensatory ideology of almost pathological proportions. True, some warning voices are beginning to be raised, but on the whole we surrender to this kind of displacement mechanism and arrogantly believe we have rid the world of death. In making the death concept taboo we have, however, deprived life of its vitality. Our whole attitude to life is out of balance; we are intent only on savoring what we think of as the good and pleasurable, but reality catches up with us again and again—at the crematorium or under the surgeon's scalpel. This characteristically Western attitude toward death is almost without parallel in recorded history.

Nowadays the shaman—an expert in death and dying, a messenger from the Beyond—is gradually coming to be recognized as one of the most capable explorers of an inner world which, in turn, is but the outer appearance of another realm. The tribal medicine men are the living representatives of both preindustrial and postindustrial psychology. Their knowledge goes way beyond the narrow confines of conventional psychology, which at best manages to unravel the conflicts arising from the interrelationships of human beings. The transpersonal psychology of the shaman, however, arrives at diagnoses and forms of healing that overcome the shortsightedness inherent in forms of analysis confined to the individual, the family, or the immediate human environment. The new psychology will show the conflicts in our lives to be related both to the here and now and to the Beyond. Based on this superior insight it will strive for therapeutic solutions that might be somewhat unusual and incomprehensible in the eyes of ordinary people.

In its search for more comprehensive criteria of diagnosis and treatment, Western psychotherapy has passed through several phases. It has abandoned the notion of the isolated individual and has related the pathological disturbances of the patient to a wider area of cause and effect. However, the shaman, having mastered all this, goes one step further. He transcends the level of the material and enters into the spiritual realm, into pure consciousness.

The shaman "dies," he anticipates his death and with his soul visits the Beyond to explore the geography of the realm of death. This is an extremely dangerous undertaking and all too often we hear of shamans who did not come back, whose bodies were not reactivated by the life force but remained corpses without a soul. The journey into the other dimension is therefore fraught with many perils, so that only someone who has prepared himself through long practice and who is armed with thorough and precise knowledge can expect to meet and overcome them. The shaman's art calls for supreme control of awareness, thought, and feeling, and culminates in a separation of the soul from the body. This process has been given many names, such as astral journeys, soul-excursions, ascents into heaven, descents into hell, journeys to the Beyond, and out-of-body experiences (OBEs), etc. The latter represent a special state of consciousness, characterized by the unique separation of body and self-awareness, and are therefore different from all other states of altered consciousness.

The intentional separation of consciousness, of the sense of identity, of the thinking "I"—in short, of the soul—must be counted among the most mysterious attainments of the human psyche. The traditional lore of tribal cultures makes a careful distinction between those who are qualified to heal, to diagnose, or to teach rituals and those who, over and above that, are able to communicate with the powers of the Beyond by shedding their body. A medicine man may be capable of telepathy, clairvoyance, or precognition, but he will remain incomplete and in need of further training as long as he has not entered the postmortal realm.

The shaman, then, is a master of death; he actually dies and is actually reborn. He is "dead" for a limited period of time, but his return from the realm of the dead is uncertain. Through his practices he finds himself constantly on the edge of the abyss of total extinction. Hostile circumstances may prevent him from finding his way back. Spirits and demons—but also the beautiful signs and experiences he encounters in the subtle sphere—are capable of deluding, enticing, and confusing him. Other sorcerers may bar his way back and even ambush him. Or he may simply get lost in this still unfamiliar spiritual landscape. His consciousness may be clouded, his intention lacking in clarity; or he may encounter situations for which his training did not prepare him.

Reports about shamanistic practices frequently refer to the theme of the "journey" in an attempt to describe how the soul leaves the body and travels through the landscape of the realm of the dead. This metaphor of a journey to the Beyond is a classical image of which practically all cultures make use to bring the travels of the consciousness of shamans or saints within the range of people's understanding. In the last resort, all such attempts to present subtle experiences encountered in a transpersonal dimension in terms of metaphors common to our three-dimensional world are inadequate. However, they are the only method available to us for verbalizing the inexpressible. At times, the ways in which tribal cultures describe experiences in other realms of consciousness may seem laughable and naive to us, yet their use of plainly realistic and everyday images constitutes the only practical solution if they want to convey anything about such realms of existence.

If one can speak of naivety at all, such a term should not be applied to the language used by the shaman, but rather to our inability to decipher the code for translating his words from an acausal and transpersonal level to one of personal language. Frequently our vocabulary even fails us when it comes to translating the experience of smelling into terms related to hearing or when we want to translate an optical impression into an auditory one. Worse than that: Language proves inadequate when it comes to expressing our feelings in words. The right and left hemispheres of our brain use different methods for processing data and impressions; the right hemisphere "feels" more intuitively, comprehensively, and symbolically, while the left hemisphere "thinks" predominantly in linear, logical, and rational terms. The two hemispheres thus represent opposite modes of experiencing. The difference between the experience of the here and now and of the Beyond should be seen in the same way. In the Beyond communication is not language-based but, as shamans keep telling us, takes the form of a direct telepathic and feeling-oriented exchange from person to person. Because there are, in the Beyond, neither material barriers nor corporeal limits, but only pure consciousness in the form of the soul, it is perfectly possible to participate directly in the "other" and to spontaneously penetrate the psychic atmosphere of another person or being.

If we were to attempt to find an even remotely appropriate style for describing what happens in the Beyond and what the soul experiences there we would, in all probability, have to dissociate ourselves from any allegorical interpretations and turn to the language of modern microphysics because the terminology used by that discipline is sufficiently abstract to describe things our graphic intelligence and logical thought are unable to grasp. Of course, it may not necessarily be helpful to make use of microphysical terminology, but such an approach might give us a more precise and unequivocal description than everyday language or allegory can provide. As we shall see, psychological terminology will not be of much help, because it is wholly oriented toward describing personality characteristics and, moreover, it labels transpersonal states as morbid fantasies of a schizophrenic mind.

Mircea Eliade stresses that death mythologies and geographical descriptions of the Beyond also form part of the existence of modern Western man. It has been conclusively proven that the mythical originality of these "imaginary" worlds is featured in our literature and poetry and has always been an important motif in the visual arts, including the cinema and stage. The dualisms of Here/Beyond, Life/Death, and Mind/Body exercise a natural fascination, which even educated people are unable to escape. It would seem that we are here confronted by a kind of Jungian Archetype, a true transpsychic experience, which has survived all the epochs of Man's history and again and again resurfaces in individuals, cults, and whole cultures. It is a perennial and eternal wisdom, a naive primordial experience of mankind, and Western man—as I shall demonstrate—is no more able to evade it than people living in a traditional tribal manner.

Such an experience cannot be grasped by the use of cliché-ridden contrasts between primitive and modern, sick and healthy, sane and insane. It occurs both in the sick and the healthy, in intellectuals and in emotional people, in psychotics, scientists, and artists. Recent findings show that this is a universal human experience, ultimately accessible to anyone and relatively simple to trigger—namely by placing oneself in a situation which could easily prove fatal. Whenever we are involved in a serious accident—be it at work, on the road, or during recreation—or when we become severely ill, have a fainting fit, or enter a state of trance or ecstasy, our consciousness can become independent and live through a characteristic sequence of near-death motifs. The prerequisite for such death experiences is the deconditioning and annihilation of our customary modes of perception, the interruption of biopsychic functions. In the near-death state, the out-of-body experience, and during the journey to the Beyond, we are confronted by real phenomena of consciousness and not just by symbols of the unconscious.

As examples of the attention devoted to death by earlier generations we can cite the Tibetan or Egyptian *Book of the Dead* as well as the medieval tradition of *ars moriendi*—the art of dying. These writings describe what awaits us when we die, when consciousness leaves the body and sets out on its journey to another realm of existence. Such attempts at giving people during their earthly life—and particularly during the process of dying— some idea of the Beyond and of the psychic states that await them there represent a powerful form of the "psychotherapy of death," because their main aim consists in preventing shock and postmortal breakdown.

Recently we have begun to observe dying people more closely instead of leaving them to doze in their wretchedness—lonely, isolated, and ignored. Even physicians who have traditionally ascribed all phenomena to bodily functions are starting to develop a "feel" for the psychic world of the dying and the revived. We are learning that the near-death state and process of dying are a normal state of consciousness, during which people require particularly sympathetic care and treatment. The idea of making it easier for people to die, by talking to them and by gently guiding them toward a recognition of the inevitable has been unfamiliar to most psychiatrists and psychologists or was considered unnecessary. Psychology, which after all should concern itself with all the stages of a person's life, has ignored death and banished it to the terminal wards of our hospitals. The unfeeling and unimaginative attitude toward death by Western psychology has lately been given compensatory momentum by an interest in thanatological research. All the same, so far only a few progressive and pioneering spirits have seriously begun to study what happens during the process of dying, because anyone pursuing research in this area still runs a very real risk of being confronted by a wall of silence, rejection, and even fear.

The sort of discrimination and aversion we encounter in death research can also be found in connection with studying the world of the shaman. Cynicism toward death is cynicism toward the mystic's conception of the world. If, in the course of time, the acknowledgment of death were to expand from the present small group of specialists to wider sectors of our Western society, we would look forward to a corresponding upgrading of the shaman's view of life.

On the basis of the growing empirical data provided by people that have been reanimated from a near-death state, we are now in the process of mapping the near-death realm and developing a kind of graph of the death process. The belief of tribal communities in a life after death is not simply a handed-down cosmology. On the contrary, the imagination of these communities continues to be fuelled by the shaman's accounts of his journeys to the Beyond.

One day we may find that the anticipation of death through a near-death experience, combined with a psychic rebirth, is not only the best possible preparation for actual death, but also forms an optimal basis for restoring a proper balance and harmony in the psyche. The Augustine monk Abraham a Santa Clara has said, "Someone who dies before he dies does not die when he dies." The death/rebirth process is the central therapeutic agent in all tribal religions. It forms the basis for rites of passage or initiation, which mark the passing from one phase of life to the next, and it stands at the threshold of the shaman's experiences of initiation and vocation. The intensity of a near-death experience may range from being present when someone is dying and sharing this process in mind and feeling to being brought oneself to the very edge of physical extinction. Naturally there will be corresponding degrees as far as the aftereffect and the transformative quality of such an experience are concerned.

In the course of its history, Western thought has become alienated from our inner sources of inspiration, so that reports on the experiences in the after-death state, cosmological models of the Beyond, and eschatologies which primarily were not the result of philosophical reflection, but arose out of psychic experience, were increasingly regarded as speculative expressions of discursive thought. In this way we lost our knowledge about unsuspected energy reserves of consciousness and their ability to expand and travel beyond the three-dimensional world. The increasingly materialist ideology took the various cartographies of the Beyond for descriptions of physical landscapes in remote areas.

This is not really surprising, because we know that any scientific discipline can judge another only by its own criteria, and for the materialist view the dimensions of consciousness revealed by modern research work quite simply did not exist. As a result, it inevitably misinterpreted psychic data as factual. This, in turn, led to enormous distortions and confusions in the "scientific" study of religions. This tangle of misunderstandings and false interpretations has to be rectified and unraveled step by step. Ironically, this is being done with the very methods of materialist and empirical science.

When we come to deal with the actual experiences of the shaman we shall discover an interesting parallel to this principle of externalization because they themselves frequently present their transpersonal experiences in pictures and sensory images that lead the uninitiated to assume that actual material experiences are being related. For that reason missionaries, priests, and explorers, due to their incompetence in such matters, thought that the statements made by "primitives" referred to the realities of the external world and all the more so, if the observers themselves were subscribing to a view of the world in which devils, demons, and angels were held to be material phenomena.

Religious and spiritual experience is a form of intuitive self-exploration. Our spiritual consciousness unconsciously plumbs its own depths by exposing itself to situations that alter its inner structure. If mechanistic and materialistic science manipulate the external situation and do not take into account the quality of the subjective wakefulness of the observer, "spiritual consciousness research" will pursue a diametrically opposite path: Because the investigator wishes to further develop or transform himself through his work, he manipulates the biological and psychological a priori conditions of normal consciousness in a way that leads to its deautomation and dissolution.

This leads us to the need for a new approach to consciousness research—an approach which is fundamentally different from previous strategies and therefore not just a refinement or modification of traditional methodology. We have to first realize that, up to now, science has been characterized by an inherent principle of externalization, which has led it to misinterpret all psychic facts as facts of the material world. Not only have we ignored the question, whether there is room for a Beyond, or for a realm of gods and demons in our picture of the world, we have in fact totally eliminated the very possibility of such a realm of existence by dismissing all such ideas as the product of a sick and hallucinating psyche.

It is interesting to note that an approach that, by virtue of its inner structure, closes itself off from all concern with such matters as death and dying, perforce leads to the self-inflicted limitation of the researcher. Our whole culture is an expression of this self-limitation and one-sidedness. The one-eyed paradigm of materialism is in a state of decline. It remains to be seen whether it will be able to survive its retreat from the domain of the sciences and secure its continued existence as a meaningful philosophy on the fringes of our postindustrial society. In the light of the new consciousness research its survival is, in any case, becoming increasingly doubtful.

3

The Reality of the Soul

*When the gods caused man to descend from the god Mataliki,
they were afraid to give his soul full awareness, because once it left
the body enjoying full awareness, it would never come back, and
the body would thus be superfluous. The gods therefore ensured
that the soul would see the world in a misty fashion only, that it
would be afraid of daylight and thus would have to see the world
always under cover of darkness.*[1]

*The only thing of value in a man is the soul. That is why it is the
soul that is given everlasting life, either in the Land of the Sky or
in the Underworld. The soul is man's greatest power; it is the soul
that makes us human, but how it does so we do not know. Our
flesh and blood, our body, is nothing but an envelope about our
vital power.* —Ikinilik, *an Utkuhikjaling Eskimo*[2]

*It is a thin insubstantial human image, in its nature a sort of
vapor, film or shadow. . . .mostly impalpable and invisible, yet
also manifesting physical power.*[3]

The soul consists of fine uniform atoms of a special kind.
—Demokritos

If mankind has one thing in common it is surely the belief in the
existence of a soul, of a life-bearer in the form of a consciousness only
loosely associated with a body. This notion can be found almost without
exception among all traditional peoples and cultures, and indeed also in all
modern civilizations, albeit only in subcultural groups.

Western civilization is an island in an ocean of animism and spiritualism; and even on this island there are some who do not exclude the notion
of an exsomatic soul; these people have salvaged the remnants of magico-

occult and vitalistic ideas of former times and present them to our modern age under the cloak of science.

From the renaissance onward, our culture has acknowledged the soul less and less as a nonmaterial spiritual life-principle. With the rise of economic materialism and a mechanistic, purely object-oriented science, our modern culture has come to look increasingly upon the psyche as a conglomerate of biological, physiological, and sociocultural factors. The idea of an invisible life-giving soul—or entity of consciousness—independent of the body, soon came to be seen as no more than a primitive and superstitious notion without any content of reality. Yet this notion of the soul has from the very beginning been part of the philosophical and psychological state of man; it has been present throughout the centuries and epochs and, in the last resort, has also had an impact on Western science.

Edward Tyler says in his book *Primitive Culture*: "The conception of the human soul is, as to its most essential nature, continuous from the philosophy of the savage thinker to that of the modern professor of theology. Its definition has remained from the first that of an animating, separable, surviving entity, the vehicle of individual personal existence."[4] Indeed the idea of a soul runs through the whole of Western history from antiquity to the present. Not only have occultism, spiritualism, esotericism, theosophy, and romantic as well as animistic philosophy striven to give proof of a spiritual principle which is independent of the body, but in recent times such attempts can also be detected in certain areas of parapsychology. The scientific view of the world has not succeeded in doing away with the kind of "archaic" and "mythological" ideas it abhors. In fact the contrary has turned out to be the case: Scientists today are using technological aids to capture on film the aura of the soul or of an energy body hitherto unknown to science. They claim to have discovered a new state of matter they call bioplasm, and their claims have once again added fuel to speculations about the existence of a soul.

The soul is evidently too complex a phenomenon and thus cannot be swept from the table by some brilliant stroke of theory. It is too deeply rooted in our consciousness for scientific puritanism to be capable of dealing it a death blow. An Iglulik Eskimo told Knud Rasmussen the following about the soul:

> Among us, as I have already explained to you, all is bound up with the earth we live on and our life here; and it would be even more incomprehensible, even more unreasonable, if, after a life short or long, of

happy days or of suffering and misery, we were then to cease altogether from existence. What we have heard about the soul shows us that the life of men and beasts does not end with death. When at the end of life we draw our last breath, that is not the end. We awake to consciousness again, we come to life again, and all this is effected through the medium of the soul. Therefore it is that we regard the soul as the greatest and most incomprehensible of all.[5]

The Eskimos have a straightforward and matter-of-fact attitude toward death. They say the moon spirit has revealed to them that the passage from life to death consciousness is only by a brief moment of dizziness and that immediately after that one reemerges in another world.[6] This is why the Eskimos do not disapprove of suicide; on the contrary, they believe that it has a purifying effect. There are many anecdotes about the carefree way in which Eskimos contemplate death. Typical of this attitude is the case of an old woman who hadn't heard anything from her son, who was away on a journey. After six months she was told that he was missing in his kayak at sea and was presumed dead. She couldn't expect to be looked after indefinitely by the tribe and so she cut a hole through the ice and drowned herself in order to be with her son in her spirit body.

To the Panamanian Cuna the soul—*purpa*—is an invisible double, a shadow, and the actual essence of life. For that reason they also describe the origin of something as purpa, as its primordial image.[7] In much the same way the Canadian Tlingit Eskimos refer to the soul as Quatuwu—that which feels—"when feeling disappears in someone that person is dead."[8]

The Indonesian Batak believe that all the good and bad a person experiences is determined by his or her soul (Tondi). Before a soul enters the body of a pregnant mother, the goddess Mula Djadi informs it of the destiny of the person in whom it is going to dwell. The Tondi's complete independence of the body is further confirmed by its ability to reincarnate, if it so chooses, as a medium capable of faithfully reproducing the behavior and appearance of its former existence. As a result of this the watching relatives are frequently moved to tears.[9]

In Central Malaysia it is believed that the soul (Semang) leaves the body at the moment of death, either through the toes or the head. It then remains in the vicinity of the grave for seven days, during which its face glows like a glowworm that can be perceived by other mortals. But it can also be a danger to them, because it does not want to travel alone to the land of the dead; it longs for a companion.[10]

With the Eskimos, too, the soul roams about in a lost state for three days after death and then sets out for the realm of Sedna—the mother of sea creatures—from where it can raid the settlements of mortals in the shape of a spirit creature called Tupilak.[11]

The Latin American Kamayurá believe that Ang, the soul of the dead, tries to abduct relatives during and prior to the funeral but is effectively and quickly driven off by appropriate rituals.[12]

The funeral customs and expulsion rituals that are performed after death are based on the realization that consciousness, finding itself unexpectedly disembodied, is reluctant to give up its established place in the family. It needs time to accustom itself to the new situation and thus tries to attract relatives (or rather their souls) so as not to be alone. Evidently the soul does not instantly realize that it has lost its body. Despite the fact that it has become pure consciousness it continues to roam about, no longer recognized by other mortals. The frequently very complex funeral rites are an attempt to make the soul realize that it no longer belongs with those that live in a body.

However, the soul does not only leave the body in the event of death; any shaman, if he so wishes, can cause it to part from his own body. The medicine man of the Kamayurá causes it to leave through the top of his head, especially when he is "smoking." In order to prevent it escaping unintentionally he must neither stare at others for long periods nor look at his own image in a mirror or become too excited during sexual intercourse.[13] This is because all these actions involve one-pointed concentration, which can cause a hypnoid state of altered consciousness, during which the soul might become separated from the body.

There is fairly general agreement throughout the world about the appearance of the soul. Again and again it is described as a subtle vapor or a smokelike substance. The Latin word for soul, *anima*, comes from the Greek *ánemos*, wind. The Latin *spiritus* (spirit) also stands for wind. To the Mandan Indians the soul is transparent. With the Omaha it is said to be capable of passing through solid matter. The Thompson River Salish Indians describe it as foglike. The Koyukon say it is like air or liquid. To the East Greenland Eskimos it feels soft, like a body without bones.

The ability to perceive the souls of others is mainly restricted to shamans, but ordinary people can see it in a dream or occasionally as a ghost. Among the Bear River Indians only shamans and ordinary people in a coma can perceive it. The Déné believe that the soul is particularly easy to see during an illness, and also in the dark or in an exceptional psychic state.[14]

The idea of reincarnation may be found in a few cultures. The Yugakhir believe that an ancestral spirit enters the body of the mother at the moment of birth. This is an example of the belief that reincarnation or rebirth takes place within the clan.[15] The Tungus, too, believe in reincarnation. The soul of the living (*chanjan*) has another name (*omi*) after the death of the body, which means something like "becoming, being formed." It resides in the abode of the Omi-Souls by the source of the river of kinship. In the course of time all these souls reincarnate. If a soul is not escorted by an ancestral spirit to the world of the dead or if it succeeds in escaping from its guide or escort, it will visit its living relatives, slip in through the smoke hole of the tent or enter the body of a woman, who soon thereafter will give birth to a child. With the Tungus of the Stony Tunguska we find a "shadow soul" that has all the hereditary characteristics of the clan and thus represents that which can be passed on genetically.[16] The Birarcen Tungus believe that after death the soul "goes to the world of the dead. . .and may later be returned to this world to some male or female child or to an animal, or it may remain unemployed.[17]

Similarly all Australian aboriginal tribes adhere to the preexistence of a spiritual substance that animates the body. The "ghost children" develop outside the material world and wait to be incarnated. For this they enter the body of a mother on earth, either by their own volition or without having any choice in the matter.[18]

To the Ojibway Indians man consists of a physical body that is finite and perishable, and of an immortal substance that must continue to grow while it resides in that body. Its growth is to be directed toward a harmony of heart and spirit. It is a man's duty to further develop his spirit soul. Only if he has lived in a state of goodness to the end of his allotted span does he go to the land of souls. Should he die prematurely without having achieved a "good" life he must return to earth and manifest himself once again in a physical body, unless he decides to remain in the no-man's-land between the realm of the dead and the earth.[19]

Many tribal communities believe that everything has a soul. In other words, their view of the world is panpsychic. The Senegalese Badyaranke, for instance, say that the soul can dissociate itself from the body by its own volition and is capable of transforming itself into any natural phenomena. For that reason the Badyaranke can never be certain whether the wind, animals, or insects do not bear a human soul. This belief harbors certain dangers for the magician or sorcerer; should he change himself into an animal he can be caught or killed at any time.[20]

The Indonesian Mentawai also ascribe a soul to everything: animals, plants, and all material objects. Their hunters try first of all to attract the soul of an animal by performing an appropriate ceremony, after which it is easy to catch its body.[21] Strictly speaking, killing is considered a sacrilege that—as was pointed out to Knud Rasmussen by an Iglulik Eskimo—can rebound on the hunter. The greatest danger to a hunter's life arises from the fact that his nourishment consists exclusively of animals, whose souls might revenge themselves for having been deprived of their body.

It was fashionable for a while in ethnological circles to study the "multiple soul belief" of tribal cultures. It was thought that most primitive tribes believed in the existence of several souls—a body soul, a vital soul, and a free soul. However, a closer look at such a concept shows that behind it lies the belief in a duality between body and soul. While the body soul is related to organic functions and the vital soul to psychic processes, the real soul or free soul is connected with existence in the Beyond. The various tribal people do indeed make a clear distinction between physical, mental and spiritual processes. Any confusion regarding the differentiation between the actual constituents of the soul should be ascribed rather to the interpretations of the ethnographers than to the traditional societies themselves. Shirokogorov considers the "multiple soul theory" to be an academic ethnocentrism, a European fixation, an invention of the ethnographers.[22]

The multiple soul belief is, in fact, an attempt on the part of tribal cultures to construct a model for modes of human functioning. We do not wish to dwell on this matter, but would simply point out that conceptions that make a distinction between physical, psychic, and transpersonal factors are superior to Western psychology, because they include the spiritual component. The idea of an interaction between transpersonal, personal, and organic elements gives a more precise and more realistic description of existence than a view that is limited to the notion of a communication between body and psyche. We cannot be certain that tribal cultures believe in the existence of several souls in one individual. All we know is that they make a very clear distinction between body, psyche, and spirit soul. The exoticism underlying the multiple soul theory is evidently a product of the ethnographers' imaginations.

As stated above, ideas about the nature of the soul are similar throughout the world. This fact is usually ignored or simply taken for granted. Without wishing to diminish the impact of cultural contacts and migration, it would seem that the universal conformity of the belief in a soul and of ideas about its function and nature has been confirmed and strengthened, again and again, by the actual living experience of people in all cultures and during all epochs. The belief in a soul is therefore not a tradition but a living reality. It is not our intention to give extensive proof for such a belief in all ethnic groups. This has been extensively provided by other studies. Hans Fischer, for instance, has made a comparison of all the beliefs about the nature of the soul among the peoples of Oceania. We consider the result of his investigations to be representative of all other cultures. They are, in summary, as follows:

- The soul is described as wind, vapor, a shadow, an image, a sketch, a mirror image in water, a phantom, an outline, a reflection, an echo, a double, life-spirit, spirit, a will-o'-the-wisp, that which is immortal in all humans, a form, a similarity, an appearance, a representation, a half-light, breath.

- The soul is the life-principle, it can exist without a body, it is the prerequisite of consciousness. The body only lives by virtue of the soul, is of secondary importance, and is completely dependent on it.

- When no soul is present the body is unconscious or as if dead. It continues to function in a purely mechanical manner, but is incapable of generating wakefulness. Comprehension declines and the body collapses. It is exhausted, weary, and feels cold, growth is impeded, and so on. The soul is the source of health, strength, and warmth.

- The soul is present throughout the body or only in certain parts of it, such as the head, the heart, or the belly.

- The soul can leave the body through all bodily orifices, such as the mouth, the anus, the nose, the fontanelle, the ears, the eyes, or the navel.

- Under the following conditions the soul is disconnected from the body: during sleep, in dreams, in a state of shock, fear, or unconsciousness; in battle or when excited, during the delivery of a child, in illness, and during emotional fluctuations in general.

- The soul leaves the body some time before the actual moment of death.

- The return of the soul into the body is indicated by sneezing. A sleeping person should be woken up gently to avoid startling the soul, which might be away on a journey; this applies especially in the case of shamans.

- Some people can see a person's soul before that person dies; this is a sign of impending death. When someone dies, the spirits of his ancestors are awaiting the soul. When it has completely separated from the body the relatives accompany it on its journey to the Beyond.

- After death the soul remains for some time in a human environment, near or in the place where it lives, or by the graveside— sometimes until the body begins to decompose, but never after that. It then sets out on its journey to the Beyond.

- Defensive rituals are performed because people fear the soul of a dead person. All possessions of the deceased are destroyed so that nothing remains to remind him of his earthly existence and he can thus leave the world of man without becoming homesick. The soul or ghost of a person can cause fear and misfortune; but it can also bring good luck if used as a protecting spirit.

- A distinction is made between people who have only just died, ghosts or haunting spirits, and souls of the dead. A ghost, i.e., a lost or roaming soul, will walk abroad in the neighborhood of the living. The soul that goes straight to the Beyond is called the dead-soul. It can enter people and possess them, and represents a temporary state. It has to pass through further states of existence in order to develop itself spiritually or finally dissolve completely.

- Both dead spirits and ghosts can become visible, frequently in human form, but more ethereal in appearance and surrounded by a phosphorescent aura of light. They can also reveal themselves as animals or in an amorphous form.

- The spirits of the dead can transcend space and thus are able to move from one place to another in no time. They are capable of taking on any shape. Soul substance adheres to fingernails, hair, excrement, and saliva. These can therefore be used for all kinds of diagnostic purposes as well as for negatively influencing or affecting the person in question. The soul substance adheres to all things with which the soul has been in contact.

- The souls of children and sick people can easily be abducted by spirits of the dead. The soul is never safe against abduction by spirit beings. A soul can be recalled into a corpse by magic or sorcery. As a result of this a zombie comes into being.

- Before a battle the soul can leave the body and fight its enemy in a disembodied state.

- The shaman is the specialist of the soul; with his soul he is capable of healing but also of causing harm. It is visible only to seers and shamans.

- Because the soul is not bound by time and space, it receives information in an extrasensory and acausal manner. It can recognize objects over vast distances, journey quickly to remote countries, and associate with mythical beings. The soul knows the psyche of people.

- Since other beings and objects also have a soul, the human soul can establish contact with them.

- Man consists of a body, his life-force, his psyche, and his soul. The life-force (vital soul) is identical with our bodily functions, such as the circulation of blood and energies as well as biochemical processes.[23]

Many notions of magic may be derived from the idea of a subtle energy body. Let us, in conclusion, summarize them:

1. Other living entities such as animals or plants—but in our understanding also dead bodies—have a second body, which is of a spiritual nature.

2. The cause of illnesses resides in the soul body. Healing must therefore concentrate on harmonizing this soul body.

3. The Beyond, in which the soul lives, is subject to laws and conditions of space, time, and causality known in our world, but at the same time embodied in the qualities and capabilities of the soul.

4. Since all material forms not only possess a soul body but at the same time are bearers of the spiritual essence—mana, power,

ch'i, prana—our soul is directly connected with them: the soul and the ensouled universe are a whole.

5. By altering the structure of their consciousness, people of all cultures acquire access to the soul body, to the Beyond, and to a nonmaterial cosmic reservoir of energy.

4

Soul Journeys and Teachings about the Beyond

I rose above the limits of the world . . . my feet were walking on the far side of heaven. —A Chuckchee Shaman [*Bogoras* 1956]

You ask me, but I know nothing about death; I only know life. I can only tell you what I believe; either death is the end of life or it is a passing-over to another form of life. In either case there is nothing to fear. —An Eskimo Woman[1]

We define an out-of-body experience (OBE) as a form of perception, in which all objects are arranged in such a way that the observer perceives them from a point that is not identical with his physical body. Because of their differing phenomenology we must make a clear distinction between OBEs and other similar states, such as might occur during sensory deprivation, in a hypnoid condition or in imaginative and dreamlike states. Nevertheless, OBEs can be triggered by such states, for they are, as it were, a bridge leading to them. Celia Green has established that there is a marked difference between a lucid dream in which the dreamer is aware of dreaming and a genuine OBE.[2] On the whole an OBE is identical with a near-death experience. As was pointed out already, thanatological research has mapped the course of death experiences in which the separation of consciousness from the body forms a central link in an apparently consistent chain of events.

The feeling of being outside of one's physical body can arise in all altered states of consciousness, during autogenous training, under hypnosis, during intense daydreams, or under extreme physical or psychic stress. But this is still a long way from a genuine OBE. For one thing, the characteristic chain of events observed in near-death experiences is absent. The OBE is thus a psychic experience that differs from the normal phenomenology of altered states of consciousness.

The experience of leaving one's body and of undertaking journeys of consciousness is probably one of the oldest underlying principles of religion and magic. Wherever there is a belief in a soul we also find the parallel notion that the soul separates from the body. This is understandable, if we remind ourselves that in near-death situations people frequently go through a spontaneous OBE.

Ideas about the soul and about such states as OBEs are therefore not founded on abstract thought; their origin lies in genuine psychic experiences. C. G. Jung believed that the world of the dead was not a "spiritual invention," but a living experience, no less real than the experiences we have in the material world. This also explains why the spiritual point of view is found all over the world. A central feature of that view is the belief that there is a life-substance independent of the body and that the primordial domain of this life-substance is the realm of the dead or the Beyond. The environment experienced during an OBE is identical with our traditional descriptions of the Beyond, the world of the dead, heaven, or hell.

The term OBE is slowly gaining ground in ethnological circles. Some authors, such as Bourguignon,[3] Dobkin de Rios,[4] Harner,[5] and Halifax[6] have already accorded it ethnological status, and Dean Sheils has tried to produce a transcultural compilation of OBEs.[7] We shall now give descriptions of several OBEs of people from traditional cultures.

A Samoyed in the Underworld

The explorer Kai Donner once asked a member of the Samoyed tribe what he knew about the underworld and received the surprising reply: "Why should I not know about it? I have been there myself." The man went on to describe how, when suffering from a severe illness, he had been prematurely pronounced dead. While the funeral ceremony was already under way, he had traveled to the underworld and finally returned to his own body. Here is his narrative:

> I had been sick in bed for a long time, and the heat (fever) had plagued me badly. Finally my spirit left its body and flew away. I came to regions where I had never been before and the further I went, the duskier it became. I crossed a large ocean through wondrous forests

and high mountains. Finally I reached a ridge of high hills from which I could see a black river. There were many people in the black river all trying to escape from it. Some of them sank ever deeper into the stream and they tried in vain to work themselves out. Others climbed the smooth mountain slopes until their bloody hands were no longer able to continue and they would fall down again. In the river there was a tremendously high pole which many climbed. Large birds were flying around the pole and terrified the people so that they would lose their grip. Others drove back and forth on the river without trying to escape but fished and had a good time on the sandbanks.

In the forests above the river, people were hunting and living just like on earth. A few of them were there with their entire families; others waited for their wives and children. After I had looked around, I walked on for a while and then went to sleep. When I awakened I found myself back on earth and the sun was just rising. Its rays awakened me and I felt completely healthy. Only when arising did I notice that I had been dead, for my mother had dressed me beautifully, brought me outside and covered my corpse with a bark mat, as one is accustomed to do with the dead. My mother told me later that I had died toward evening but that the rays of the sun had given me new life.[8]

Although this narrative contains only a few characteristic elements of the Beyond, the description of the black river with its desperate swimmers is nevertheless quite informative. The souls on the far side of the river seem to lead a comfortable life—at least as comfortable as their life on earth—while the newly-arrived souls are trying to cross the stream and endure great hardship in doing so. It would seem that the water represents a kind of purgatory that has to be gone through before one can enter the world of the Beyond .The water symbolizes the cleansing from the conditions of earthly existence. If a person's consciousness leaves the body only temporarily, however, it can fly across the river without difficulty or sometimes cross a bridge unhindered—an image that can be found in numerous descriptions of OBEs. A near-death candidate's journey to the Beyond would thus appear to be much less complicated than it is for someone who has actually died.

An Arctic Journey through the Air

Our next example comes from Knud Rasmussen's book *New People*. It tells of the Eskimo Angakok (shaman) Kritdlarssuark, whom white seafarers told about Eskimo tribes who were said to live in a faraway place on the other side of the ocean. After long reflection, Kritdlarssuark decided to set out in search of this mysterious country and its unknown inhabitants. To his tribal members he confessed: "Can you understand my longing for new countries? This longing to see new people?" He could find no rest and performed great rituals to summon the spirits, in which all the members of his tribe participated. Accompanied by his protecting spirits, his soul undertook many long journeys of exploration in search of the distant land, until one day he announced that he had found it. He persuaded some of his tribal brothers and sisters to actually set out with him on a journey to these distant and strange people. Being a strong and skillful hunter, Kritdlarssuark acted as leader of the convoy of sleighs during the expedition. Although his hair was already turning gray he proved tougher and quicker than many of his younger fellow travelers. It was said that those traveling behind him saw a white flame shining over his head at dusk. That is how great his power was. When they had been traveling several years and only a fraction of the party had survived the cold, the hunger, and the exhaustion, they reached the great ocean at springtime. Kritdlarssuark told them to make camp; he then summoned the spirits to find out exactly where these new people—whom he felt to be quite close—lived and hunted. While his soul was traveling through the air and over the ocean, his body remained behind as if it was dead. He returned with the good news that they had only to cross the water to make the long-awaited encounter. And so it turned out: When they arrived on the other shore, they found huts and dwellings, but not a human soul was to be seen. They continued their search and in the end found the strangers they had sought for so many years.

According to Rasmussen this long journey is perhaps the only authentic example of an Eskimo migration, extending over several years, from one polar region to another. Kritdlarssuark's report not only throws light on the status and influence of the shaman within his culture and on his role as an existential and spiritual guide, but also explains to what extent people, under the harsh natural conditions of the Arctic region, rely on extrasensory and clairvoyant abilities to overcome the obstacles and hardships of their environment.

A Soul's Flight across the Atlantic

The best known OBE in ethnological literature is that of the Sioux medicine man Black Elk. We shall therefore only quote relevant extracts. While touring as a showman in Europe, Black Elk suddenly became unconscious during breakfast with his friends in Paris. The actual experience begins somewhat dramatically: The ceiling starts moving, the house begins to turn, and rises into the air with everybody in it. It returns to the ground without Black Elk, who remains on a cloud in the sky. He then follows the shipping route across the Atlantic to his home and from a cloud watches his mother at her work. Later, when he actually returned home, she confirmed his observations and felt that she too had been aware of his presence. Black Elk was unconscious for three days. Here is how he relates his experience:

> Then I was alone on this cloud, and it was going fast. I clung to it hard, because I was afraid I might fall off. Far down below I could see houses and towns and green land and streams, and it all looked flat. Then I was right over the big water. I was not afraid any more, because, by now, I knew I was going home. It was dark, and then it was light again, and I could see a big town below me, and I knew it was the one where we first got on the big fireboat and that I was in my own country again. I was very happy now. The cloud and I kept on going very fast, and I could see towns and streams and towns and green land. Then I began to recognize the country below me. I saw the Missouri River. Then I saw far off the Black Hills and the center of the world where the spirits had taken me in my great vision.
>
> Then I was right over Pine Ridge, and the cloud stopped. I looked down and could not understand what I saw, because it seemed that nearly all of my people of the different bands were gathered together there in a big camp. I saw my father's and mother's teepee. They were outside, and she was cooking. I wanted to jump off the cloud and be with them, but I was afraid it would kill me. While I was looking down, my mother looked up, and I felt sure she saw me. But just then the cloud started back, going very fast. I was very sad, but I did not get off. There were streams and green lands and towns going backward very fast below me. Soon the cloud and I were going right over the very big town again. Then there was only water under me, and the night came without stars; and I was all alone in a black world and I was crying. But after a while some light began to peep in far ahead of me. Then I saw the earth beneath me and towns and green land and houses all flying backward. Soon the cloud stopped over a big town, and a house began coming up towards me, turning around and around as it came. When it touched the cloud, it caught me and began to drop down, turning around and around with me.

It touched the ground, and as it touched I heard the girl's voice, and then other voices of frightened people.

Then I was lying on my back in bed and the girl and her father and her mother and her two sisters and a doctor were looking at me in a queer way, as though they were frightened. The English-talker came from the show and he told me how it was. While I was sitting at breakfast, they said I had looked up and smiled, and then I had fallen like dead out of my chair. I had been dead three days, except that once in a while I would breathe just a little. Often they said they could not feel my heart at all. They were sure I would soon be really dead, and they were getting ready to buy my coffin.[9]

The Ghost Dance Movement, which spread through all the tribes of the Great Plains, aimed at restoring the ancient traditional way of life of the Indians. During the Ghost Dances many of the dancers went into a trance and in their visions received advice for a better life. Black Elk, too, became unconscious and his experience is characteristic of an OBE:

After a while I began to feel very queer. First, my legs seemed to be full of ants. I was dancing with my eyes closed, as the others did. Suddenly it seemed that I was swinging off the ground and not touching it any longer. The queer feeling came up from my legs and was in my heart now. It seemed I would glide forward like a swing, and then glide back again in longer and longer swoops. There was no fear with this, just a growing happiness.

I must have fallen down, but I felt as though I had fallen off a swing when it was going forward, and I was floating head first through the air. My arms were stretched out, and all I saw at first was a single eagle feather right in front of me. Then the feather was a spotted eagle dancing on ahead of me with his wings fluttering, and he was making the shrill whistle which is his. My body did not move at all, but I looked ahead and floated fast toward where I looked.

There was a ridge right in front of me, and I thought I was going to run into it, but I went right over it. On the other side of the ridge I could see a beautiful land where many, many people were camping in a great circle. I could see that they were happy and had plenty. Everywhere there were drying racks full of meat. The air was clear and beautiful with a living light that was everywhere. All around the circle, feeding on the green, green grass, were fat and happy horses, and animals of all kinds were scattered all over the green hills, and singing hunters were returning with their meat.

I floated over the teepees and began to come down feet first at the center of the hoop where I could see a beautiful tree all green and full of flowers. When I touched the ground, two men were coming toward me, and they wore holy shirts made and painted in certain way. They came to me and said: "It is not yet time to see your father, who is happy. You have work to do. We will give you something that you shall carry back to your people, and with it they shall come to see their loved ones."

I knew it was the way their holy shirts were made that they wanted me to go back. They told me to return at once, and then I was out in the air again, floating fast as before. When I came right over the dancing place, the people were still dancing, but it seemed they were not making any sound. I had hoped to see the withered tree in bloom, but it was dead.

Then I fell back into my body, and as I did this I heard voices all around and above me, and I was sitting on the ground. Many were crowding around, asking me what vision I had seen.[10]

In this passage the physiological symptoms accompanying Black Elk's OBE are of great interest. He says that it felt as if his legs were full of ants and that this feeling spread until it reached the region of his heart. This phenomenon is characteristic of a numbness slowly spreading through the body, culminating in the feeling of having lost the ground under one's feet and being drawn out of one's body. The sense of being on a swing is also rather descriptive. As if catapulted from a swing he glides through the air at great speed. Many people who have had OBEs report that their movements simply continued as if nothing had happened, although their body fell to the ground. Black Elk's body, too, continues the motion of the swing and flies into space. Altogether, this feeling of being on a swing is a very vivid image for separating from the body.

Frequently mentioned phenomena about life in the Beyond are that the people there have sufficient food and that the landscape is bathed in radiant light. In another OBE—also during a Ghost Dance—Black Elk again is aware of this wondrous atmosphere:

I saw again how beautiful the day was, the sky all blue and full of yellow light above the greening earth. I saw that all the people were beautiful and young. There were no old ones there, nor children either—just people of about one age, and beautiful.[11]

Life without aging and illness and the fountain that bestows eternal youth and beauty are further classical features of existence in the Beyond. They should, therefore, not just be thought of as a visionary fulfillment of our dreams. To complete our picture of journeys to the Beyond we have chosen two more examples from Black Elk. In the first of these he finds himself in a settlement in the Beyond, where he encounters a noble chieftain clothed in light, who tells him about the unity of all things and then fades away. Black Elk describes him as follows:

> He was a very fine-looking man. While I was staring hard at him, his body began to change and became very beautiful with all colors of light, and around him there was light.[12]

On the way back to his earthly body Black Elk flies over a black river— obviously the frontier between this world and the Beyond:

> I started to walk, and it seemed as though a strong wind went under me and picked me up. I was in the air, with outstretched arms, and floating fast. There was a fearful dark river that I had to go over, and I was afraid. It rushed and roared and was full of angry foam. Then I looked down and saw many men and women who were trying to cross the dark and fearful river, but they could not. Weeping, they looked up to me and cried: "Help us!" But I could not stop gliding, for it was as though a great wind were under me.
>
> Then I saw my earthly people again at the dancing place, and fell back into my body lying there. And I was sitting up, and people were crowding around me to ask what vision I had seen.[13]

Like others who have only temporarily visited the Beyond, Black Elk crosses the River of Death without difficulty. It would seem that only people who have actually died encounter problems at this point, because the river appears to represent their individual burden of transgressions.

Black Elk's narrative contains many characteristics of a near-death experience: he loses consciousness; he is taken for dead; he falls back into his body; he has supersensory perceptions (which are later confirmed by his mother); he flies through the air; he is told that he has to return to earth because his time has not yet come; the scenery of the Beyond is beautiful, radiant, and similar in appearance to that on earth; he encounters a figure of light; and he flies over a black river.

A Journey to the Beyond Refused

In 1882 the famous anthropologist Frank Hamilton Cushing was traveling with some of his friends from Zuni—an American Indian settlement in

New Mexico—to the American East Coast. In the course of this journey, his adoptive father Palowahtiva, who was the governor of Zuni, related to Cushing an important episode in his life. When he was a young man, he had been critically ill and had left his body and encountered his deceased uncle, who wanted to escort him to the realm of the dead. At the beginning of this experience the daylight had faded and he was cloaked in darkness, followed very soon after by radiant light, which seemed much brighter than ordinary daylight. His spiritual body then rose from a prone position—his weak physical body would have been incapable of this—but he did not go to the realm of the dead because the journey his uncle invited him to take was prevented against all expectations. Here is Cushing's description of the episode:

> And I became worse and worse, day after day, and it was said that it was finally not well with me, and the message was sent to my elder relatives and others in Taya and Heshota-tsina. Before they had time to come, I was dying, it seems, for I was become but bones with skin over them, and weak of breath, and very slow of heart. And thus I was lying one day in the afternoon, and the light was coming in through the window at the end of the room, but I did not see it. In daylight it grew dark, and it was bad for me but a very short time, for I had forgotten all things. Then I saw again, and the light was coming through the window at the end of the room, brighter than before, so that all things were clear to me, very clear. I looked around the room, wondering that everything was so much better than it had been for so long, but still lying there by the side of the fireplace, feeling that I no longer need lie there.
>
> I saw a broad-shouldered, god-sized man coming toward me, he having opened and passed through the door. I did not know him. He was dressed in the ancient costume of my people. He came toward me, holding in one hand, which was extended toward the door, a riata (lasso), as though he had led a horse behind him. Then he stood over me, and looked down at me and smiled, not greeting me in the least except by this word, "Keshi" (which may be translated "Is everything arranged?" or "Is it all in readiness?"). Then he said to me, "Would you like to go with me?" And I looked at him and said, "Why not? But I do not know you," said I, looking at him as though against a strong light, with my hand shading my eyes. "I seem to know you, yet I do not."
>
> "My child," said he, smiling, "it is not surprising that you do not know me. I am your grand-grand-uncle, and went away from Zuni a

long, long time ago, long enough surely before you were in the womb of your mother."

"Ah, yes!" said I.

"Now, are you ready to go with me?"

"Yes," said I.

"It is well," said he. "In order that this journey, which is long, might not seem strange to you, I have brought a couple of fine horses, such as my people used and I see your people use constantly nowadays. Everything is in readiness for you. The horse is saddled and bridled, and is a good horse. Come, let us go." And he turned to gather up the riata and lead me toward the door.

I was rising from my bed easily enough, when there appeared, not coming through the wall opposite, but already through the wall, the form of a little old man, dressed in the most ancient costume of my people. White was his apparel, with leggings of knotted cotton, soft and in figures, fringed down the front of the leg, with embroidered breech-clout, and embroidered wide-sleeved cotton coat; and his hair was as white as snow and very long, falling down either side of his head in front, and done up in a strange old-fashioned knot behind. His face was surely pleasant, but very old, and he was short, not as high as the lower part of the window. Though so very old, he walked with an easy and majestic tread, noiselessly, more so than the wind.

He came toward my uncle, reached out his hand and laid it on my uncle's sleeve, and said to him "What are you doing here, my son?"

"I have come for this, our child," replied my uncle.

"Why!" said the old man, looking at him not sharply, but in a commanding way, "He is not ready yet. You must not take him away. Go back! Go back, my son!" said he. "For many years he will not be ready."

"But he is ready," said my uncle, dropping his head on his breast and beginning to gather up the riata.

"We are not ready, if he be," said the old man. "Leave him and go."

My uncle turned, not sadly, but thoughtfully, and disappeared through the door.

Then the old man turned toward me and came to where I was lying, looking at me. "My son," said he, "it is not time for you to go yet. We do not wish it. One sometimes learns wisdom through great illness. Therefore you have been ill. You have been ill so that it has been said, 'He will go.' But you will not go, no. For many a long year you will not go; you will become old, even as I am, before you go. Your hair will be white, your face will be wrinkled, and you will grow shorter as you have heretofore grown taller, year after year. Were you to go now, one fewer would be those in the world where so many once dwelt who give us those attentions which we cherish, who sacrifice plumes of worship to us, as was directed in ancient times, who pray to us and greet us, and show that our children among men have not forgotten us. These things are most acceptable to us; we would not miss them from one individual, so few are they who are left among our priests, whose time is not measured out and who has not properly and in a finished manner reached the dividing line of the light of his life. Live, my child! Live many a long year, until you, even as I am, are old. A few days, and your flesh will begin to gather upon your bones, and as you were, so will you become again. And although it may not be pleasant to you to think that you must endure illness and suffering, and many unhappinesses, yet know it is best that this should be so. Live! Become well! And when the time has come for you to go, it will be said, 'Yes,' and we will come for you. Farewell. Be it even as I have said." And the little old man turned and I lost sight of him, and everything grew dark again, and in a moment I heard the people crying, crying, crying about me, and they began chafing my hands and feet, for they thought I had even died.[14]

The cultural framework of this adventure is as instructive as it is confusing. Palowahtiva's uncle is dressed in traditional Zuni costume and the small old man, too, wears clothes of days long past. The uncle has horses at the ready—not so as to lighten the journey, but to make it seem quite ordinary. The journey to the realm of the dead was not to frighten him or be any different from a normal everyday horse ride.

Just as visionary experiences are marked by characteristics specific to the culture in which they occur, so near-death experiences also have a strong cultural and subjective imprint. Our cultural and social conditioning continues to manifest itself even in an altered state of consciousness. It is very hard for the human spirit to escape this conditioning, so it could be said that our history continues to catch up with us. Surrounded by the shadows of its own imagination, our spirit—even while in the Beyond—conjures up countries, places, people, animals, and customs which have their origin in its terrestrial environment. It is the task of science to unveil or unravel this conditioned perception. Transpersonal anthropology specifically aims at tearing away this veil of cultural expectation.

However, Palwahtiva also experiences a number of motifs closely related to OBEs: the tunnel, or rather, the entry into radiant light; the encounter with a deceased relative and with higher spirit guides; the separation from his body; the preparation for the journey to the realm of the dead; his being called back by an important spirit person; predictions about the remainder of his life; the statement that his illness had been ordained so that he might learn to respect the wisdom of his people's traditional beliefs; and, finally, his resubmergence into darkness and recovery of consciousness, in the presence of his mourning relatives.

The Birth of a Prophet

The Seneca Indian seer Handsome Lake was very ill for several years before the gates to the realm of the dead opened for him. As a result of this experience, he began to devote himself to the revival and refoundation of American Indian religion.

Handsome Lake collapsed unconscious during a ritual dance and was caught by three men in ceremonial dress. They said they were messengers from the creator, because he was to be cured of his illness as a reward for the patience with which he had borne it. The message sent by the creator can be put in a few words: People who drink whiskey and make use of evil sorcery, love potions, and medicines that cause an abortion or sterility, must pay for their transgressions.

Later a fourth angelic messenger appeared to him in one of his visions of the Beyond. This fourth messenger he took to be the Great Spirit, who had come to collect him. Handsome Lake made no reply, but quickly asked his relatives not to put his death clothes on him—even if he appeared to them to be dead—and to carefully avoid any contact with his body. He said he would leave them, but would return, because his people still needed him.

He related afterward how he had spent seven hours in the land of the dead. In the company of a guide, who was dressed in blue and armed with a bow and arrow, he had visited heaven and hell and was given information about the nature of the cosmos. These experiences became the basis of the new religion propagated by him. He said that as he was standing on the earth, surrounded by his guide and the three messengers, the Milky Way suddenly moved rapidly toward him and he was able to perceive the traces of the human race as footprints in the form of individual stars of varying degrees of luminosity.

Soon after that a brilliant light appeared. This was the path to the realm of the dead and he found himself walking along it in the company of many other human beings. A number of visions, which his guide explained, had appeared to him, and he came to realize that the Christian religion was bad for the Indians. Later, he and his companions met Jesus, who said that the Indian people would only survive if they turned away from the religion of the white man. After this encounter with Jesus they came to a fork in the road, where the individual souls were told which path to take by judging spirits. The broad path led to hell and the narrow one to heaven.

He took a fleeting glance into the hell realm with all its punishments, and saw alcoholics who had to swallow molten metal; quarrelling couples who argued until their eyes stood out of their heads; and witches being cooked in a cauldron. On the road to heaven he met his dead son and the dog he (Handsome Lake) had sacrificed. His guide had once again given him important advice and prophesied that he would not meet the three messengers again until he actually died, when they would come to collect him and escort him for good to the realm of the dead. Then his guide left him and Handsome Lake returned as a prophet to his small village on the banks of the Allegheny River.[15]

In this very brief summary of Handsome Lake's journey to the Beyond, characteristic themes follow each other with astonishing consistency: unconsciousness, encounter with heavenly messengers and spirit guides; the parting of the ways, where the souls are judged, with one road leading to heaven and the other to hell; a brief view of the torments of hell; walking along the road to heaven; visions about the cosmic origin of mankind; revelations about the nature of the cosmos; and the characteristic promise of the messengers to return at the time of the actual death of the traveler. In addition, Handsome Lake was shown his future heavenly dwelling place but not allowed to enter it, because had he done so, he would not have been able to return to earth.

Prophets and seers frequently receive their inspiration during a journey to the Beyond. Handsome Lake is by no means an exceptional case. On the contrary, it would seem that such experiences form the basis for the revelation of many religions and philosophies. It is worth pointing out, however, that an ascent to heaven or a journey to the Beyond of the kind experienced by, say, Emanuel Swedenborg, Jesus Christ, or the prophet Mohammed should not be confused with a near-death experience, because in their cases the characteristic sequence of events found in such experiences is absent.

I Walked through Rolling Hills

Essie Parrish, Kashia Pomo shamaness, was the leader of Bole Maru, a religious movement combining Christian and traditional American Indian elements. She was a Maru, a dreamer who conducted ceremonies and dances revealed to her in her dreams. She had her first spiritual experience at the age of seven, when she encountered a man wearing a magic cloak of feathers. She was unconscious at the time.[16] We quote her description of this journey of consciousness in the following passage, which contains many typical features of an ascent to heaven and convinced her that it was vitally necessary to revive the religion of her people.

And so I went. Through rolling hills I walked. Mountains and valleys, and rolling hills, I walked and walked—you hear many things there in those rolling hills and valleys. I walked and walked until I came to a footbridge, and on the right side there were a whole lot of people and they were naked and crying out, "How'd you get over there, we want to get over there, too, but we're stuck here. Please come over here and help us cross. The water's too deep for us." I didn't pay any attention, I just walked and walked, and then I heard an animal which sounded like a huge dog, and there was a huge dog and next to him a huge lady wearing blue clothes, and I decided I had to walk right through. I did and the dog only snarled at me. Never go back.

I walked and walked and came to only one tree, and I walked over to it and looked up at it and read the message: Go on, you're half way. From there I felt better, a little better. And I walked and walked and walked and walked and walked and I saw water, huge water—how to get through? I fear it's deep. Very blue water. But I have to go. Put out the first foot, then the left, never use the left hand, and I passed through.

I went on and on and on, and I had to enter a place and there I had to look down: it was hot and there were people there and they looked tiny down there in that furnace running around crying. I had to enter. You see, these tests are to teach my people how to live. The fire did not burn me.

And I walked and walked and walked and walked. On this journey you will suffer. I came to a four-way road like a cross. Which is the right way? I already knew. East is the right way to go to heaven. North, South and West are dangerous. At this crossroad there was a place in the center. North, you could see beautiful things of the Earth, hills and fields and flowers and everything beautiful and I felt like grabbing it but I turned away. South was dark, but there were sounds, monsters, and huge animals. And I turned away. I walked eastward and walked and walked and there were flowers, on both sides of the road, flowers and flowers and flowers out of this world.

And there is white light at the center, while you're walking. This is the complicated thing: My mind changes. We are the people on the Earth. We know sorrow and knowledge and faith and talent and everything. Now as I was walking there, some places I feel like crying and some places I feel like talking and some places I feel like dancing, but I am leaving these behind for the next world. Then when I entered into that place I knew: if you enter heaven you might have to work. This is what I saw in my vision. I don't have to go anywhere to see. Visions are everywhere.[17]

This journey, once again, contains many familiar themes: the bridge; the naked people helplessly thrashing about in the water, unable to reach the other side; the guardians of the other world—the dog and the tall woman; and then the tree, reminiscent of the World Tree, from which the traveler takes strength and courage. After running through rolling hills, fearlessly passing the guardians and crossing a large expanse of water, she reaches a kind of hell, but is not touched by the hellfire. Then we come to the frequent motif of the parting of the ways. Essie Parrish chooses to continue toward the East, along the road to heaven, lined with flowers not to be found on earth. During her long journey she is accompanied by a white light which—as we know from all traditions—enlightens and elevates.

Parrish says that "if you enter heaven you might have to work." This is because someone who has penetrated into heaven soon begins to experience in himself an urge to bring others into contact with the spiritual, to show them that "visions are everywhere," which seems to imply that the other reality and the true nature of things can be perceived wherever you are. For that reason she is able to say: "I don't have to go anywhere to see."

Miriru: The Mating with the Ungud Snake

All the OBEs so far described display a clear structure, in that the mechanism of consciousness being either projected from or leaving the body features vividly in all of them. However, in many reports about OBEs it is not so easy to trace this motif of the soul journey, because some cultures have so thoroughly integrated this theme into their symbolism that the actual psychic experience behind it has become all but unrecognizable. We shall illustrate this by an example from Australia.

The medicine men of the Unambal tribe in Northwestern Australia are generally capable of separating the soul from the body. In this state—known as *miriru*—they consort with the spirits of the dead. The soul (*yàyari*) of the medicine man slips out of his body, climbs a tree, and then ascends to the land of the dead along a thin cord. The helping spirit of the medicine man escorts the soul, and they both watch the dances of the dead, which are then taught to the members of the tribe back on earth. The same applies to the death chants, known as Corróborees, which migrate from tribe to tribe and in this way spread over quite large areas. To bring back a Corróboree from the land of the dead is referred to as "finding a Corróboree."

It even happens that whole groups of tribesmen travel to the land of the dead together, sitting, one behind the other, on long dancing poles, with a medicine man at the front and rear, and are connected to each other by a cord made of human hair. Other tribesmen crouch around the group on their haunches and chant continuously until those sitting on the dancing pole have entered a trance state. If, after the return from the Beyond, the dancing poles show smears of blood, it means: On our journey we encountered dangers and as a result the spiritual substance of the poles was wounded.

The medicine man causes his soul to leave his body and ride through the air on the mythical Ungud Snake—a symbol of regeneration, spirituality, and transcendence—which emerges from his phallus. Before the flight, the medicine man has a feeling that he is climbing a tree, from which he rises into the air together with the Ungud Snake. Although the Ungud force leaves the body, it remains connected to it by a thin thread emerging from the man's penis. After he awakens from the trance and returns from his OBE, the medicine man remembers his flight as if it had been a dream.

During the flight he copulates with the Ungud Snake. Medicine men often report that they were traveling through the air between two Ungud Snakes who copulated with each other during the flight. This can only be observed by the inner perception of another medicine man.

The equation of Ungud Snake and erection, that is to say the combination of regenerative, spiritual, and sexual energies, is reminiscent of the Hindu notion of Kundalini energy, which rises in the form of a snake along the spine and, winding its way from chakra to chakra, promotes the development of higher consciousness. The copulation of the Ungud Snakes, between which the medicine man flies through the air, provides a further vivid image for the arousal of psychic energy, which evidently helps the soul to separate from the body and thus experience its flight through space. The medicine man first climbs a tree—most likely a symbol for the World Tree—before ascending to the Beyond along a string or cord.

There is no reason why an OBE should not be preceded by such a vision of a cosmic tree, which symbolizes the breakthrough to another level of consciousness and existence. This beautiful, deeply symbolic, and mythic description of an altered state of consciousness can be found all over Australia and must be counted among the higher achievements of Australian culture.

Contact with a predominently Western civilization harbors many dangers for Australian aborigines. One tragicomic feature of this acculturation is the comparison many aborigines make between the native blackfellow doctors (bàn-men) and Western physicians. The white doctor comes flying in an airplane. He opens the body of the patient, examines its insides, and then closes it up again. This has many similarities with what native doctors do: they, too, can fly and open the body of a patient, and then perhaps place something inside or even take something out, after which they press the wound together again. Yet, the essential difference—namely, that the bàn-men, as opposed to the white doctors, carry out this operation in an altered state of consciousness—is ignored by the natives. Paradoxically then, the present-day methods of the white doctors reinforce and strengthen the belief of the natives in the powers and abilities of their own traditional healers.[18]

5

The Body/Spirit Connection:
Ropes of Air and Invisible Threads

Many traditional tribes, as well as Western occultists and esoterics, believe that after the soul leaves the body it remains connected to it in a characteristic manner by a string, rope, an invisible band, or a thread as delicate as that of a spider's web. Although only a few examples from a small number of cultures are quoted here (ethnographic literature has scarcely paid attention to this aspect), it can be assumed that this belief exists in very many tribes. In our Western tradition of magic, the experience that the soul (or consciousness) remains connected to the body is particularly well documented. The relevant literature mentions without exception the phenomena of an "astral band." During an OBE, people sense a cable or rope that connects their spirit body to their material body, rather like the umbilical cord between a newborn child and its mother. However, the point of connection can vary greatly; the cord may indeed start at the navel, but can also emerge at the fontanelle, the neck or other central points of the body.

Eliade has devoted a whole article to this phenomenon, in which he compares it to the archetype of the Cosmic Rope that holds together heaven and earth and has a symbolic function similar to that of the World Tree or World Mountain.[1] He furthermore is of the opinion that the Indian rope trick and reports of a thin live worm emerging from the mouths of Australian medicine men can be explained in the same way. However, as Ronald Rose has pointed out, the latter phenomena are more likely due to a kind of hypnotic effect and therefore should not be discussed in the context of the soul.[2] The experience of soul and body being connected by an extremely thin thread arises exclusively in an altered state of consciousness and is felt only by persons who set out for the Beyond or go on a dream journey.

The data collected by Crookall and Green show that during an OBE, Westerners, too, are aware of such an elastic connecting thread.[3] Evidently, we are here dealing with a universal experience. The comparison of this thread to the umbilical cord often gives rise to rather rash explanations, such as that psychic experiences of this kind are nothing more than a reflection of the material connection between mother and child. Irrespective of whether the experience of a body/spirit connection is interpreted as an archetype, a hypnotic delusion, a symbol, or as a real—albeit immaterial—link between body and soul it is a transcultural experience which arises spontaneously in all epochs, particularly in an altered state of consciousness. Given our limited knowledge about such matters, it would be premature to try to arrive at a conclusive explanation of this phenomenon. In the following we give examples from several cultures in which the idea of such a link is highly developed.

The Patagonian Selk'nam describe a psychic vision or an out-of-body experience as an "eye" that leaves the body of the magician and flies in a straight line to the desired location, but remains connected to the physical body throughout its flight by an extremely thin elastic thread, which contracts as the "eye" returns to the body.[4]

In her book *Magic and Mystery in Tibet*, Alexandra David-Neel mentions a Tibetan woman who had become ill some years before she met her. She had remained inanimate for a whole week. During that time she had been agreeably astonished by the lightness and agility of her new body and the extraordinary rapidity of her movements. She had only to wish herself in a certain place to be there immediately; she could cross rivers, walk upon the waters, or pass through walls. There was only one thing she found impossible—to cut an almost impalpable cord that attached her ethereal being to the material body, which she could see perfectly well sleeping upon her couch. This cord lengthened out indefinitely but, nevertheless, it sometimes hampered her movements. She would become "caught up in it," she said.[5]

The Dolgan and the Evenke of the Stony Tunguska (Siberia) believe that an invisible thread connects Man in a straight line to the hand of Main, the supreme God of Fate.[6]

The Washo Indians say that during sleep, unconsciousness, or in a trancelike state, the soul leaves the body, but remains connected to it by a thin thread made of the same substance as the soul. If a sleeping person is awakened roughly, there is a danger that this fragile thread connecting the soul and the dreamer will be broken while the soul is on one of its nightly excursions. In that case, the body and soul are irreversibly separated and death ensues.[7]

The Iglulik Eskimo shaman Aua told Rasmussen:

> Old folk declare that when a man sleeps, his soul is turned upside down, so that the soul hangs head downward, only clinging to the body by its big toe. For this reason also we believe that death and sleep are nearly allied; for otherwise the soul would not be held by so frail a bond when we sleep.[8]

The Huichol shaman Ramon Medina Silva says the soul or life-force is connected to the body by a fine thread as thin as the silky thread of a spider.[9] Similarly, some Australian tribes believe in a thin silk-like thread that emerges from the mouth, and connects body and soul.

The medicine men of the Rai (Northwestern Australia) travel through the air and below the earth on a "rope of air."[10] With the Ungarinvin, for instance, a fine thread emerges from the penis when the soul (yà-yari) leaves the body; the shaman (bàn-man) draws himself upward or, as he says, "on top." This thread not only forms when the medicine man chants about his genitals while in a state of miriru but also during an erection. The soul then goes on a "walkabout," but throughout this dream journey remains connected to the body of the bàn-man by that thread.[11] In a state of miriru devil-doctors can ascend to the realm of the dead along this thin thread.[12]

The shamans of tribes in Northern Dampier Land travel "on top"— that is, to heaven—with a specific aim, such as to cause a rainfall. For this purpose, the shaman carries "a thread like a stroke of lightning" inside himself. When he manipulates this thread, a stroke of lightning comes from his body and thunder is heard, by which the life-force of the shaman is liberated and follows the lightning.[13] The "doctors" of the Australian Kulin and Kurnai also cause a fine thread to emerge from their body. It comes out of their mouths like a spider's web and they climb to heaven on it.[14] The medicine men of the Murring ascend to heaven along a thread the thickness of a stalk of grass.[15] If the "doctors" of the Northwestern Australian tribes and the Theddora (New South Wales) want to visit heaven they produce from inside themselves a barely visible thread along which they clamber up.[16] The Kurnai further believe that the spirits of the dead lower this thread down from heaven. For the Wiradjuri that mysterious thread is attached to the tail of Gunr, the Tiger-snake.[17]

The Parang Negritos see the connection that enables the shaman to travel to heaven in a more symbolic way:

> During a seance of healing, the shaman (Halak) . . . holds between his fingers threads made of palm leaves or, according to some sources, very fine strings. These threads or strings reach up to Bonsu, the celestial God who lives above the seven stories of Heaven. For as long as the session lasts, the Halak is in direct connection with the celestial God by these threads or strings which the God lets down and retrieves after the ceremony.[18] This amounts to saying that a cure is effected by the shaman while he is in communication with the celestial God and, in the last analysis, gives thanks to this communication.[19]

Western mediums also experience a cord connecting body and soul. Robert Crookall has collected a large number of such experiences, not only from mediums but also from ordinary people. The body/spirit connection is described by them in many ways: thread, band, pipeline, arm, cord, luminous silver thread, cord of light, light beam. Some people mention several connecting threads. Others describe the thread as vibrating, alive, and radiating a silvery glow. At the start of an OBE the connecting cord is strong but gets thinner with increasing distance from the body and finally becomes as thin as a hair and is no longer visible.[20]

6

The Out-of-Body Experience

The fact that out-of-body experiences do not only occur in a trancelike and comatose state has been well-documented by the researches of Celia Green. She collected data from people who observed themselves from a vantage point outside their body while engaged in everyday activities such as riding a motorcycle, making a speech or singing a song on the stage.[1] It is worth noting that these activities require one's complete attention so that critical self-reflection is eliminated. As is well known, one-pointed attention is an indispensable prerequisite for all states of altered consciousness. In some people the OBE is preceded by a state of extraordinary wakefulness; in others by a deep relaxation, sometimes accompanied by a feeling of numbness or paralysis. Frequently an OBE occurs as a result of stress, sickness, or physical trauma.

The first reaction to an OBE is, in most cases, one of astonishment and amused surprise. All the same, some people promptly terminate the experience as soon as they catch sight of their own body. The shock of the unaccustomed brings them back to waking consciousness. Most people describe their position during an OBE as "above the body" or have the experience of floating just below the ceiling. Some "fall through their bed" during sleep; others report a lowering of their legs until they are in an upright position, or they simply float upwards. Some even develop a certain curiosity and a desire to explore; they may actually experiment in order to discover the nature of their unfamiliar state.

Objects retain their solid appearance during an OBE, but colors are said to be incomparably brighter and more luminous, as if alive. If an OBE occurs at night the whole room is filled with radiant light and the outside is brighter than daylight. The environment, too, frequently appears to be different from the way it is experienced after the return to normal consciousness. These differences in perception particularly occur during deliberate

OBE experiments. Some people experienced 360-degree vision, were able to see through solid objects, and perceived things over long distances. Yet others report that they had a more comprehensive view of happenings and events, access to extensive information, and the feeling of knowing without having to think—a kind of omniscience and omnipotence. Any question they asked themselves was immediately answered. They also felt that they could "traverse" the whole universe in a flash. This "traveling clairvoyance" allowed them to explore any place in the universe.

The intellectual capacity, too, is enhanced. Ideas arise quick as lightning and thought processes are more active and alive. Despite this, the OBE is not felt to be an analytical experience but is generally described as being passive and observing. People can remember their normal consciousness and believe that the OBE has brought them to the very limits of their attentive capabilities. According to Green, 56% of the people tested reported enhanced wakefulness and concentration. They described the OBE as natural, complete, real, light, exhilarating, free, lofty, energetic, and healthy. At the same time, however, they experienced a certain fear of not being able to get back into their body, by either traveling too far from it or losing control.

Charles Tart has tested OBEs under laboratory conditions and discovered the following prominent features:

1. A floating feeling
2. Seeing one's own body
3. Suddenly being at a place of which you have just thought
4. The belief of having a nonphysical body
5. Absolute certainty that the experience was not a dream

Tart is of the opinion that for most people an OBE will occur, at best, only once in their life. Hardly anyone seemed to have a clear idea as to what triggered the experience; they were astonished and unable to classify their enhanced mode of perception. Tart considers it an unwarranted simplification to equate an OBE with a dream, because "dream" is too clumsy a term to account for all the states that occur during sleep.[2]

It is very difficult to measure brain wave activity during an OBE. To do so, one would have to find people capable of leaving their body at will. The EEC readings taken by Tart were inconclusive because they were confined to only a few people. Tart suspects, however, that low alpha wave activity and a dream-free phase are characteristic of OBEs. As a prerequisite for inducing an OBE he mentions, first of all, a dream-control technique by which the dreamer becomes aware of the fact that he is dreaming and then tries to transform the dream into an OBE. As a second method he suggests the use of the hypnogogic phase preceding sleep, from which, according to him, one might well be able to enter an OBE. As a third possibility he mentions the development of a trancelike state.

In one person tested by Tart the OBE was marked by flat alpha wave activity, a normal heart beat, absence of rapid eye movement (REM) and no significant change in skin resistance. These findings are not only incompatible with the Western tradition of occultism—that connects a comatose state with slow respiration and a reduced pulse rate—but they also contradict the situation found in near-death experiences occurring under extreme psychophysical conditions. Evidently there are many different triggering mechanisms. In some cases people remain in a stable physiological state; in others their biological functions change abruptly.

The out-of-body experience need not end with a characteristic near-death sequence. The following report by the American medium Eileen Garrett is a typical example for another kind of extra-corporal experience. Garrett projects part of herself to other places to gather information. That may sound like an OBE, but her narrative is more reminiscent of what is known as clairvoyance or "remote viewing." Garrett writes:

> I experience an impression of "flowing" within me, and at the same time something moves out from me to an object, yet remains an individual part of myself. By means of an indescribable contact which takes place between the object and me, its "Life" becomes clear. I *"know"* the nature of a tree or a flower or a rock, partly through the occurrence of this sensation. The process is instantaneous and timeless. It takes far longer to describe it than it takes to occur.
>
> I can project a part of myself to distant places and into the presence of people I know—a process which began very early as a game to relieve weary days in bed during the long winters when I was often ill. It has since developed, and is now a phase of my psychic capacity. Within the quiet of my own room, I could extend the nebulous me into the outer world.[3]

The scientific study of the OBE has only just begun. As yet we have no clear idea about its typical physiological features, nor do we know its place within the framework of higher states of consciousness. Is an OBE a unique psychic state or no more than a variant of an alternative state of consciousness? We only know that an OBE can occur in an awakened state, during sleep, in a dream, in the hypnogogic phase preceding sleep, and in other transpersonal states. One thing, however, is certain: The out-of-body state is a prerequisite for the experience of consciousness in the Beyond—an experience which has decisively influenced the religious beliefs of all cultures. Because of that, it holds a central position in the ethnology of religions and, as such, calls for broadly based research.

7

The "True Earth"

In his *Phaedros* Plato describes the place where souls reside after death. He calls it the True Earth. It is the highest region of being; here, disembodied and in indescribable bliss, live those who are wholly liberated but—despite their extremely subtle existences—not yet completely free of human problems. The True Earth is situated in the Pure Ether where everything is clearer, lighter, healthier, and happier. To the Greeks the ether was just as much a metaphysical power as ch'i is to the Chinese or prana to the Hindus. In this realm of existence the seasons are of a pleasant temperature, there are no illnesses, you live much longer, the subtle organs are more transparent than ours, the air is purer than water, and the ether cleaner than air. Let us summarize what we know about this heavenly realm of being, this True Earth.

The few, but nevertheless representative, descriptions of OBES and of the geography of the Beyond permit us to sketch a prototype of this non-material dimension. Certain stereotypes and consistently recurring themes and experiences are found in all cultures. Gayton has demonstrated that the Orpheus myth is widespread in North America.[1] His comprehensive collection shows that both myths and the subjective experiences of shamans show consistent and unvarying features: helping spirits from the Beyond who escort the soul to the other world; the overcoming of obstacles (rivers, bridges, temptations); the presence of a guardian at the entrance to the world of the dead; attributes of existence in the Beyond, such as bliss; similarities with life on earth, and so on.

While some of these themes may be missing in this or that culture, it would be shortsighted to conclude that they are completely unknown to individuals and in the traditions of these cultures. Let us be modest and assume that ethnographic knowledge is as yet incomplete. Quite apart from that, there is a vast difference between the level of experience of a shaman as a specialist in the field of entering another state of consciousness and the tradition passed on by ordinary members of a culture—a fact generally ignored by anthropologists. The spectrum of the transpersonal experiences of any one shaman is too differentiated and specific to be squeezed into the standard framework of a particular culture. The belief that shamanic experiences can simply be subsumed under the prevailing religious tradition is due to the shortsightedness of ethnological theories, which fail to take into account those shamanic insights which activate values and symbols beyond that which is culturally acknowledged.

Furthermore, the early ethnographers did not have access to modern thanatological findings, and even present-day anthropologists have up to now hardly bothered to give due appreciation to the conceptions and cosmologies of death that are being developed. We have tried to demonstrate that no essential difference exists between the death experiences of Westerners and those of members of tribal cultures. We have further attempted to highlight the basic identity of such experiences but the gap resulting from cultural methods of codification is, of course, still very large. We are particularly concerned to ensure that "primitive" conceptions of the soul and the Beyond are not looked upon as hallucinatory artifacts or maybe even as traditions handed down within a particular culture. We are of the opinion that they are the result of true transpersonal experiences which are just as much part of the repertoire of the human psyche as any ordinary sensation or cognitive process.

Modern research into NDEs has restored the long-ignored connection between such experiences and tribal religions. The circle has been closed and the unproductive, unfruitful, and artificial distinctions between the civilized and the primitive mind are beginning to dissolve into thin air. Near-death research has thus not taken us further away from "archaic" cultures; it has led us back to them. We can no longer look upon tribal religions and their ideas about the World of the Dead as limited conceptions. In fact, we are beginning to realize that they have to be seen as a result of expanded experience. The narrow confines of purely discursive thought have been split open and expanded. We are beginning to consider it possible that mankind can have access to a spectrum of spiritual and psychic possibilities exceeding our wildest hopes and dreams. This realization has led to a new type of anthropological field research, in which the investigator approaches shamans as a pupil rather than as a knower, because he is aware of their greater range of experience.

Knowledge about the realm of the dead cannot only be acquired through myths, archetypes or the study of whatever psychological theory of hallucination happens to be fashionable: In every human being there is the possibility of consciousness separating from the body and penetrating the nonphysical world of the spirit. Science is not yet in a position to say much about the nature of such an experience. In any case, for the present it is enough to know that such a possibility exists: anything beyond that leads to speculations that go beyond empirical principles.

Bertrand Russell's *Religion and Science* contains the following passage on the development of science:

> The sciences have developed in an order the reverse of what might have been expected. What was most remote from ourselves was first brought under the domain of law, and then, gradually, what was nearer: first the heavens, next the earth, then animal and vegetable life, then the human body, and last of all (as yet very imperfectly) the human mind.[2]

The exploration of consciousness by consciousness itself is a very strange kind of odyssey from which traditional science was completely debarred by its very methods. But this was not the case with traditional tribal communities. They were the first to unveil the secrets of the self, and it would seem that, to this day, they have remained the true custodians of the mystery of consciousness.

Bertrand Russell's remarks are correct only in the context of the Western world. We have just begun to seriously explore the deeper layers of existence and have a lot of catching up to do as far as the exploration of consciousness is concerned. This is why the study of what is most exotic and wayward to our understanding—namely the inner world of the shaman and magician—has become so important and urgent, for it is we who should be the apprentices of these past masters of the art of entering altered and expanded states of consciousness. In the meantime, consciousness research has already come to realize that structures that were hitherto believed to be objective are beginning to dissolve—that "inside" and "outside," "I" and "you" are so interrelated that they cannot be disentangled and there is no way of measuring the objective "external" world, because all we are measuring are our own yardsticks so that our measurements are no more than observations of our own consciousness.

In the cosmologies of most communities the Beyond is structured in the same way as the terrestrial realm. This is why the Washo Indians believe the Here and the Beyond are mirror images of each other. The souls of the

dead live in the Beyond, and their feelings and actions are in no way different from those of the living. That is also the reason why the living fear visitors from the spirit world, because the souls have not discarded their
human emotions and are capable of inflicting great harm on them. In consequence, the Washo and many other native peoples wipe out all traces
and former belongings of the dead which could give them a clue to their
past. The former houses of the dead are burned down or converted, anything that might trigger a memory is erased, and any reference point that
might lead the departed to trace relatives is carefully removed.[3]

The Yugakir, too, believe that the souls live as they did on earth but that
their world is one of shadows, a world in which shadow souls live in shadow
tents and hunt shadow animals.[4]

The Buryat (near Lake Baikal, Siberia) compare life after death to life
on earth but believe that in the land of the dead there is no pain and suffering, although those living there continue to follow their trade as they
did on earth. Those who could sew go on sewing, and those who knew
how to write continue to write.[5] The world of the Beyond does not, however, need to be an exact mirror image. Many tribal peoples believe in a
sort of "upside down world," essentially not very different from our own,
but with certain things reversed. The Eastern Yugakir say that we look toward the outside with our eyes in this world, but the dead direct their
gaze inwards. The Lapps believe that the soles of the feet of the dead are
pointed away from the earth when they walk. For the Samoyeds, rivers in
the Beyond run "backward," the tips of the trees grow downward, the sun
rises in the west and life begins with old age, so that after birth you get
younger and younger.[6]

To the Cuna Indians the relationship between white people and Indians
in the other way around in the Beyond, so that after their death the Cuna
come to own all the luxury goods formerly in the possession of the white
people, who in turn have to accept whatever subordinate role they imposed on the Cuna during their life on earth.[7] Otchala, a Gold shaman of
the Southern Tungus in Northeastern Siberia, describes the way to the
Beyond as being divided into eighteen sectors, where the scenery and
places show no great difference to what we know on earth.[8] The journey
itself, like all journeys to the Beyond, is marked by difficulties, obstacles
and trials of many kinds; in fact, it seems more like a path of mystical initiation than an ordinary journey.

The traveler to the Beyond faces a great variety of dangers, of which the
river marking the frontier between our world and the Beyond consistently

occurs in all cultures. According to the Haida Indians the dead person, once he has reached the shore of an ocean bay, calls to the other shore from where a figure carrying a red staff sets out on a raft to take him to the other side.[9] In Borneo they believe in a city of souls situated on an island in the Sea of Fog. The traveler has to use a vessel made of iron to reach it, because on the way there hot whirlpools of fire must be crossed. Sinners become very thirsty, because of the tremendous heat, but are only offered a pitcher of molten lead to quench their thirst, whereas virtuous people suffer fewer torments.[10] With the Yugakir, there is an old woman standing on the bank of the river who asks whether the soul wishes to cross for good or only temporarily. The traveler then has to cross the river in a boat and is met by a dead relative on the other shore.[11]

According to the Cuna Indians, there is a house at the mouth of the river where the Guardian of the River lives. A choice of eight different canoes is available, and the river has to be crossed in one of these, all according to the kind of life the traveler lived on earth.[12] In the Solomon Islands, the soul of the dead reaches Totomanu, the river of Living Water, in which it bathes and is thereby transformed into a true spirit of the dead.[13] For the Semang (Malaysian Peninsula) the road to the land of the dead at first has ordinary scenery, but then gets lost in spheres that are increasingly unearthly. A river appears, which marks the frontier between this world and the Beyond. After the soul has washed itself in this river it becomes aware of its destiny, picks a few flowers and then loses the longing to return to the earthly life. The Lakhers (East India) call this river "Lungo," which can be translated as "without feeling," and thus might be an allusion to the loss of the human status as a result of crossing it.

With the Malay Rengma Naga there is a guardian at the entrance to the realm of the dead who extinguishes the memory of life on earth by a slap on the face. With the Lakhers the guardian of the Beyond acts also as a judge of the dead and questions the souls about their lives. With the Malay Sangtam Naga, admission to the realm of the dead depends on passing a particularly dangerous test: A "Mother that devours with her claws" orders the soul to remove parasites from her hair. If it fails to pass the test of the Great Mother, the archetype of regeneration, it remains a ghost.[14] With the Nung (Malaysian Peninsula), the soul also reaches a river in the underworld. The guardians posted there will not allow the souls of sinners to pass, who are either detained or thrown off a bridge and have to expiate their sins before being allowed to cross to the other shore.[15] The Semang (Malaysian Peninsula) believe that at the entrance to the realm of the dead a fearsome guardian awaits them who separates the good souls from the bad, but only after all souls have gone through a kind of purgatory. The way to the land of the dead leads over two bridges: the first of these is like a springboard that catapults souls up into the firmament, while on the second bridge they are pushed into the ocean by a creature called TaPed'n.[16] To reach the underworld (Hades) Aeneas had to cross the river Styx. Charon, the ferryman and guardian of the river, wanted to refuse him the crossing but in the end allowed him to cross as a result of the entreaties by the sybil accompanying him. Similarly, the Egyptians believed in an ocean or sea that separates our world from the underworld, and Sumerians had to cross a large ocean before reaching Sheol, the world of the dead.

The Ojibway Indians, too, have an ancient Orpheus myth, in which a river plays a central role. It tells of the man Geezhig (Cedar) and the woman Wabun-anung (Morning Star) who are planning to be married, when Wabun-anung unexpectedly dies. Geezhig is so distressed that he wants to follow her to the Land of Souls. He roams around aimlessly but cannot find it anywhere. His quest takes him through forests and over mountains until one day he meets a wise old man who tells him that he has been expecting him and knows what he seeks, but he cannot permit him to enter and exhorts him to go back and live out his life, because his time has not yet come, since his spirit soul is still joined to his body.

Geezhig entreats him so fervently that in the end he agrees to help him providing Geezhig will only spend a short while in the Land of Souls. The man then gives him some good counsel and says it is easy to find a way across the river, which seems deep and wide to some, and narrow and shallow as a brook to others. He also promises to guard Geezhig's physical body while his soul is away on its journey. Geezhig should go with the spirits of the dead to the other side. An adamantine bond that can only be severed by death itself would continue to connect his soul to his body. By this link Geezhig would return.

Geezhig falls to the ground and feels a mystic force lifting his soul from its abode within the tissues and fibers of his body. Now his journey to the Land of Souls can begin. Somehow he feels as if he still possessed a body with legs to walk and eyes to see. Geezhig reaches a broad expanse of turbulent water which he tries to cross in a canoe he finds moored to the bank. He guides his craft carefully and senses that he is being watched. Soon he is surrounded by others who are also bound for the other side. Close to him he beholds his beloved Wabun-anung. As their eyes meet, all the loneliness, sorrow, and sadness are washed away as if they had never been.

Geezhig tries to steer his craft to her but cannot alter his course as she paddles steadily for the other side. As Geezhig draws near the farther side, the water becomes more turbulent, full of eddies and jutting rocks. Many of the travelers are overcome, as Wabun-anung's canoe moves serenely ahead in gentle waters. As Geezhig reaches the other shore he is called back to return to the Land of the Living. He turns his canoe around and recrosses the river which has suddenly shrunk to a small brook.[17]

Ruth Landes has recorded an Ojibway narrative of a journey to the after-death or shadow realm, in which the soul reaches a river with a strong current. There is a bridge in the form of a fallen tree; its roots touch one bank of the river and the branches the other. The bridge sways dangerously up and down. As the soul gets nearer it realizes that this apparent bridge is, in fact, a gigantic snake whose head is on the same side of the river as the soul. Members of the esoteric Midéwiwin Order of the Ojibway have no difficulty in crossing the river, because they know the special formula that has to be recited. Others must expect to meet considerable obstacles, because for some the snake will remain still as if lifeless, while in the case of others it will contort itself dangerously over the raging torrents.

Rivers, however, are not the only kind of obstacle. The Haida believe that the dead have to pass through up to five countries in the Beyond. Each crossing from one country to the next signifies a further death.[18] Among the Sima-Sima of Central Ceram (Indonesia), the soul leaves the body and wanders to the World Mountain which rises over nine levels. At each level the soul is interrogated by spirits and may only advance to the next if it has led a blameless life.[19]

According to the California Chumash Indians, the soul rises from the grave three days after burial and continues to roam for a further two days near where it used to live. When it realizes that all its property has been destroyed, it sets out for Similaqsa. Soon it sees a light and goes toward it through the air and thus reaches Similaqsa. The old people of the Chumash say there were three lands to the West: Wit, Ayaya, and Similaqsa. These were somewhat like purgatory, hell and heaven. At first the soul comes to a deep ravine through which it must pass. In the ravine there are two huge stones that continually part and clash together so that any person caught between them will be crushed, but souls can pass through unharmed. Past the clashing rocks the soul comes to a place with two gigantic birds (qaq), each of which pecks out an eye as the soul goes by. The soul quickly picks two of the many poppies growing there in the ravine, inserts them into its eye sockets and so is able to see again immediately.

When the soul finally gets to Similaqsa, it is given eyes made of blue abalone shell. After leaving the ravine the soul comes to La Tonadora, the Woman-who-stings-with-her-Tail. She kills any living person who comes by, but merely annoys the soul which passes safely. The soul finally reaches a body of water that separates this world from the next. There is a bridge that the soul must cross to reach Similaqsa. The souls of murderers and poisoners never reach the bridge but are turned to stone from the neck down and have to watch the other souls pass. As the soul crosses the bridge two huge monsters rise from the water on either side, attempting to frighten it, so that it falls into the water, where the lower part of it changes to that of a frog, turtle, snake, or fish. However, the soul of anyone who has regularly attended the traditional toloache rituals (toloache: leaves from a narcotic plant) has nothing to fear and may pass the bridge safely to reach Similaqsa. There are two roads leading from the bridge—one goes straight ahead and the other to the left.[20]

The Chumash journey to the Beyond thus consists of a series of dangerous encounters. Once again we meet the theme of the river and, in addition, the closing rocks, the gigantic birds, the bridge, and the watchman. But the soul overcomes all these obstacles without difficulty once it has seen the light of the Beyond. True, its eyes are pecked out, but even that turns out to be an advantage, because upon arrival in heaven—which we may take as a symbol of the transformation from a profane to an inner mode of perception—it is given new eyes, which better equip it for seeing in the Beyond.

The dangers are not so great for people who have participated in religious ceremonies and who have made contact with altered states of consciousness by the use of psychedelic substances—in this case the leaves of the toloache plant. It would seem that because of this they are psychically better prepared for the adventures their consciousness encounters in the Beyond. The unprepared, on the other hand, can have great difficulty in overcoming the tests and trials they meet in the Beyond, because they are unacquainted with mechanisms of psychic projection and with the archetypes of the psyche. As in the case of the shaman, a psychotherapeutic and ritual preparation is a prerequisite for a successful spirit journey to the Beyond.

Paul Radin has described the soul journey among the Winnebago Indians. The first obstacle the dead encounter is a deep ravine, the beginning and end of which are out of sight and which you cannot bypass. The only thing to do is to jump straight into it. There is no other way to get to the other side without being hurt or without difficulty. The journeyer then has to penetrate the undergrowth. Here, too, he will only succeed if he walks into it without fear. He next encounters cunning birds who try to confuse him with their wild chatter. It is important to just listen to them in a state of relaxation. Finally, horrible revolting slime rains down upon the soul which it must not try to shake off but must patiently endure. In addition to that, the soul has to run through burning earth and climb a vertical wall without showing fear or doubt. The soul thus must overcome all these obstacles fearlessly and with complete self-confidence.[21]

The psychological principle behind this impressive sequence of obstacles and trials is that one must retain one's equanimity in the face of what appear to be very real threats. The best way would seem to be to walk fearlessly into the danger without a thought of possibly being killed. Whoever can do that will find that the dangers and trials are just a reflection of his own timid psyche. In this way our consciousness learns to overcome and destroy self-hallucinated barriers.

The structure of the Land of the Dead would thus seem to be the structure of our consciousness. Mental discipline and knowledge of the mechanisms of mental projections are the first principle of orientation; otherwise we get lost in the images of pseudomaterial realities we have conjured up, and in consequence have to pass through the torments of hell. It therefore depends on the psychic maturity attained during one's lifetime whether the entry into the Beyond causes us pain or transforms us into a blissful state.

The hallucinations of material obstacles in the Beyond are nothing more than the anthropocentric and culturally conditioned visions of an ego which is still caught in the grip of social and cultural models of the imagination and has not yet learned to adapt to the new environment. The dangers and threats that arise are created by the ego itself. In the Beyond, our pure primordial consciousness is confronted by our thoughts. During such a confrontation we can either react emotionally to the abhorrent slime and the chatter of the crafty birds or we can dismiss them as hallucinations.

All cultures attach crucial importance to the behavior of the hero, the shaman, or the temporary visitor during their travels to the Beyond. The traveler must not become intimidated by the monstrous creatures and natural dangers he encounters, otherwise he is swallowed up by them and thus becomes the victim of his own projections. The best way of countering this danger is a relaxed form of attention that does not get carried away by fear. This kind of attention is typical of the meditative state of Zen monks. They, too, may become aware of unconscious archetypal images. However, by remaining emotionally detached from them they do not invest them with sufficient energy to be overcome by them. The Zen monk allows the images to come and go; they pass his all-pervasive wakefulness without leaving emotional traces in his consciousness. We could say he treats the visions that arise like soap bubbles.

The passage from life to death often occurs almost unnoticeably. The body collapses and consciousness moves on without it. What survives is the psychic presence of mind, a conscious being, while the body, the carnal sheath, is shed by the spirit.

Paul Radin has recorded the death experience and subsequent reincarnation of a warrior of the Winnebago Indians who was killed in a battle, but at first was completely unaware of this; he simply kept on fighting. Only much later, when his relatives did not react to his presence and he saw his dead body on the battlefield, did he become aware of his situation. The fact that his relatives could neither see him nor hear him speak was typical of his out-of-body experience, as was the seamless passage from a state of consciousness dependent on the body to one independent of it as well as the inability to correctly assess the new situation.

Here is how the Winnebago warrior described his experience:

I come from above and I am holy. This is my second life on earth. Many years before my present existence, I lived on this earth. At that time, everyone seemed to be on the war path. I also was a warrior, a brave man. Once when I was on the war path, I was killed; it seemed to me, however, as if I had merely stumbled. I rose and went right ahead until I reached my home.

At home I found my wife and children, but they would not look at me. Then I spoke to my wife, but she seemed to be quite unaware of my presence. "What can be the matter," I thought to myself, "that they pay no attention to me and that they do not even answer when I speak to them?"

All at once it occurred to me that I might in reality be dead. So I immediately started out for the place where I had presumably been killed. And surely enough, there I saw my body. Then I knew positively that I had been killed. I tried to return to the place where I lived as a human being, but for four years I was unsuccessful.[22]

For the Winnebago, then, death is just like "stumbling," after which consciousness moves on without the body. Not until the warrior sees his own dead body does he become aware of the new situation. Among the Siberian Buryat the soul, after having roamed around its former dwelling place for three days, must step into the ashes of the fireplace; if it leaves no impression there, it becomes aware of its new state and sets out for the land of the dead.[23]

In almost all traditions the soul remains for a while near its former home. During this period many tribes try to guide the soul onto the right path to the Beyond by certain psychotherapeutic techniques, recitations, chants, and prayers. For a short time after death, the soul continues to be in a receptive state. In their reports about near-death experiences (NDEs) Western people, too, confirm that clear awareness continues during the NDE; the physical environment is clearly seen and the voices of those present are clearly heard. On the basis of such knowledge many cultures have developed what we might call post-mortem therapies. The Tlingit Indians, for instance, say that the dead like to be sung to; it helps them to find the right path.

The Midéwiwin Order of the Ojibway have collected reports about mastering the realm of the dead. The Ojibway shaman Will Rogers has given Ruth Landes a set of birch bark scrolls on which details about the spirit realm are recorded.[24] According to these scrolls the spirit rite of the Midéwiwin is conducted after the death of a person. The soul continues to carry out its habitual tasks even after death; it washes itself, goes to the spring to drink, and demands attention from its former relatives. The spirit ritual aims at appeasing and, ultimately, ousting the dead, so they will not take revenge on the living or torment their enemies in their dreams. The soul must then set out on a path of dangers that can only be overcome with the help of the Midéwiwin ritual.

Many funeral and death rites, during which people frequently behave as if the soul of the departed were present, are a reflection of such beliefs. The Tibetan and the Egyptian *Book of the Dead* as well as the medieval tradition of *ars moriendi* are likewise attempts to give final instructions to the dead. The dead person should calm down, dissociate himself from his earthly life, attune himself to the new situation, and in particular learn to confront his expectations and conceptions in a detached manner. The geography of the Beyond portrayed in these writings should not be seen as a naive description of other landscapes, other ways of conduct, and other conditions of life, but as an attempt to make the surviving consciousness aware of the fact that it itself constitutes the world of the Beyond. Seen from this point of view, near-death therapy can be described as the most refined and most effective form of psychotherapy, because it shows that what happens to us is no more than a reflection of our individual thoughts and emotions and it teaches us to deal with our projections.

There is no realm of death as such. Instead, the Beyond consists of all those properties particular to our consciousness once it is independent of the body. And so the spirits encountered there are described as omniscient, knowledgeable of past and future, and capable of finding lost objects. The drama of life on earth is revealed to them as a fixation on a limited space/time scale. They perceive past, present, and future to be an inseparable whole, because they see from a cosmic perspective. Unlike people living on earth they do not experience a continuous sequence of time intervals but can comprehend the complete process of an action or a life. They are therefore in a position that is not subject to our conventional notions about time and space. That is also the reason why people try to make contact with celestial spiritual entities. They want to find out more about their destiny in order to be able to deal effectively with the course of worldly events.

However, life in the Beyond is not only beautiful, wondrous, full of celestial light, and eternal. As the hell experiences of all traditions tell us, it can also be painful and replete with infinite suffering. Sinners are punished by having to relive their wrongful actions and attitudes in a greatly intensified way. Hell is often nothing more than an expression of psychic passions in an extremely densified form. The intensification of earthly experiences in the Beyond is an intensification of thoughts and feelings manifesting themselves free from the three-dimensional reality of corporal existence. Consciousness is left completely to itself and indulges in bizarre dimensions. Its unfulfilled desires now move to their climax and, free from any restriction, precipitate each other in a state of unbridled excitation.

These emotional excesses of consciousness could be said to represent hell, just as the idea of a judgmental review of one's life, the admission of guilt and the confession of one's transgressions may be expressions of the emergence of psychic consciousness. The Ojibway believe that on its way to the world of shadows the soul will encounter an obstacle for every transgression in its former life. To overcome these obstacles, it is necessary to expiate one's guilt. For instance, a man whose life was marked by sexual transgressions will carry with him the vaginas of all the women with whom he has coupled and, in the same way, a woman must carry with her the sexual organs of all the men with whom she had intercourse outside of marriage.[25]

In search of a parallel for the way consciousness is experienced outside the body, we should look at data of experiments in sensory deprivation. During these experiments, people who are kept in a room insulated from light, sound, and variations in temperature, lose contact with their sensorial structure and thus with normal reality. Within a few hours they are submerged into an ocean of hallucinations displaying a whole phalanx of magical and paranormal sensations. During these hallucinations consciousness remains closely connected with the body; all that is happening is an alteration and dissolution of the accustomed bodily limitations. If the deprivation continues, a feeling of floating or of being outside the body may arise. However, these experiences and sensations are only a pale image of the much more intense states encountered after death.

According to southern Korean beliefs, after death people must pass through ten gates, at each of which a judge questions them about certain areas of their lives and praises or rebukes them accordingly. They then come to an eleventh gate where all their good and evil deeds are weighed against each other, so that a balance of their life is struck. At a twelfth gate it is decided where the soul is to go. Each soul is accompanied by a counselor or mentor who—like the defending counsel in a courtroom on earth—supports the soul at the eleventh and twelfth gate and tries to plead mitigating circumstances for its bad deeds.[26]

People who travel temporarily to the world of the Beyond and wish to return to earth must not identify too strongly with what happens there. Many legends and descriptions of experiences in the Beyond warn us that the consciousness of a temporary visitor must not surrender too much to the lifestyle of the dead. Visitors should not eat their food or participate in their games, because to do so could mean that they will be detained or expose themselves to the risk of sensual absorption. The traveler to the Beyond must move as carefully as a tightrope walker, detached and in full control of himself. This detachment of consciousness is the supreme rule in both heaven and the underworld.

A Guajiro shamaness has described her journey to the Beyond and the dangers that awaited her there as follows:

> I know the "other world." I was dead; at least that's what everybody thought. I was unconscious; no pulse could be felt and my hands were cold. While I was in this state the spirits took me with them to a

place where there were many dead. I saw many dead people there. Some I knew, sisters and other relatives as well. There were Wayú (name of a tribe) and Civilisados (Whites), but they were separated from the Wayú. I couldn't eat the food of the dead. They eat better than we do; there were enormous amounts of melons (a delicacy in the arid Guajira region) and lots of meat. They have everything there. I was not allowed to eat. I could only walk around and look. Nor was I allowed to touch anything, and I couldn't speak with the dead. Only the spirit that acted as my guide spoke to them.

Many of the dead wanted to talk to me, but my spirit guide forbade me to answer. When I noticed a relative, everybody began to talk. If one of them wants to talk they all come along and want to have a little fiesta, to laugh and tell stories. But I was not allowed to do that, because they would have kept me there and not let me go away again. I could have died. My spirit guide told me that I should just look around but pay no particular attention to the dead.

The dead look like people here. They live the way people used to live on earth, and the place we went to in the Beyond is just like here. There are cold and hot regions, places with water and places without water, rich and poor, sick and healthy. It is just like here.[27]

Many beliefs about what happens after you die feature a whole series of disagreeable experiences through which the individual has to pass: the agonizing crossing of the river of the dead, various painful and confusing states in a kind of hell, and finally, a psychic judgment at which one's whole life is reviewed—a sort of lightning psychotherapy that allows a person to assess his life. These "adventures" of consciousness are generally followed by a positive phase in which another world appears—a world full of radiant light, like our idea of paradise. We must, of course, remember that there is one important difference between an NDE and a genuine death experience: as a rule the out-of-body state is experienced as agreeable during an NDE, even illuminating, and contains mystical elements that should not be overlooked.

Travelers to the Beyond have witnessed horrific sufferings and pains of hell, but did not have to endure these themselves because they were only visiting. They crossed the river of the dead without difficulty and were allowed to take the easy road to heaven. The only obstacles met by them were that sometimes the guardian at the river of death would not allow them to cross at all or that they had to leave heaven sooner than they wanted. On the other hand, their temporary journey to the Beyond does feature a series of adventures and trials, but these are not experienced as torments, tortures, or punishments but rather as tests of the traveler's capacity for psychic and spiritual insight.

In many cultures there is not just *one* heaven and *one* underworld but a number of levels in either—three, seven, nine, or even an infinite number. These levels the soul must attain in succession. They are evidently either stages of psychic development, or insight, or simply phases of life in the Beyond. The descriptions of the Beyond all point to an endless journey of consciousness, such as is spoken of by the people of Pukapuka (Polynesia) who believe in an infinite number of underworlds.[28] The Yuma Indians believe that the soul (Metr'ao) remains for a while near its earthly dwelling place. In the course of its subsequent journey it must pass through three levels before reaching the land of the dead, which is very much like our world except that people do not die there. Nor are there any cold seasons, so that everything grows and flowers all year round. The first level is on the earth itself. The second level (Ampo't) is full of fine dust and situated not far above the earth. The third (Asa) is a world of mist, and the fourth is the actual realm of the dead. People who die prematurely spend a longer period of time in each of these spheres so that relatives dying after them can catch up with them and they can all reach the land of the dead together.[29]

In the cosmography of the Tungus there is a Lower World, a Middle World, and an Upper World. In the Upper World live the stars, the sun, the moon, and a few spirits and souls. The Middle World, our earthly realm, is populated by spirits, humans, and animals. In the Lower World, which is similar to the earthly realm, live the souls of the dead. The Manchurian Tungus believe in nine heavens; the first three are populated by spirits, in the fourth lives the sun, and in the remaining five the stars and planets. In this way the physical and mental universes unite to become *one* world.[30] Plato's universe contained three levels: the sensory realm of our earthly world; the etheric realm or the realm of spirits, demons, and gods—the classical Beyond and the realm of ideas which leads to pure light and all that is good. This latter realm is external to all material existence and thought processes.

Asked about the origin of their knowledge of the Beyond, the members of the various cultures say they gained this knowledge from the experiences of those that have returned and from their shamans. In our Western culture we would have to answer such a question by saying that our knowledge of the Beyond stems from the narratives of reanimated accident victims who went through a near-death experience. The mythical reports of cultural and archaic heroes of their journeys to the Beyond and about the flights of shamans (which are repeatable at any time) provide the members of a culture from early childhood onward with psychological guidance and behavioral models which also help the dying to pass safely to a new realm of consciousness. The epic tales of all peoples are in the form of orally transmitted rituals of initiation or Books of the Dead which prepare man for the great drama beyond death. The time has come for anthropologists to develop new models of understanding that allow them to recognize such reports about journeys to the Beyond as a method of spiritual training. Anthropology must become more open to the possibility of the existence of a consciousness that is independent of the physical body.

It remains to be seen what kind of psychic cosmology transpersonal science will present us with and into what kind of a framework it will place human consciousness in the light of the extension of our spiritual potential. We are certain that this new concept of the world will in every way be capable of holding its own beside the model of the world presented to us by physical science.

PART TWO

Shamanic Initiation

The great sea has set me in motion,
Set me adrift,
Moving me as the weed moves in a river.

The arch of sky and mightiness of storms
Have moved the spirit within me,
Till I am carried away
Trembling with joy.

—Uvavnuk, an Eskimo shamaness
[Ramussen 1946]

8

Suffering Kills, Suffering Enlivens: Sickness and Self-Healing

Western culture and medicine have declared total war on sickness and death: on death because it signifies the end of our earthly existence, and on sickness because it impairs our enjoyment of life. We look upon sickness as bad, something to get rid of as quickly as possible, to put an end to. We see it as something invading us: a virus, a bacillus or whatever, and so we experience it profoundly as an alien process that incapacitates, paralyzes and destroys our body internally, as an unnatural state of affairs that should be suppressed by every conceivable means. In short, sickness and death are the gargoyles of our civilization.

Sickness to us is a blemish, a dirty spot on the self-deceiving mirror of our technological megalomania. Suffering and sickness are seen by our culture as something that emerges from a source hostile to the body, and so our fight against sickness, death, suffering, and physical pain is felt by us to be completely natural. Our static view of the world abhors any kind of change, except perhaps economic and technological. In particular we resent any alteration of consciousness and ontological change.

If we were able to understand sickness and suffering as processes of physical and psychic transformation, as do Asian peoples and tribal cultures, we would gain a deeper and less biased view of psychosomatic and psychospiritual processes and begin to realize the many opportunities presented by suffering and the death of the ego. Our long and continuous battle against death and sickness has so deeply taken root in our consciousness that even modern psychology has felt compelled to take up the cudgel against physical weakness and dying. Consequently, psychic and physical suffering have remained unacknowledged as a means of altering consciousness and as forces and mechanisms of transformation and self-healing.

In recent years a general revaluation of consciousness—that essence which pervades all our actions in life—has taken place, accompanied by a more positive attitude towards states of altered consciousness. Science has thus begun to reassess the sacred knowledge of past cultures and traditional societies which do not regard sickness and death as primarily evil and hostile, but acknowledge their positive internal dynamism. For these traditional cultures sickness, suffering, and death are manifestations of the body's inherent wisdom, to which we only have to surrender to reach areas of perception capable of revealing the true basis of our earthly existence.

They look upon life in the Beyond and on death as a way of regenerating and recovering from our earthly existence. They also see sickness as a process that cleanses us of the bad habits we have accumulated by our false attitude to life. To die and to suffer a severe sickness are part of the basic experience of the shaman's path. This does not mean that every shaman has to undergo this kind of initiation—there are several other possibilities —but in the later stages of shamanic development they are a means of further transformation. We therefore have to let go of the prejudices we have held for generations and of our pessimism towards pain and suffering. We must learn to look death in the face and come to understand sickness as something resulting from an inner imbalance. Only then will we discover its true meaning in the context of our existence. Sickness is a call for self-realization, self-development, and in extreme cases—as the following narrative shows—a variety of shamanic initiation.

On his travels through Siberia, the Hungarian explorer Vilmos Diószegi collected many reports about shamanic vocations experienced as a result of sickness. Once he asked Kyzlasov, a former shaman of the Sagay tribe from Kyzlan on the river Yes, how he had acquired his powers. Kyzlasov reacted with a stony silence. But then his wife began to tell her husband's story:

> How did he become a shaman? Sickness seized him when he was twenty-three years old and he became a shaman at the age of thirty. That was how he became a shaman, after the sickness, after the torture. He had been ill for seven years. While he was ailing, he had dreams: He was beaten up several times, sometimes he was taken to strange places. He had been around quite a lot in his dreams and he had seen many things. . . . He who is seized by the shaman sickness and does not begin to exercise shamanism, must suffer badly. He might lose his mind, he may even have to give up his life. Therefore

he is advised, "You must take up shamanism so as not to suffer!"
Some even say, "I became a shaman only to escape illness."[1]

Sunchugasev, another shaman who was present, added:

> The man chosen for shamandom is first recognized by the black
> spirits. The spirits of the dead shamans are called black spirits.
> They make the chosen one ill and then they force him to become
> a shaman.[2]

Suzukpen, a former important shaman of the Siberian Soyot community near the Suy-Surmak River, narrated the following about his long illness and his calling to shamanism:

> It has been a long time. With two of my brothers, the three of us went
> to hunt squirrels. Late at night we were crossing a mountain, going
> after the squirrels, when suddenly I saw a black crow right in the mid-
> dle of the road.
> We were advancing in single file. I was the first. I came nearer, but
> the crow kept crouching in the middle of the road. It stayed right
> there and waited for me.
> When I reached it, I threw some snow toward it from a branch.
> It never moved.
> Then I hit its beak with my stick.
> Kok-kok. The knock resounded loudly.
> What was all this? What was going to happen to me? Because
> the night before—before seeing the crow—I had already felt miserable.
> Next day I went back to where I had seen the crow. Not even a
> trace of it was to be seen, anywhere! Although the others, that is my
> brothers, had seen it too.
> From then on, from the time I hit the beak of that crow, I became
> very ill. My mind was deranged.
> I have been suffering for as long as seven years.[3]

Among the Siberian Soyot most prospective shamans become ill—girls
between the ages of ten and twelve and young men at the age of twenty to
twenty-five. They suffer from headaches, nausea, and loss of appetite.
When a shaman is called to attend them he says that one of the mountain
spirits wants to turn the sick one into a shaman. One shaman by the name
of Sadaqpan from the Ulug Dag region was ill in bed for a year prior to his
initiation. He suffered from a heart condition, frequently screamed out in
pain and behaved like a madman. He was thirty years old at the time. The
Soyot call the time during which a spirit torments a future shaman "albys."

This period frequently remains a blank in the shaman's life; he cannot remember what happened. He gabbles confused words, displays very curious habits of eating and sings continuously.

The son of a shaman called Sandyk from the area near the Sistig-khem told how his father experienced his call to shamanism:

> At first, my father was sickly; he had a weak heart and so suffered from attacks. That is why people thought he might start practicing the shaman's art. A spirit appeared to him, or rather two spirits: Säräl čoydu and Tämir qastaj. The first one was what we call a "great spirit" (Uluy aza). Near the Khamsara lived a famous shaman of the Aq čódu tribe, called Amyj or Taqqa. He was brought to see my father and told him, "On the fifteenth of this month you will become a shaman." Amyj was a great shaman.[4]

Among the Siberian Tofa, too, shamans become sick before their initiation and are tormented by spirits. A shaman called Anjataj suffered for three years from headaches and pains in his arms and legs. In his dreams the spirits asked him to become a shaman. He slept for three days in a row. When he felt better he followed his calling. The shaman Vassily Mikailovic of the Amastayev clan, who was initiated at the age of eighteen, was so dangerously ill that he could not rise from his bed for a whole year. Only when he agreed to the demands of the spirits did his health improve.[5]

Franz Boas has recorded the experiences of a Kwakiutl Indian, who became a healer after having always doubted and been critical of shamans. One day he went out hunting with some others, paddling in a canoe along the coast. He saw a wolf on a boulder which jutted out from the rock face. The wolf was rolling around on its back and scratching its mouth with its paws. To everybody's surprise the wolf did not run away as they came closer but appeared to be very trusting. There was a deer bone stuck in its bloodstained mouth; it looked at the hunters as if it expected help from them.

The young hunter soothed the wolf, saying, "You are in trouble, friend. Now I shall be like a great shaman and cure you, friend. I will take out your great trouble and set you right, friend. Now reward me, friend, that I may be able, like you, to get everything easily, all that is taken by you, on account of your fame as a harpooner and your supernatural power. Now reward my kindness to you, friend. Go on! Sit still on the rock and let me get my means of taking out that bone." Later he dreamt about this wolf which appeared to him in the form of a harpooner. It told him where the seals were to be found and assured him that he would always be a successful hunter.

As time passed, he always managed to bring home a good kill. One day other members of his tribe found some crates full of food and clothing that did not seem to belong to anyone. But the contents of these crates had been contaminated with smallpox (perhaps intentionally by white settlers). All his hunting companions died and he was lying among them without hope when two wolves came trotting along and began to lick him. They vomited foam all over his body, which they then licked off again, only to vomit more foam over him. They continued to do this until he felt stronger. Then he recognized the wolf he had once saved.

Restored by the wolves, he continued to roam around with his brother wolves. One day, however, his wolf friend pressed its muzzle against his chest bone and vomited all its magical force into him. He fell into a deep sleep and dreamt that the wolf changed into a human being and told him that he would now be able to heal the sick, to project energy that makes people ill, and to catch souls. When he awoke he was trembling all over. Now he was a shaman. It felt good and he was all the time in a sort of delirium and sang the four sacred songs the wolf had bequeathed to him.[6]

Here is a somewhat similar story about Lebi'd, another Kwakiutl Indian. Lebi'd was ill for a long time, three winters in a row. When he finally died it was bitterly cold outside. The snow and the storm continued unabated so he could not be buried. Again and again the people had to postpone the burial ceremony. Suddenly he was heard singing a song, and the wolves that began to gather around his corpse were howling with him. Then the people knew that Lebi'd had become a shaman.

He followed the wolves into the forest, and although the people looked for him they could not find him. On the second day, a song could be heard from far off. In the meantime his house had been cleaned and all were waiting for his return. They had started a fire in his hearth, and the people beat the drum three times. Then Lebi'd appeared, stark naked. He sang a sacred song:

> I was taken away far inland to the edge of the world,
> by the magical power of heaven, the treasure, ha, wo, ho.
> Only then was I cured by it, when it was really thrown into me,
> the past life bringer of Nau'alakŭmē, the treasure, ha, wo, ho.

Lebi'd danced and danced and when all the people had withdrawn and only the other shamans remained, he began to relate what had happened to him, as is the custom.

When he died, a man had appeared to him and invited him to go with him. He had risen to his feet and had been surprised to see his body lying on the ground. They had run far into the forest and soon entered a house where he was given a new name by a man called Nau'alakŭmē, who had transferred his shamanic power to him by vomiting a quartz crystal over him. Singing his sacred song, he had caused the crystal to enter him (Lebi'd) through the lower part of his chest bone .That is how he had become a shaman. The wolves, meanwhile, had changed into humans. As Nau'alakŭmē sang, he pressed Lebi'd's head, first with his left hand, then with his right, and finally with both. Then he passed his hands all over Lebi'd's body and shook the illness out of him. He did this four times.

All the other creatures present then took off their wolf masks and approached his dead body. As Nau'alakŭmē breathed his breath into him, the wolves licked his body. Before that, they had caused his soul to shrink to the size of a fly. His soul was then reintroduced into his body through his head. Immediately after that, his body came alive again. He started to sing a sacred song and—this time in his physical body—set out with the wolves into the forest where Nau'alakŭmē taught him not only how to cure illnesses, but also to send out sickness against others. He had also prophesied that Lebi'd would always dream about him and that he could come to him for advice whenever he was in need of it.[7]

These examples of how two Kwakiutl Indians experienced their calling feature an encounter with helping spirits in animal form—in both cases wolves, who were actually humans in disguise. The wolf vomits his magic strength into the Indian who—as is often the case in an altered state of consciousness—becomes euphoric. In most cases the experience of being resurrected after terrible torments, sickness, and near-death is accompanied by a feeling of euphoria, because the suffering has annihilated all former characteristics of the personality. The sickness is a cleansing process that washes away all that is bad, pitiful, and weak. It floods the individual like a raging river and cleanses it of all that is limited and dull. In this way the sickness becomes a gateway to life. In all cultures people who have a near-death experience encounter beings that represent the resurrection of life. These beings bestow life; they are bearers of divine power. After the sickness—providing it was sufficiently severe and frightening—a new life, a transformed existence, begins.

Lebi'd's story shows another typical NDE characteristic. As he "dies" and leaves his body, he is met by a being from the Beyond and taken to a "house"—symbolic of a transcendent state—where he is not only given a new name to confirm his inner transformation, but quartz crystals—symbols of transparence, illumination, and magical power—are placed into his chest. The life-giving spirit splits off these crystals from himself and spits them out, thereby allowing Lebi'd to share the nature and the living strength of the spirit.

What happens next reminds one very strongly of methods of magnetopathic treatment, the laying on of hands by which negative energy—the illness—is stroked away or literally shaken out of the body. This practice is common to psychic healers the world over. The restored Lebi'd is now the possessor of higher knowledge. The wolves and the life-bringer accompany him to his dead body and cause his soul to reenter it. Thereafter the life-bringer is Lebi'd's helping spirit who will stand by his side whenever he heals anyone. Lebi'd became a shaman with the help of the essence of life itself, supported by wolves representing the forces of the animal realm. He became a Chosen One, capable of seeing life and nature undistorted, because the mask of earthly ignorance and delusion was removed from his eyes.

A comparable experience is that of the Paviotso shaman Reno who dreamt that he visited the realm of the dead. Often, when dreaming of places in the Beyond, he felt weak and miserable. For a whole year he was close to dying. During his dreams his body became as rigid as a board, and the souls of the dead came to steal his soul. All this he related after his dream journeys. He began to realize gradually that he was meant to be a shaman and that he had to accept the power. However, his health did not improve until his father, also a shaman, healed him by tremendous efforts which almost cost him (the father) his life.[8]

Reno, then, was brought close to death by terrible sufferings. His body became cataleptically rigid, as often happens in a deep trance, and the souls of the dead were out to steal his soul. This occurred several times during his long sickness. We may assume that he acquired basic knowledge of shamanic ways of seeing during his journeys to the Beyond.

On the Indonesian Mentawai Islands, the calling to shamanism is also preceded by a sickness—in this case malaria—sent by the heavenly spirits. The person destined to become a shaman dreams that he ascends to heaven or goes into the forest to look for monkeys. If the spirits abduct someone chosen for shamanism to heaven he is given a beautiful new body like that of the spirit beings. After his return to earth, the spirits help him with his healing. In this way a new seer is born, known as a Si-kerei, some-one who possesses magical powers: "seeing eyes" and "hearing ears."[9]

At this point we might properly ask whether the sickness is sent by the heavenly spirits themselves or whether it should be seen as a byproduct of a person's spiritual growth, of a process aimed at revealing to the sick initiate the heavenly—respectively, his inner—world. Be that as it may, in many tribal cultures the initial impetus towards transformation comes either from heaven or from the underworld, because that is where you are given a new body—the spirit body of the beings in the Beyond which equips the initiate with their knowledge and powers and enables him to transcend matter, space, and time.

Among the Zulus someone destined to become a shaman (Inyanga) suddenly becomes ill, behaves in a curious manner and is unable to eat normal food. He will only eat certain things. He continually complains of pain in various parts of his body and has the most incredible dreams—he becomes a "house of dreams." He is quickly moved to tears, weeping at first softly to himself and then loudly for everyone to hear. He may be ill for several years before he sings his first great song. When that happens, the other members of the tribe come running and join in. Now everyone is waiting for him to die, which might happen any day. The whole village finds hardly any sleep at night, because someone about to become an Inyanga causes a great deal of unrest. He hardly sleeps. And if he falls asleep, he soon wakes up and begins to sing even in the middle of the night. He may get it into his head to climb onto a roof and jump around like a frog, shaking himself and singing. His helping spirit keeps whispering into his ear and promises him that he will soon be able to give advice to those that come to him. He can hear the whistling of the spirits and converses with them in the language of the humans. Often, however, he does not im-mediately realize what they are trying to tell him.

At this point it is still unclear whether he suffers from a sickness that will turn him into an Inyanga, or whether he is just crazy. If the people think that he is destined to become a shaman they say, "Ah, now we can see. It's in his head." The helping spirit (Itongo) is at first perceived rather vaguely by the sick person, who cannot properly understand it. For that reason, the other members of the tribe must help him to disentangle what he has seen and heard. Soon the Itongo will say, "Go to so-and-so and he will give you medicine." After that the initiate improves. When the helping spirit finally promises to stand by him he says to the sick person, "It is not you that will talk to people but we will tell them everything they need to know, whenever they come for advice." If the relatives of the sick man do not want him to become a shaman they summon another recognized healer and ask him to appease the spirit. In that case the spirit may leave the man but in all likelihood he will be plagued by sickness for the rest of his life. Even if he does not become an Inyanga, he still has higher knowledge and the people say of him, "If he had become a seer he would have been a great seer, a first-class seer."[10]

We shall now relate the story of James, a Zulu, who unexpectedly left the Mission Station because he felt very weak but did not want to be treated by the Mission doctors as he feared that he might be sent to a place for the insane. So he went back to his native village. The first signs of his sickness consisted of a tingling and drawing feeling that spread from his toes and fingers, through his arms and legs, to the whole of his body and made him feel as if there were a heavy weight on his shoulders.

> But it is not that only; but now there are things which I see when I lie down. When I left home I had composed three songs, without knowing whence they came; I heard the song, and then just sang it, and sang the whole of it without ever having learnt it.
>
> But that which troubles me most now is that there is not a single place in the whole country which I do not know; I go over it all by night in my sleep; there is not a single place the exact location of which I do not know.
>
> I see also elephants and hyenas, and lions and leopards, and snakes and full rivers. All these things come near to kill me. Not a single day passes without my seeing such things in my sleep.
>
> Again I see that I am flying, no longer treading on this earth.

He was then asked whether he still believed in the Lord. He answered:

> No. To do so is death to me. If I try, saying "Let me pray," it is as if I summoned all kinds of death to come and kill me at once. The Lord's tidings are plucked out of me by this disease. It alone has now the dominion over me.[11]

The Mundu mugo, the shaman of the Kenyan Kikuyu, receives his calling and his spiritual support from God (Ngai). It is however assumed that he has an inborn disposition for healing. The impulse for the initiation as a Mundu mugo arises from a sickness characterized by dramatic dreams, hallucinations, inability to concentrate, weak eyesight and abnormal forms of behavior. At the same time his family is visited by a series of misfortunes and accidents. If another Mundu mugo then describes all these signs as meaningful, the initiation is confirmed and publicly sanctioned.

This is followed by the initiation ceremony. If the novice is poor and cannot afford the expensive festivities involved, a ritual is nevertheless performed to relieve his suffering and to accord him the status of an "unconfirmed" Mundu mugo. If he is rich and can pay for the appropriate festivities, he becomes a fully recognized Mundu mugo. Thereafter he specializes in particular skills such as prophecy, diagnoses of illnesses, knowledge of herbs, restoration of the fertility of women, unmasking of sorcerers, or curing mental illness.[12]

According to Harvey, the calling of Korean shamanesses expresses itself in various physiological disturbances, conspicuous forms of social behavior, outrageous activities, impoliteness, and a lifestyle that inverts traditional cultural values. For instance, the prospective shamaness may wear winter clothes in summer, bathe in cold water in winter, reveal secrets which are taboo to mention, or begin to tell the fortune of anyone who happens to be passing in the street. This illness is known as Sinbyong, "caught by the spirits" or "the spirits have descended," and may be accompanied by visual and auditory hallucinations. At first the relatives find it difficult to establish whether such a woman is really mentally deranged or whether they are dealing with a vocation for shamanism, because in many cases the initial symptoms are practically indistinguishable. The Koreans believe that the spirits visit especially those whose maum (heart or soul) are "split" and upon whom a tragic fate has been bestowed.[13]

In Korea, shamans (Mu dang), 60,000 of whom are at present organized in a professional association (the number of nonregistered shamans is estimated at over 140,000),[14] are no longer accorded a high social status but find themselves on the lowest rung of the social ladder, together with prostitutes, shoe menders, soothsayers, Buddhist monks, and dancing girls. Many more women than men feel called upon to become a Mu dang, although there are some men or hermaphrodites who feel attracted to shamanism. On the Korean mainland, 90 percent of practicing shamans are women; on Cheju Island, up to 60 percent. The behavior and dress of male shamans is extremely effeminate.

The calling for shamanism occurs in three ways:

1. By birth into or adoption by a Mu dang family
2. By Mu dang apprenticeship
3. By a spontaneous feeling of vocation

The most frequent case, the psychic experience of a calling, begins with a sickness that cannot be cured by customary methods of treatment. The person concerned hears voices, speaks in tongues, can only absorb liquid nourishment, and grows as thin as a skeleton. Bouts of depression and a manic compulsion to dance until unconscious alternate. The sick person goes on long walks into the mountains or to the sea and has dreams in which helping spirits give instructions and reasons for founding a new cult. The novice shaman is overcome by visions of the native pantheon of Gods or may acquire his objects of power by suddenly falling to the ground. After a tragic event such as the death of a relative, an epidemic, famine or economic ruin, a person may become a Mu dang apprentice if the Buddhist monasteries, to which the mentally ill go to be cured, are unable to alleviate the symptoms of the sickness. In such cases the spontaneous calling is followed by an apprenticeship, extending over several years, with an older and experienced Mu dang.[15]

We would like to illustrate the genesis of this sickness with reports about the calling of two Korean shamanesses:

> Mrs. Lee Kum Sun's boyfriend died at the age of twenty, which greatly distressed her. Shortly before that, her parents had arranged for her to be married to her present husband but her dead boyfriend kept appearing to her in her dreams. At the age of thirty-two she began to see him in her dreams continually and developed the first signs of her sickness. One day she dreamt that she ran barefoot and completely naked to the foot of a mountain where a white-bearded man appeared to her and promised her health and good fortune. At the age of forty she was initiated by an old shamaness. After that everything went well and her health was restored.

> Mrs. Oh Un-sook disliked her husband from the very beginning. After several years, unusual symptoms developed. She lost her appetite, was unable to eat meat or fish, only drank cold water, and developed headaches. She spent most of her time alone. These symptoms lasted about ten years. When she was forty years old she dreamt of thunder and lightning and of a pillar of light that struck her head three times. Thereupon three old men from heaven appeared to her in a dream. One day she saw a vision of a great general riding on a white horse who approached her. Thereafter she dreamt many times that she went to bed with this general. At the age of forty-seven she was initiated as a shamaness and all her symptoms disappeared.[16]

In one of these two shamanesses the calling was triggered by the tragic loss of a lover, in the other by an unhappy marriage. Psychologists would no doubt say that these are clear examples of a desire to escape an unsatisfactory reality. However, such a conclusion would be somewhat premature. We must not overlook the fact that an unhappy marriage and the death of a lover are traumatic experiences which can provide fertile ground for entering an altered state of consciousness. Traumatic shock can cause the collapse of psychic structures, whereupon a more subtle and paranormal sensitivity begins to grow from the ruins of normal consciousness. Lee Kum Sun met a white-bearded old man—the archetype of wisdom— and Oh Un-sook had a vision of a Korean cultural hero—also a symbol of wisdom and strength. Moreover, Oh Un-sook shares the General's bed—a further pointer to her intimate connection and fusion with the transpersonal. At the same time this love affair reminds one of the type of spirit wedding discussed in a later chapter.

Oh Un-sook's vision of a pillar of light also reinforces the impression that we might be dealing with an illuminating manifestation which afforded her contact with the Beyond and heavenly beings. These two simple narratives indicate that we may not be confronted by abstruse creations of a deviant mind but rather a high form of intuitive insight.

Eduardo Calderón, a Peruvian healer (*curandero*), began to be plagued by disquieting dreams and visions in his childhood:

> During my youth from more or less the age of seven or eight years I had some rare dreams. I still remember them. I remember dreams in which I flew, that my ego departed from the state in which it was, and I went to strange places in the form of a spiral. Or I flew in a vertiginous manner: ssssssssssss, I departed. I tried to retain myself and I could not. Strange dreams, strange. I had these until the age of more or less twelve or thirteen. . . .
>
> I have seen things as if someone opens a door and the door is closed. I have had nightmares, but not ordinary ones. I have seen myself introduced through a hole in the air, and I went through an immense, immense void. I have felt numbness in all my body as if my hands were huge but I could not grasp. I could not hold up my hand.[17]

He began to follow his call to serve mankind at an early age. However, his ambition to study medicine was frustrated by the poverty of his family. So he had no other choice than to earn a living by the use of his artistic talents.

At the age of twenty-one he developed a typical shamanic illness that modern medicine was unable to diagnose or treat therapeutically:

> In Lima I was studying fine arts and suddenly I began drinking and spending everything on drink. I came down with a rare sickness. It happened that on one occasion I saw a cat on my left shoulder. It was enough that with that impression of a cat everything that I did was overturned . . . and I lost the power to hold things in my hand and to stand up. I completely lost all my strength. I could not hold myself up in a standing position and walked like a sleepwalker, according to what they tell me.[18]

Eduardo's family had faith in the health abilities of curanderos and called in a woman healer conversant with the properties of herbs. She gave Eduardo a mixture of juices extracted from plants, whereupon he vomited up a dark brew despite the fact that he had not drunk any other liquid. He immediately improved. On the basis of his experiences during his sickness he decided to become a healer. He supported himself by working as a longshoreman and by producing pottery at home. At the same time he became the apprentice of a local curandero. He also studied with various shamans in Chiclayo, Mocupe, and Ferranafe in northern Peru. For several years he acted as assistant to these curanderos until finally his teacher in Ferranafe pronounced him fully qualified.

He was twenty-eight years old at the time and had served four years as an apprentice shaman. He swore never to misuse his powers and to apply them only for the benefit of mankind. Eduardo considers shamanism to be a simple matter of "seeing," a skill or trade anyone is capable of acquiring providing he regularly trains himself in it. It is however open to question whether such training and practicing alone will ensure success, because Eduardo—as his life history shows—was called to his trade by a higher power. Moreover, we must not exclude the possibility that he inherited certain shamanic propensities because both his grandfathers were shamans.

From a description given by Sieroszewski we can gain an idea of the liberating and healing qualities of the shamanic seance when the shaman himself feels stricken and debilitated by illness. The Yakut shaman Tüsput, who was critically ill for more than twenty years, could only find relief from his suffering whenever he conducted a seance during which he fell into a trance. In the end he fully regained his health by this method. However, if he held no seances over a long period of time he once again began to feel unwell, exhausted, and indecisive.[19] In general, the symptoms of an illness subside when a candidate for shamanism enters a trance. The same phenomenon was observed by Shternberg in the case of a Siberian Gold shaman that even his colleagues were unable to cure. Only when he learned how to enter a trance state did his illness leave him.[20] Similarly, Sancheyev mentions a shaman who at first refused to follow his calling but was forced by illness to consort with the spirits and hold seances, which in the end led to his recovery.[21]

The story of the Yakut shaman Uno Harva also features a relief from illness once he agreed to take up shamanism:

> I became ill when I was twenty-one years old and began to see with my eyes and hear with my ears things others could neither hear nor see. For nine years I fought against the spirit, without telling anyone what had happened because I feared they might not believe me or make fun of me. In the end I became so ill that I was close to death. So I began to shamanize, and very soon my health improved. Even now I feel unwell and sick whenever I am inactive as a shaman over a longer period of time.[22]

Adrian Boshier describes the illness of Dorcas, the daughter of a Methodist preacher, who is now a recognized Zulu shamaness (sangoma). For three years she was bedridden and during this time could only absorb small quantities of food and drink. At night she left her body and visited distant places; in this way she traveled everywhere. Even the white doctors were at a loss. Then one night her dead grandfather appeared to her in a dream. He said he would enter her body and continue his work on earth in this fashion. Being a devout Christian she did not agree to this. After that, other shamans appeared in her dreams, scolded her, and called upon her to become one of them. These visions became more and more frequent, passing before her inner eye like pictures on a cinema screen.

One night several famous sangomas came to her bedside. Chanting a song, they seriously advised her to submit and make a shamanic headdress for herself. She still failed to understand what was happening and wanted to be cured by ceremonies and rites of the Apostolic church. She was taken to a river to be christened. They guided her into the water, and just as they were about to submerge her she was lifted up by a gigantic snake under her feet—her grandfather! Her mother then took her to an aunt who was herself a shamaness. Soon many other healers and shamans assembled, beating their drums and exhorting her to get up and sing. She then danced and sang hour after hour. That was the beginning of her training, and from then on she followed the instructions of the spirits.[23]

A refusal to follow the call leads to unnecessary suffering. The South American Guajiro shamaness Graziela, for example, was asked by her helping spirits to travel with them to the other world. But she says:

> I do not like traveling to these distant places. My spirits often invite me to go there, but I prefer not to go with them. Sometimes I say to them, "I do not want to go with you." Whenever I turn down such an invitation I develop a fever and become very ill. That is my punishment. Then I must chew manilla to get better again. I receive many invitations.[24]

Every sickness is an attempt at healing and every healing an attempt to escape from the everyday neurosis of ordinary consciousness so as to arrive at a more subtle and, in the last resort, superhuman form of perception. The sicknesses that arise as a result of a calling are surely the highest form of illness—a sacred illness which by its power makes it possible for mystical and metaphysical insights to arise. As we have seen, this frequently happens without regard to the feelings and wishes of the chosen one who, in most cases, is not aware of the fact that his body is undergoing an initiation. To resist such a process of transformation is a natural reaction to that which is unaccustomed, mysterious, and without limit. The initiate struggles both against his pain and suffering as well as the future social functions he will have to perform as a shaman, which all too often will deprive him of the possibility of leading a normal everyday life.

Resistance to psychophysical change and a disintegration of the normal structure of existence has always been part and parcel of the transformative process. Because of this, it forms at least a partial aspect of every rite of transformation. Rejection of the new and unknown is a standard human response. True, existence itself is change, but the leap from three-dimensional to multidimensional perception and experience is the most fundamental change. To reach a translogical form of knowledge or realm of wisdom, celestial beauty, and spiritual essence is one of the most ancient experiential goals of mankind.

The central issue raised by this chapter is therefore: Why do we have to become ill before we can accept a new insight? Why is the entry into a more comprehensive level of experience so frequently marked by sickness or, one might say, a cleansing process? Purification plays a prominent role in the life of all communities that are close to nature. While our culture attaches primary importance to physical cleanliness, other cultures still have knowledge of psychic and spiritual methods of purification which might well be compared to our psychotherapeutic techniques. We see life as a relatively uniform and continuous process marked by merely peripheral changes, whereas so-called primitive cultures tend to see personal development as a series of leaps from one mode of existence to another. This is clearly shown by the traditional rites of passage conducted not only at birth, puberty, and death but especially at the breakthrough from everyday existence to a spiritual dimension, as experienced by religious adepts—the leap from the human to the superhuman.

The important stages in a person's life are connected by periods of inner purification so that the individual, being properly prepared and in a clear state of mind, undistracted by customary thought processes and memories, may progress to a new and unburdened existence. This purification may take many forms: either purely physical such as vomiting, perspiration, fasting, pain, fever, and cleansing of the body with water, or intense psychic isolation during which the memory of the constitution of one's ego is shed; extreme exhaustion which disrupts the regular functioning of the organism and the psyche; and actual sickness which brings internal obstacles and defilements to the surface and, indeed, expels them, thereby producing a heightened sensitivity for the process of being—a sensitivity that ultimately enables the shaman to diagnose and heal the illnesses of others.

Frequently the shaman enters a patient's state so thoroughly that he himself experiences the symptoms and pains of the illness and, in this way, acquires special knowledge as to its cause. There are several reports about shamans who went so far as to take a patient's illness upon themselves in order to destroy it. In the course of their painful existence, many shamans have physically experienced countless illnesses and are therefore conversant with a wide range of physical and psychic reactions.

Modern Western medicine might consider it superfluous, even somewhat obscure or eccentric, for a healer to involve himself so intensely in the process of an illness. Nevertheless, the logic of doing so can hardly be doubted. It is based on the premise that someone who has himself experienced and overcome the pain and suffering of an illness, will best be able to diagnose and effectively treat it. Western medicine, of course, rejects the image of the wounded healer, the sick doctor who has cured himself. It places too much stress on the purely technological manipulation of the patient and has therefore become increasingly alienated from the actual experience of the patient's condition.

If we wanted to summarize the effect of a long psychosomatic sickness on a shaman, we would have to say that the essential criterion lies in his talent to enter into an intensified exchange with reality, thereby transcending the material demarcations between objects and people. It lies in the very nature of the shaman to perceive the pulse of the universe in himself and others and, by going along with it, to influence and change it. His approach is based on empathy and unity with actual life-forces and therefore is inimically incompatible with the dichotomies and codified differentiations of a materialist philosophy.

A sickness that is understood as a process of purification, as the onset of enhanced psychic sensitivity giving access to the hidden and highest potentials of human existence, is therefore marked by very different characteristics than those ascribed to pathological conditions by modern medicine and psychology—namely, that suffering has only negative consequences. According to the modern view illness disrupts and endangers life, whereas the shaman experiences his sickness as a call to destroy this life within himself so as to hear, see, and live it more fully and completely in a higher state of awareness.

The symptoms of shamanic sickness are in most cases confused, undefinable, and follow no known pattern. Moreover, physical, psychic, and social reactions are closely interwoven. Particularly noticeable are forms of behavior that reject, and even deride and ridicule, accepted customs and standards. Initiates become holy fools who systematically put the world on its head or indulge in unworthy, shameless, and perverse behavior incompatible with established morality.

The fool exposes the limitations of human criteria, confronts us anew with the undefined nature of our cosmic existence, leads us backstage to make us aware of the artificiality of our cultural values, and then shows us a world without limit, because it is neither categorized nor ordered in accordance with artificial opposites. The sick jester removes these opposites, tears down external and internal barriers and causes us to tumble head over heels from our tailormade world of lines and demarcations into a more comprehensive and holistic dimension that has no beginning or end.

We have seen that often not only the shaman himself but his whole family are visited by misfortune, as for instance in the case of the *kikuyu* or the Korean shamanesses. In Siberia, too, the relatives of a shaman are "sacrificed" as soon as signs of shamanic sickness appear in a member of the clan. The effects of the call to shamanism are wide-ranging, and sacrifices have to be made for that call.

The Koreans talk about a "bridge of people" (*indari*) that comes into being when a member of the family is chosen to be a shaman and another member has to die as a result of this. They refer to this process as "spanning a bridge over a human being" (*indari nonnunda*). A God has "entered into" the shaman and, in return, demands another human life. However, if the clan is willing to submit the member destined to become a shaman to the requisite ceremony of initiation as soon as as the first symptoms of obsession or sickness manifest themselves, indari is not inevitable. But most families are unwilling to have a shaman in their circle, so the Indari phenomenon occurs quite frequently. According to the investigations made by Cho Hung-Youn, indari occurs on average seven or eight times in every twenty cases of shamanic vocation.[25]

Frequently we find a combination of sickness and out-of-body experiences. The suffering drains the organism of its will to live, whereupon consciousness feels itself freed of the body and sheds it like a lifeless container. The dying are led to far and distant places. "There is not a single place the exact location of which I do not know," says the Zulu shaman James. Again and again we are told, "At night in my sleep I go everywhere." The Peruvian healer Eduardo flies "into the air through a hole," and Dorcas, the Zulu sangoma, leaves her body at night to fly through space.

If the near-death experience deepens, the person concerned establishes contact with supersensible entities. The journeyer enters a world which presents itself to him symbolically in many different ways: as "a house of life," a "wise old man with a white beard" or a spirit animal that transmits a new understanding of life to him. Sometimes the spirits furnish humans with a body in their own image, as is reported by the natives of the Mentawai Islands, or the bringer of life—as in the case of Lebi'd—vomits a crystal into the adept which fills him with supernatural strength.

His journeys to the Beyond often take the shaman to what he calls "the edge of the world," which we can take to mean the limits of human existence. Equipped with qualities normally found only in spirits or spirit animals, and made sacred by his contact with wise men and bringers of life, the shaman now truly has "eyes that see and ears that hear." He now has "a split soul and a split heart" or feels like "a house of dreams." The sacredness of the world has given him power and thereby has chosen him, sometimes against his own will, to act in accordance with his expanded knowledge of being and to introduce this knowledge to our human world. He has been caught by the spirits and must serve the spiritual world.

9

Rituals of Dismemberment and Bone Displays in the Underworld

To my left I saw an angel in bodily form . . . its face so fiery that it seemed to belong to the highest of angels, who appear to be all flame; they must be the ones we call Seraphim. . . . In its hand I beheld a long golden spear at the point of which a small flame seemed to flicker. I felt as if the angel pierced that spear several times through my heart, that it penetrated to my bowels, which were extracted when the spear was withdrawn, leaving me all aflame with an immense love for God. The pain was so great that I had to groan, but the sweetness that came with this violent pain was such that I could not wish to be free of it, to be content with anything less than God. The pain is not physical but in the mind, although the body partakes of it to a high degree. The ensuing caressing between the soul and God is so sweet that I implore God to allow anyone to taste it who may think that I lie.

—Saint Theresa [Underhill 1928]

Initiation always signifies death and resurrection. This is as true of the rites of passage marking the entry to a new phase of life as it is of shamanic initiation. The former life must be destroyed and erased. During the rites of puberty performed in tribal cultures, the initiates, after their period of isolation, often speak a new language when they return to the village, or they have lost their memory, forgotten their previous existence. That is why they are given new names and in some cases have to be reintroduced to the rules of their culture. During their initiation shamans may also acquire a secret esoteric language that brings them into contact with higher powers. They converse with each other in this language, which is not understood by the other members of the tribe. This sacred speech as well as sacred songs, sacred objects of power, sacred symbols, and sacred drugs make the initiate part of the magico-religious universe.

The period of initiation strips the shaman of all his social and mental habits as well as his religious and philosophical ideas. To use a more graphic expression: he is skinned, his bowels are torn out, and as happened to Saint Theresa, the flesh is cut from his bones. He is literally chopped into pieces, cooked, grilled, or fried. Eskimo shamans must be able to see themselves as no more than a skeleton before they may accommodate the transitoriness of our egocentric world. Tibetan yogins are said to meditate upon death in charnel grounds until they experience a decomposition of their bodies and perceive themselves as skeletons. For that reason many yogins use human bones as ritual objects and the skirts of Siberian shamans are embroidered with a skeleton.

In many traditions the spirits of the underworld not only take the body of the initiate apart in a most gruesome way—they also put it together again, but in a curious manner which endows the person subjected to such a dismemberment with superhuman powers. Such "bone displays" lead to a heightening of the spiritual state, a liberation from the blind causality of everyday life. Bone displays are thus a source of the true life and represent a mystical rebirth.

Traditional Western psychology, however, does not want to know about such matters as the death of the ego; the pain and suffering entailed in it are too enormous. The psychotherapeutic patient, too, does not wish to endure such suffering; nor would the therapist be able to provide adequate support. Modern psychologists consider the bone displays and experiences of dismemberment described in this chapter to be archaic experiences of the soul, which are so brutal that no modern patient could be expected to endure them. But a critical and truly healing experience cannot be brought about by either psychoanalysis or the clearing up of ego disturbances, social conflicts, mother complexes, or by any other fashionable humanistic group therapy. True transcendence calls for a willingness to suffer a genuine death of ego and not merely an imaginary death experience, to which we might perhaps be willing to submit.

The experience of dismemberment presupposes either an intense psychic crisis or a near-death experience, in which the return to life remains uncertain. Of course, the extinction of the "I" may reach different levels of intensity. As in the case of all transpersonal experiences, themes of the ego death can be discerned even in dreams or daydreams, albeit only in extremely diluted form. The shaman's is an ego death that may miss real death by no more than a hair's breadth. We are not referring here to a mytho-poetical imagination of death in the form of allegories and archetypes. The death experience of the shaman is a dangerous walk on a tightrope between this world and the Beyond. It is not a hallucinatory pseudovision of death.

Many shamans were critically ill, socially unacceptable, and psychically confused over periods of several years; during their time of suffering their body and psyche adjusted themselves to an alternate mode of perception. This continuous biopsychic process of transformation often culminates in experiences of dismemberment, which represent the zenith and turning point of inner change toward a spiritual state of being. The experience of dismemberment is only one of many possibilities of gaining access to the paralogical world of the transpersonal. Journeys to the Beyond, contact with animals and spirits of the Beyond, visions, and the acquisition of objects of power are other effective ways of exploring the limitless realm of consciousness.

To us the experiences of the shaman may often appear exotic or mythical, but we should remember that death/rebirth experiences have occurred at all times and are the source of every form of spirituality and religion. Christ died in agonizing pain and thereafter rose from the dead. Mohammed traveled to the Beyond. Tantalus killed his son Pelops and offered him as food to the gods, who thereupon caused the youth to regain life by cooking him. Similarly, many European mystics and even some of our contemporaries have emerged from the experience of dismemberment in a rejuvenated and newborn state. We are here confronted by a transpersonal principle of the highest order, a principle that represents the very core of all mysticism and introspection.

Our first example is of Chikō, a Japanese priest, who was seized by unworthy feelings of jealousy for the saintly priest Gyōgi, upon whom the emperor had lavished special favors. Soon after that Chikō fell sick and told his disciples that, if he were to die, they should wait nine days before cremating his body. Soon after, he died as expected and his disciples, according to his instructions, locked his body in a room. When they opened the door at the end of nine days, they found that he had come to life again.

He said two messengers had come for him, and together they walked along a road to the west which led to a golden palace with two awesome fig-ures on either side of the entrance. But the fearsome guardians allowed them to pass and told them to take the road to the north. Soon Chikō began to feel a scorching heat burn his face although he could not see any fire nearby. Then a pillar of red hot iron appeared before him. "Clasp that pil-lar," the messengers ordered. Chikō did so and all at once his flesh was burned away, so that only his skeleton remained. The messengers came back after three days with brooms and brushed the iron pillar, crying, "Come back to life, come back to life."

Chikō revived and they continued their journey northward until an-other pillar rose before them, even hotter than the first, and this time made of brass. Once again the messengers ordered Chikō to throw his arms around the pillar. He did so, and again all his flesh was burnt away. Again the messengers returned after three days and conducted their rit-ual of revival.

After Chikō had been revived a second time, they continued their jour-ney northward and came to a fiery cloud—so hot that birds fell down dead from the sky. "What is this place?" Chikō asked. "The Avici hell where you are to be burned," the messengers replied, seizing him and hurling him into the fire where he remained for another three days until they returned and brought him back to life.

When, on their way back, they reached the golden palace, the two guardians by the gate told Chikō that he had to endure these torments to wipe out his jealousy of Gyōgi Bosatu. After he had recuperated from his ordeal, Chikō visited Gyōgi and confessed his former jealousy. He was for-given and thereafter led an exemplary life.[1]

This dramatic death experience features several themes of the Beyond: the way to the west, the guardians at the entrance to the other world, tor-ments of hell, and the spiritual messengers. Its central theme is Chikō's de-struction by heat and fire. Only his skeleton remains—a symbolic indication that he has reached a higher level of consciousness. He rises from the fires of hell just as the phoenix rose from the ashes: reborn and cleansed of bad feelings and intentions. He is now able to resume his duties in a purified state. The fire has literally burned away all evil and represents a universal motif of the restoration of balance and purity. Whether fire it-self is no more than a symbol of transformation or whether, over and above this, it represents an actual biochemical process that is experienced as inner heat—similar to Kundalini energy—will have to be left to future physiological investigation. We hope that such research will give us experimental access to the experiences of the shaman by the use of acknowledged scientific methods.

In Indonesia the shaman must also allow his body to be torn to pieces before he can serve the spirits. The Dayak of Borneo has his head severed from the body during initiation. Then the brain is removed from the skull, washed, and reinserted, so that the future shaman will have a clear and undisturbed mind. However, it is only after the spirits have blown gold dust into his eyes that he becomes a seer and perceives the world of the Beyond. His heart is pierced by an arrow to arouse in him compassion and gentleness toward the ill. During the actual Dayak ceremony, a coconut is smashed above the initiate. This may well be their way of demonstrating the "spiritual brain surgery" in a visible manner.[2]

As we can see, the psychic dismemberment results in a clear mind, enhanced perception, greater capacity for compassion, and true gentleness toward our fellow beings. It would seem that only self-borne suffering will stimulate true tolerance and genuine compassion.

/Garugu //Khumob,* the highest ranking medicine man and sorcerer of the South West African Hain //om, suffered a severe sickness before the age of sixteen. He almost died. It started in his knees and rose relentlessly through the rest of his body. Several times he fainted, and for a short time his soul ascended to //Gamab, the supreme deity. The sickness subsided when he reached his sixteenth year and was trained as an herbal healer by his uncle, who was a great shaman.

One day when he was alone in the bush /Garugu //Khumob heard cawing sounds and a woman appeared to him. Her name was Khaendaos, and she had been sent by //Gamab. She declared her love for him and asked him to take her as his wife. /Garugu //Khumob resisted her invitation by saying he would prefer to marry a human woman. He would not even be swayed when Khaendaos promised to bear him four children. She then became angry and gave him a beating. She was stronger than he and rummaged for four days in his innermost soul and finally dismembered his body. She took his soul with her to //Gamab's abode. After five days she brought it back and /Garugu emerged from a deep unconsciousness. He was wearing a headband, and on his chest and back sat the four children of Khaendaos. While he was unconscious he came to the World Tree where the souls of unborn children and the dead abide.

---

*The oblique strokes (/ and //) represent clicking sounds typical of the language of some African tribes.

At home the brother of /Garugu's mother asked him, "Was it Khaendaos who dismembered you thus?"

"Yes."

"Was it raining when this happened?"

"Yes."

"Did it burn like fire?"

"Yes."

"I see you have four children by her."

"Yes."

After this experience he began to work as a healer of his own free will. He keeps the four children in a container which he always carries with him when he conducts his healing ceremonies. Khaendaos protects him against alien spirits, but for this he must pay her. If he annoys her she seizes him by the throat and almost strangles him.[3]

Initiations by a female being who declares her love for the initiate and later becomes his protecting spirit follow the pattern of the spirit wedding, in which a human being and a celestial entity become united, whereby sexual polarity transcends two levels of existence. There can be no doubt that this is one of the reasons for the acquisition of special powers as a result of such a process. In our narrative /Garugu //Khumob is also dismembered, his spirit bride rummages in his soul, and even takes it to the highest deity. His sickness evidently brought //Garugu very close to death, as a result of which he traveled to the Beyond to the source of wisdom, where he came to the World Tree symbolizing the ultimate unity of cosmological levels or forms of existence. He is given a spiritual bride and four powerful spirit children—an almost unique treasure of mystical experience when one considers that /Garugu was only sixteen years old.

The apprentice shaman of the Ammassalik Eskimos (eastern Greenland) sets out for the mountains of the mainland after rubbing his whole body with a special kind of seaweed. In the mountains he looks for a large grinding stone with a flat surface, against which he then rubs a smaller stone. Crayfish and other crustaceans are often placed between the two stones. Hour after hour, day after day, the apprentice rubs the small stone in a circular manner against the grinding stone, fasting all the while, whereby his power of concentration is increased. Every summer he resumes his lonely practice. After a certain period, according to tradition, a bear rises from the sea. The bear is so emaciated that all its ribs can be seen (the skeleton theme). It devours the apprentice alive, but only to vomit him up again. Thus the initiate "dies" or loses consciousness.

Soon after the bear has spit him out he awakens, his bones are once again covered with flesh and blood, and his clothes come flying toward him. He stands there fully dressed. He continues fasting and rubbing the grinding stone every summer until he has accumulated a sufficient number of helping spirits. During this period of training and initiation, the apprentices are taught a special language by the spirits—the secret language of the shaman. All of this training is carried out in secret. Neither the neighbors nor his own family should know of it until the apprentice, after ten to fifteen years of such practices, one day asks his family to extinguish the lamps because he wants to hold his first ceremony for summoning the spirits.[4]

The continuous rubbing of stones against each other may be seen as a simple way of inducing a trance. Monotony, loneliness, and repetitive rhythmic movement join with the desire to encounter a helping spirit. This combination is so powerful that it erases all mundane thoughts and distracting associations—just as the crustaceans placed between the two stones are obliterated. In the same way the spirit bear then devours the apprentice, tearing him to pieces with its teeth. The fasting is another important factor. It strengthens the power of concentration and weakens the body, or rather sensitizes it, because in the absence of digestive and metabolic processes it is more readily inclined toward the desired goal. The normal rhythm of mind and body is disrupted, and consciousness is pervaded by the monotonous circular movement of the arm and the continuous sound of two stones grinding against each other. Ultimately, the sense of ego pales and dies. Its death is due to the absence of any kind of stimulation, any kind of reference point by which to grasp the world.

The polar bear then arises from the sea and devours the body of the initiate. His ego is wiped out. As the bear gnaws every shred of flesh from the bones, the consciousness of the initiate is cleansed and purified, which is the ultimate aim of all spiritual experience and the basis of every form of shamanic power and concentration. The rubbing of the grinding stone, by its very simplicity, demonstrates to us the basic mechanism of arriving at an altered state of consciousness.

But the framework of our ego is not only broken by monotonous mechanical activities. In many tribal cultures nature herself plays an important role. During his initiation, the apprentice is often cut off from his fellow beings. He seeks the loneliness of the mountains, the forest, or the tundra, where he completely surrenders to the sacred powers of plants, animals, and rocks. To live in complete harmony with nature, to learn its ways and become conscious of its greatness and power is an inherent characteristic of initiation. So we should not be surprised that a bear or other animal—rather than an abstract deity—acts as a bridge to higher consciousness. However, this kind of "shamanic psychotherapy"[5] is only of limited significance for our own culture, because we no longer have any contact with bears or wolves. We know of no Western medium using animals as helping spirits. In any case, the dissolution of the ego does not necessarily have to be experienced in every culture as a process of dismemberment.

On the other hand, we should not see this dismemberment as a mere reflection of the behavior of the hunter who also dismembers, disembowels, cooks, and eats animals. In the past, many ethnologists were inclined toward such an interpretation which is no more than a purely superficial and accidental analogy, because the experience of psychic dismemberment is a universal transcultural and transpersonal symbol. That the initiate is often dismembered by animals is an aspect of the specific lifestyle of particular tribal communities.

The Iglulik Eskimo shamans have to see their own skeleton. The North Alaska Eskimos speak of a "worm test." Worms eat the flesh of the adept, whereby he is internally cleansed and begins to glow. A similar belief is found among the Aivilik Eskimos. In western Greenland the apprentice permits all sorts of worms to drain his blood until he becomes unconscious. This method is said to produce highly gifted shamans.[6]

It has been reported that the initiates of the Saint Lawrence Islands Eskimos fall prey to madness for five days during which they take neither food nor drink, but nevertheless become as strong as a bear, so that not even ten grown men can restrain them. During the training the candidate is sick and confused, but not really mentally ill. The other members of the tribe are well able to tell the difference. He remains in the open, away from habitations of the tribe, out on the tundra, exposed to wind and snow, to receive from the spirits and the forces of nature his shamanic knowledge and powers. Without sleeping, he beseeches the spirits, asking them for "the power to bring the dead back to life." In the course of his lonely wanderings, the initiate five times breaks the bones of a bird which he has to restore to life again[7]—a clear indication of what he will later have to endure himself.

The lonely struggle with the forces of nature, during which one is at their mercy for better or worse, is a requirement of shamanic training, because only when the apprentice becomes aware of his smallness and helplessness, when he becomes modest and humble, can his spirit blend with these tremendous forces. An awareness of the interwoven mystical unity of nature is an essential experience during initiation and of the shamanic view of the world in general. Exposed to wild animals and the stormy elements, deprived of sleep and food, his thoughts constantly directed toward the spirits and the sacred, the shamanic apprentice—once his ego identity has collapsed—experiences himself to be one with the world, the universe, nature, animals, and plants. The experience of a transpersonal self is the reward. He now represents the bridge between the world of man and the world as such, the sacred existence revealed to those who are willing to be dismembered and thereby shed their former human nature.

Among the Australian Arunta the person destined to become a medicine man seeks out a cave inhabited by the Iruntarinia, the spirits of the ancestors who lived in Alcheringa, the Dreamtime. He lies down at the mouth of the cave and sleeps until one of the spirits appears, piercing him with a spear through the back of the neck until the spear emerges at the mouth, perforating the tongue. This perforation of the tongue does not heal and is accepted as a physical sign of a medicine man. How the hole in the tongue comes about is unclear, but in any case it is big enough to put one's little finger through it. The spirit ancestor then pierces the head of the initiate with a second spear, sideways from ear to ear.

The initiate is taken into the cave, where the Iruntarinia operate on his body, taking out the organs and replacing them with new ones. He awakens in a state of madness, but this disturbed phase does not last very long. He is returned to his tribe by the ancestors and thereafter has the gift of seeing the spirits. In addition, he owns a collection of Atoongara (stones given to him by the ancestors) which he projects into the body of a patient during healing ceremonies in order to fight the evil forces within the body.[8]

During the sacred Dreamtime, the material limitations and physical restrictions of ordinary people do not exist. The novice returns to his primordial state by contacting the spirits of the ancestors. He thus gets a taste of the sacred nature of being, of a timeless age, accessible to anyone who knows how to open himself to it. To be in the company of these ancestral spirits is an experience of such transcendental force that it could be said to be tantamount to death or self-annihilation.

Upon his return to this world, the novice is mentally disturbed and has difficulty readjusting to his human environment. Catapulted out of sacred space, he gets the standards of earthly life all muddled up and only gradually succeeds in reassembling this nonsensical mosaic. He enters our world from the timeless world of the "eternal now" where the space/time continuum is magically present. He is therefore unsure of himself and behaves in a socially and mentally abnormal manner. Yet this is the way a medicine man is born. The sacred Dreamtime has turned a man into a healer.

The Corrobóree poets of the Australian Unambal receive their inspirations, songs, and dances through their contact with the dead of the underworld, the Shadows or Bangumas. These helping spirits protect the poet, show him the way to the other world and return him to his body after the journey to the Beyond. If such a poet loses or neglects the contact with these spirits, a therapeutic ceremony is held; all the men of the tribe unite to restore the severed connection to the dead ancestors. They crouch around the Corrobóree poet, who lies on the ground, and massage his body until he goes into a trance. His soul (*jajaru*) sets out to seek the spirits of the dead.

If the poet meets such a spirit (who, in turn, was dispatched to look for the poet), he says that he lost his way in the underworld as well as all his songs. The spirit, who may be the dead father of the poet, then helps him; he calls many other spirits who chop the poet's soul to pieces. Each spirit takes one of the pieces to the underworld, where the soul is reassembled. The poet is now once again able to travel to the Beyond where he can collect songs and chants, which he teaches to the members of his tribe.[9]

Similar to the Corrobóree poets, the Northwest Australian Ungarinyin have a devil doctor who is initiated by Águla, the shadow skeleton of the dead. This initiation takes place quite unexpectedly, such as when a prospective devil doctor is walking around in the bush. There is thus no long and difficult period of initiation. The skeleton spirits cause him to become "silly along head," they drag him to the spirit realm, take his brain out and replace it by a new one which renders him capable of seeing the Águla himself. They, too, teach him songs—Corrobórees—which he communicates to the members of his tribe and which are passed on to many other tribes. These dream Corobórees play an indispensable role in the life of the aboriginal community. At the same time, however, they are subject to fashionable trends and are periodically renewed.[10]

Dismemberment, exchange of internal organs or the brain, and the introduction of crystals into the body of the initiate are metaphors of inner change; allegorical and culturally oriented symbols for an introspective, psychic rebirth. Shamans from all traditions emerge with great regularity from this process of transformation chanting or singing. One is led to conclude that it is easier to communicate intuitive experiences by music or poetry than in the words of everyday speech.

If the connection of the Corrobóree poet to the spirits of the underworld has been severed, it becomes necessary for him to reexperience the sacred. A therapy takes place. While in a trance, he is dismembered by the spirit of the dead and put together again in order to refresh, sanctify, and heal the memory of the other world. He returns from this experience with new dream Corobórees, the ultimate purpose of which is to acquaint the other members of the community with the atmosphere and nature of the underworld so that people who lead lives that are restricted by the framework of the material world may experience a richer existence.

We have seen that the extinction of ego consciousness is described by a great variety of cultural metaphors. In South Australia, the passage from life to death, and to rebirth, is brought about by the rainbow snake, which connects the cosmological level of heaven and earth like a rainbow. The initiate is swallowed by it, and so begins his journey from the earthly to the heavenly realm. All cultures see heaven as an expression of that which is higher and more exalted, and there is hardly any tribal tradition that does not make use of heaven as a symbol of transcendence and heightened insight. The same applies to the realm situated below the earth—the underworld. For the modern researcher into consciousness, heaven and the underworld, or being swallowed by the rainbow snake, are expressions of an altered state of consciousness.

The medicine men of the Australian Yualai take a boy selected to follow their profession to a tribal burial ground, tie him down and, at short distances around him, light some fires of fat. One novice reported that after he had been left tied down, a big star fell beside him and from it came an iguana—his totem—which ran all over him and then went away. After that a snake, the hereditary enemy of the iguana, crawled on him, frightening him. Next, a huge figure came and drove a yam stick right through his head, placing a sacred stone in the hole made by the stick, with the help of which much of the initiate's magic was to be worked in the future. Then came the spirits of the dead, chanting songs fulls of sacred lore related to the art of healing. He was away from his tribal camp for about two months and was not allowed to become a practicing medicine man until he was some years older.[11]

In Dampier Land and in the area around the Lower Fitzroy River medicine men are created by Rai spirits who slit open the initiate's body and hang up his entrails as well as his lungs, heart, liver, and kidneys. His body is placed over an earth oven with magical cooking slabs of stone. Later his entrails and organs are replaced and the body is closed up again. Thereafter he can fly through the air like a bird and travel to the innermost regions of the earth. Magical stones are placed into his navel and between the eyes and ears. The Rai also equip him with the "inner eye" that enables him to transcend time and space.[12]

In southern Australia medicine men are "made" near a large water hole associated with a great snake known as Wonambi. The initiate is taken to the water hole by a doctor (*kinkin*). After he has departed from the tribal village he is mourned for as someone who has just died, because he is going to be "cut into pieces." At the water hole the initiate is blindfolded and given to the monstrous snake who swallows him whole. He spends an undefined period of seclusion inside the snake and is finally spat out again. In the course of a later ceremony, the "doctors" once again dismember the initiate symbolically. He is made to lie full length on his back and said to be dead. The head doctor proceeds to break his neck, dislocates his wrists and joints at the elbows, knees, and ankles. A black stone is used to "cut" these parts of the body during this rite. In actual fact the operator does not amputate these parts but makes a scarlike mark with the stone. The doctors insert a maban shell into each cut, as well as into his ears and the angle of his jaw, so that he will be able to hear and speak to everything—spirits, strangers, birds, and animals. More shells are pressed into his forehead so that he can divine and see through anything, and into his neck so that it may be turned in all directions. His stomach is also filled with maban to make him invulnerable to attack by any weapon. He is then "sung" back to life by the *kinkin* and revives. On arrival in the main camp a further test is held. All the fully initiated men, at the order of the head kinkin, throw their spears at the postulant. They glance off him though, because he is full of maban, the sacred shell. He is now kinkin and can practice his profession.[13]

The best known examples of dismemberment come from Siberian tribal communities. Among the Buryat the shamanic apprentice is visited by the Utcha, his shamanic ancestors. They take his soul (*amin*) to heaven and place it before the assembly of the Saajtani, who torment him in a horrible fashion, poking around his belly with knives, cutting whole chunks of flesh off him, and throwing them about. During these tortures the shaman can hear his heart beat, but his breath subsides and his skin becomes dark blue. The spirits cook his flesh to "ripen" it. The initiate acquires his inner knowledge during this procedure and thus becomes conversant with the rules of shamanic wisdom.[14]

Among the Tungus shamanic ability or potential is passed from one generation to the next. When the spirit of a dead shaman selects a successor from the people within his clan, it is said, "He was found by a former shaman." The dead shamans then train the neophyte. They abduct his soul, dismember it, and grill its flesh over a fire or on a spit.

Here is how the shaman Semyon Semyonov describes his own dismemberment:

> When I shamanize, the spirit of dead Ilya (a brother, who was himself a shaman) comes and speaks through my mind. I was forced to become a shaman by my shamanic ancestors. Before I began to shamanize, I lay ill for a whole year. I became a shaman at the age of fifteen. The sickness that forced me to become a shaman caused my body to swell up and I frequently fainted. When I began to sing, the sickness usually passed away. After that, my ancestors made me into a shaman. They set me up like a wooden pole and shot arrows at me until I became unconscious. They cut the flesh off me. They separated my bones and counted them. My flesh they ate raw. When they counted my bones, they found that there was one too many. Had there not been enough bones I could not have become a shaman.[15]

Another shaman called Pyotr, who was mentally disturbed for three years, also had to suffer dismemberment. His sickness was marked by alternating phases of convulsive chanting and complete apathy toward his environment. Sometimes his convulsions were so strong that he had to be tied down. After all this suffering, he showed signs of shamanic gifts at the age of twenty-five. Because his soul was brought up in the lower world, on the twelfth level of the shaman's tree, his animal mother, who cares for the egg containing the shaman's soul, traveled to the middle world to dismember his body. In this way Pyotr won his helping spirits. His main helper is a dead female relative but he may also call upon a bear and a wolf.[16]

A shaman of the Avam Samoyed was seized by a gigantic blacksmith in the underworld and torn into small pieces. His bones were boiled for three years in a cauldron until all the flesh fell off them. The blacksmith fashioned the shaman's head on an anvil, instructing him at the same time how to heal people. Later the blacksmith reassembled the bones, covered them with flesh, and gave him new eyes to make him see better. His ears were pierced with the intention of making the conversations of plants audible to him.[17]

When the shaman of a clan of the Siberian Evenk dies, his soul (*chargi*) travels downriver to the clan territory of the spirits of ancestral shamans in order to inform Mangi, the oldest of the dead ancestors. Mangi then orders the spirit of the ancestral shaman, whose turn it is to reenter life, to travel upstream and choose a suitable young man or maiden from among the members of the clan. The person chosen is overcome by intense apathy or, in desperation, escapes into the forest. He must give up all work and becomes emaciated. His soul journeys to the mountain of the shamanic ancestral spirits, to the roots of the shaman tree. There he is swallowed by his animal mother, to be reborn as an animal. In other words, the animal mother creates an animal double which later becomes his protecting spirit and lives in an isolated tree in the vicinity of the clan's abode. The shaman himself is dismembered and reassembled by the animal mother.[18]

It should be noted that the shaman tree stands on a mountain so that its topmost branches reach into the upper world, while its roots go down into the underworld. The trunk represents our earthly realm, the middle world. Near the roots live the spirits of the shamanic ancestors and the animal mother. In the middle world we find humans, and in the upper realm the as yet unborn clansmen in the form of birds. The motif of the animal mother and the birds shows that the origin of the clan and mankind as a whole is perceived as lying in the animal realm. That is the reason why all myths speak of a primodial connection between humans and animals.

The World Tree manifests a threefold cosmography; all three levels of existence are sacred by virtue of the whole tree being so. In many myths this World Tree standing on the World Mountain is also the center of the world. It thus symbolizes both the World Axis and the world as a whole. The connection between shamanism and the World Tree may appear strange and incomprehensible to the modern mind, but the theme of such a World Tree can also be found in psychotherapeutic data. The Tree offers itself to our consciousness as an ideal symbol for a connection between all cosmological levels and, in one form or another, forms part of the description of the world in all cultures. We might ask ourselves whether such poetic images do not, in many respects, appeal to our feeling and intuition to a much greater degree than the rational and abstract geographies of the soul developed by modern psychology.

In many cases shamans become healers after a ceremony of dismemberment. The Yakut, however, say that a shaman can only cure those illnesses whose evil spirit has partaken of the shaman's flesh during initiation. It is indeed the case that many practicing shamans can cure only those illnesses they themselves have experienced. If, during the ceremony, the spirits devour the leg of the shaman he will later treat diseases of the leg. During the actual dismemberment, his flesh and bones are divided among the spirits themselves. If there is not enough flesh for all the spirits, the shaman will not be able to heal all illnesses. Any illness, the spirits of which did not partake of the shaman's body, may only treated once by him.

It is also said that a shaman's power is related to the intensity with which he experiences his dismemberment. According to the Siberian tribes, unimportant shamans are only cut to pieces once or not at all. Mighty shamans, on the other hand, are dismembered several times. There is a saying, "He was dismembered thrice—he is a great shaman." Only those that have sacrificed themselves and have experienced all the phases and symptoms of the various illnesses have a true calling to become healers. After his resurrection the newly ordained shaman is to be surrounded by innocent maidens and boys. This again shows that shamanic illnesses and the dismemberment ceremony are seen as a process of purification, from which the shaman emerges newly born and untainted by the mundane concerns of human existence.[19]

Vilmos Diószegi has recorded the dismemberment experience of Sunchugasev, a former Sagay shaman:

> The candidate loses consciousness while sick. During this time he presents himself to the shaman-ancestor of his clan. When he gets there, they seek his excess bone. They cut up his whole body into pieces, they separate the heart and the lungs and examine each piece by the light. Meanwhile he sees himself cut up, he sees as his whole body and his viscera are being measured, while they are looking for the excess bone. . . .
>
> They chopped me up and then threw me into the kettle and I was boiled. There were some men there: two black and two fair ones. Their chieftain was there too. He issued the orders concerning me. I saw all this. While the pieces of my body were boiled, they found a bone around the ribs which had a hole in the middle. This was the excess bone. This brought about my becoming a shaman. Because only those men can become shamans in whose body such a bone can be found. One looks across the hole of this bone and begins to see all, to know all, and that is when one becomes a shaman. . . . When I came to from this state, I woke up. This meant that my soul had returned. Then the shamans declared: "You are the sort of man who may be-

come a shaman. You should become a shaman, you must begin to shamanize."[20]

The motif of the excess bone is fairly common among Siberian tribal communities. In the absence of a more profound explanation, we might say this excess bone implies an anatomy different from that of ordinary humans and thus expresses the special status of a shaman. As he looks across the hole in this excess bone, other worlds are instantly revealed to him. His abnormal anatomy symbolizes a correspondingly different mode of existence that transcends the average. Such a hole or orifice is also a very widespread theme of entry into another realm, as for example, the holes leading to the underworld or to heaven, as well as the long, dark tunnel so often mentioned in near-death experiences.

As in the case of all shamanic experiences, the actual psychic transformation is described with concepts and images taken from the material environment. For that reason, many theoreticians maintain that "primitives" are unable to separate material reality from psychic reality, and that this allows us to conclude that the mental formation of tribal cultures is inadequately developed.

Psychic transformation, however, cannot be conveyed by language alone, so it would certainly seem more appropriate to borrow concepts from the everyday world than to construct a new and complicated psychological terminology. Many cultures are intuitively aware of this and therefore describe the internal by the use of metaphors borrowed from the external world.

Seen in this way, the excess bone with its hole, the introduction of crystals into the body, or the boiling and grilling of the initiate's flesh are very descriptive and impressive images of mental states. Images that go beneath the skin. The scenes of dismemberment follow a transpersonal symbolism to be found in many cultures. What is being described is the extinction of accumulated knowledge and the collapse of the ego. But the images used to convey these processes are taken from the material world we know and understand. We have tried to free these shamanic metaphors from the sphere of the exotic and irrational to which traditional anthropology has banished them, and to show that they represent psychic motivations common to all mankind. Conventional psychology, because of its self-imposed scientific strictures and its unwarranted fear of that which cannot be measured, has so far refused to recognize these motivations.

The experience of physical dismemberment does not require an elaborate interpretation—it is an expression of inner healing, of a psychic cleansing process and of an ecstatic peak experience rather than an experience of destruction, as the shamanic images might at first sight lead us to suppose. True health, we are being told, can only be achieved through destruction, followed by reconstitution and reformation. The subsequent rebirth is experienced as an inner liberation from entrenched habits and standards. No matter whether we speak of a "rebirth" or a "resurrection," these words are just concepts pointing to a psychic and psychosomatic reanimation that grants us a second existence after we have been "dismembered" and so brought back to the primordial state. This second existence is marked by forces and powers that are much more complex and integral than those of ordinary men, of those that are born only once and not allowed, during their one life, to return to the sources of primordial wholeness and cosmic unity.

10

Imaginary Friends, Partial Personalities, and Genuine Spirits of the Dead

It is not enough for a shaman to be able to escape both from himself and from his surrounding. It is not enough that, having the soul removed from his eyes, brain, and entrails, he is able also to withdraw the spirit from his body and thus undertake the great "spirit flights" through space and through the sea; nor is it enough that by means of his powers (qaumanEq) he abolishes all distance, and can see all things, however far away. For he will be incapable of maintaining these faculties unless he has the support of helping and answering spirits. . . . But he must procure these helping spirits for himself; he must meet them in person. He cannot even choose for himself what sort he will have. They come to him of their own accord, strong and powerful.[1]

No, to see spirits is relatively easy. All you need is a pure soul.
— The Huichol Shaman Pedro De Haro[2]

I asked these spirit figures if I was seeing them or if I was seeing what was in my own brain. They answered, "Both."
— Eileen Garrett[3]

I am well aware that many will say that no one can possibly speak with spirits and angels so long as he lives in the body; and many will say that it is all a fantasy, others that I relate such things in order to gain credence, and others will make other objections. But by all this I am not deterred, for I have seen, I have heard, I have felt.
— Emanuel Swedenborg[4]

Strain, tiredness, and exhaustion as well as physical and mental loneli-ness cause our consciousness to produce, of its own account, images that are independent of the environment. We all know the phenomenon of an inner dialogue—a conversation with ourselves—which can be clearly observed whenever we are alone for an extended period of time, walk through a desolate landscape, or have to make decisions with which no one can help us. Then we begin an inner conversation with ourselves. We split ourselves into two or more partial personalities and allow them to talk to each other. Normal thought processes become a dialogue in the form of arguments for and against.

This chapter aims at providing an inner understanding of the helping spirits and protective deities of the shaman without getting caught up in simplifying psychological explanations. If we are to arrive at such an inner understanding we have to begin with a central principle of consciousness research—the continuum of consciousness. The spontaneous inner dia-logue arises from monotonizing factors such as mental isolation and physi-cal confrontation with vast unchanging expanses of water, snow, or sand, and as a result of artificially produced sensory deprivation. Monotony causes psychic energy to withdraw from its customary engagement with external stimuli so that it becomes available for the exploration of deeper levels of consciousness. The internal dialogue is only one of the projec-tions that then arise from the depth of the soul.

The more intense and extended the monotonous conditions are, the more varied will be the projections produced by our consciousness, and the more realistic the inner partial personalities derived from them. If ex-ternal stimuli are completely cut off—as for instance in the case of a miner buried underground or during experiments aimed at reducing sensory stimulation when test subjects are made to wear special gloves that prevent them from distracting themselves by playing with their fingers, as well as during experiments in which people are placed into a tank of salt water at body temperature in a room that is insulated against sound, light, and vari-ations in temperatures so that the test subject completely loses all sense of bodily demarcations and becomes a kind of thought creature—the "real-ity" of the figures imagined is greatly enhanced so they are barely distin-guishable from "actual" people. Here we have the first stages in the creation of helping spirits. We shall illustrate by a number of examples how these partial personalities can become helpful partners when life is endangered or critical existential decisions have to be made.

The story of Captain Joshua Slocum, who circumnavigated the world alone at the turn of the century, is well known. As he crossed the Atlantic a heavy storm broke, and he saw a bearded man who took hold of the wheel while Slocum himself, weakened by illness, had to remain below deck in his cabin. At first he thought that the bearded man was a pirate until the stranger identified himself as the former helmsman of the *Pinta*, one of the ships of Columbus. He said he always came to the help of people whenever they needed it. Despite the fact that this stranger looked completely real and lifelike Slocum knew that he was a hallucination.[5]

The well known mountaineer Reinhold Messner also tells of an encounter with a phantom companion:

> During my solo ascent of Nanga Parbat in 1978 I had invisible companions. I conversed with them in four languages although I only speak three. In my diary is the following entry under the eighth of August: "In this burnt-out state, this suffering, thoughts are suddenly extinguished, before I have had time to think them. It may be that my infinitely lonely situation is bearable only because of that. I suddenly feel as if someone were sitting beside me. I cannot see who it is, but out of the corner of my eye I seem to sense that it is a girl. It is high time for me to erect my tent, otherwise we shall perish in this heat. She watches me as I trample the snow flat, and I am thinking to myself it is nice to know that she is there. . . . In between I observe children around me, as well as men and women. I do not recognize them, nor do I particularly want anything from them. They are just there, coming and going. And I converse with them.[6]

People who, later in life, develop a talent as a medium often seem to have had imaginary friends during their childhood. Children who spend a great deal of time alone and have no playmates generally tend to create imaginary friends for themselves, who immediately disappear as soon as other (real) children or adults enter the scene. I quote below a childhood experience of the well-known medium Doris Stokes. She was six or seven years old when she encountered her secret friends, the "spirit children," after a long illness which almost proved fatal:

> Then one sunny afternoon I was parked on the path as usual, listlessly watching a butterfly flutter round the cabbage rows, when I realized someone had come up behind me. I looked round in surprise, to find a little girl standing there.
> "Hello," she said, "I'm Pansy."
> I gawked at her. She was fascinating. Her skin was black! And shiny

like father's boots. She had brilliant white teeth, tight curly hair and the loveliest dress I'd ever seen. It was like a long wrap printed in gorgeous bright blues. I'd never seen anything like it in Grantham before and I'd never seen anyone with black skin either. I thought Pansy was wonderful.

She was a bright, cheerful girl. We laughed and chattered and after a while a couple of her friends, two little boys, came over to join us. They were just ordinary boys with white skin, not black like Pansy's, but they were fun too. Soon we were all playing a noisy game of I Spy.

It never occurred to me to wonder why they weren't at school like other children. When you're very young you accept things without question.

I was completely absorbed in the game. It was my turn. "I Spy with my little eye . . ." I looked around quickly for something really difficult but all I saw was old Mrs. Rush passing the end of the path. She waved.

"Hello Doris," she called. "Feeling better?"

I nodded and, smiling, she went on. I watched her walk away, shopping bag swinging. I don't know why, there was no reason for her to have remarked on my friends, but in that moment I knew with absolute certainty she couldn't see them. . . . After a while I realized they only visited me when I was alone. At first I met them at the "garden" and later, once I was up and about again, I saw them in my bedroom. The hours passed very quickly when we were together. We chatted and giggled over childish things. They loved looking at my books and sometimes, if I was stuck over my homework, Pansy would help me. I was hopeless at Maths whereas Pansy was very quick with figures.[7]

Eileen Garrett, one of the great promotors of parapsychology and herself perhaps the most rigorously scientifically tested medium, also played with phantom companions when she was a child. She retained these companions for a number of years despite all attempts by her aunt at suppressing them. She writes:

When I was a child, far from being alone, I had my secret companions. Two girls and a boy. The boy and one girl were younger than I, and the other girl somewhat older. I called them "The Children." They sought me. I did not have to go to them in any particular place, or make any adjustments within myself in order to see them, be with them or communicate with them freely. I saw them first when I was about four years old. I was in the doorway of the house and they were in the garden. I stood staring at them. I do not know how long we may

have appraised each other, as children do, but nothing definite passed
between us at that first encounter. I wanted to go out and join them,
but I was unaccustomed to mixing with other children and I suppose
I must have turned shyly away. But next day I saw them out-of-doors,
and again we stood and examined one another intently. Nothing occurred between us other than that strange feeling by which children
sense each other's qualities and find their basis of companionship.

"The Children" continued to appear, and I accepted them. We
communicated freely, but without words. Sometimes they stayed for
hours, sometimes only for a short time. Suddenly I would realise
their presence, and as suddenly they would be gone. Everything that
I cared for was subject to change—the animals grew up and grew old,
the flowers died, the garden withered—but "The Children" did not
change. When the time came for me to go to boarding school, I was
fearful I might lose them, but they promised me that they would visit
me there.[8]

Loneliness is no doubt the reason why many children acquire imaginary friends. However, this requires also a certain amount of imagination,
and children, who live in a more mythical and magical world than adults,
find it a great deal easier to live up to this requirement. Our examples have
shown that the contact with an imaginary friend can take many different
forms. Human beings have created imaginary companions in every conceivable situation of danger and these friends, acting as benevolent spirits,
rendered them valuable assistance. Helping spirits give advice. They may
tell the mountaineer which route of ascent he should choose or where
there are dangerous overhangs. In a critical situation they may navigate a
ship through a storm, as was experienced by Joshua Slocum, or they may
converse with the lone pilot in the cockpit of his aircraft to prevent him
from falling asleep, as happened to Charles Lindbergh, who during his
solo flight across the Atlantic in 1927 was helped in word and deed by several imaginary companions.

Modern psychology, too, increasingly concerns itself with the power of
the imaginary, the fantastic, and the nature of psychedelic experiences, because unsuspected emotional, cognitive, and motivational reserves are to
be found there. Daydreams further our desire to reach a certain aim, and
inner conversation with an imaginary partner makes it easier for us to approach an impending confrontation or some other interrelational problem. In general, modern imagination therapies can provide us with a basis
for an understanding of the shaman's helping spirits. Even so, we are only

on the threshold of new insights, and such imaginary friends and helping spirits continue to appear strange and incomprehensible to us.

Let us now turn to two shamans who met their helping spirits quite suddenly and unexpectedly as a result of their great loneliness in nature, although they were prepared for this encounter by a certain psychic disposition.

The Polar Eskimo Otaq was one of the most successful hunters of his tribe and became a shaman (Angákoq) at the early age of twenty-five. He encountered the helping spirits in the loneliness of the mountains. He felt that he had only average gifts compared to other shamans but nevertheless was firmly convinced of his ability to heal others. Here is his narrative:

> I wanted to become a magician, and go up to the hills, far into the hills and rocks, very far, and sleep up there. Up there I see two spirits, two there were, two great hill spirits, tall, as tall as a tent.
>
> They sang drum songs, they went on singing drum songs, the two great hill spirits. I did not utter one word; I kept silence while they sang drum songs; I was ashamed and did not dare speak to them.
>
> The day after, I went home. And then I was a little of a magician, only a very little of a magician.
>
> But to the many people I said nothing of it. I was ashamed to speak of it, because I was still only a very little of a magician.
>
> Another time I started out again on a little ramble in the hills, hare hunting, as I had felt a longing for hare's meat. A great rock I climbed up over, and when I came to the top I laid me down to sleep.
>
> I was not sleepy, I just lay down.
>
> I lie there a little, lie and hear again the song of the hill spirits; it was the two great ones whom I heard the last time.
>
> The one now begins to speak, speaks to me, asks for a ladle of wood.
>
> I only heard that they sang and that they spoke to me; myself I said nothing.
>
> When I came down to men, neither did I tell this time what I had seen. But I carved a ladle of wood, a very beautiful ladle of wood, with no dirt upon it.
>
> The third time I heard the song of the hill spirits, I had not gone to the hills, that time it was in my house. Then they sought me of themselves, then I was beginning to become a magician, more and more, but men knew nothing of it.
>
> When I saw the hill spirits again, a great dog was running after them, a parti-colored dog; it, too, became my helping spirit.
>
> It was only when many people fell sick that I revealed myself as a magician. And I helped many who were ill.[9]

Otaq does not say whether he took over the songs of the spirits to make them his own, but we may assume that he did, because such chants are a central means of becoming a shaman. We shall hear more about this aspect in the chapter dealing with songs of power.

Otaq's narrative impresses us by its simplicity. Most researchers into shamanic phenomena are incapable of entering into an experience marked by such primitiveness of the psyche. Transpersonal experience results from the dismantling of psychic diversity, from getting off the roundabout of conceptualized stimulation. Loneliness, uniform land-scapes, monotonous behavior—in short, a meditative state of mind—are a prerequisite for higher states of consciousness. The Western re-searcher, having grown up in intellectual diversity, has little access to this kind of sensory "poverty." However, cognitive reduction is the straight gate to other levels of consciousness as diverse, intricate, and exciting as the material sphere of existence.

Spencer and Gillin describe the shamanic initiation of a Central Austra-lian Warramunga. The man was a hunter. As he was stalking an animal in the bush and about to spear it, he noticed two men in the distance. He did not pay them any more attention because he thought they were fellow tribesmen, also out hunting. After he had killed the animal he wanted to build a fire, but, to his surprise, was unable to rub the two wooden sticks to-gether in such a way as to produce a spark. When he later went to a nearby waterhole and was just about to bend down to have a drink, he again saw the two men. He was scared and ran to another waterhole only to find the two strangers sitting by its side. Now he was convinced they were after him. He hid throughout the night. At dawn he once again saw the two men. Two days later, as he was kneeling over a waterhole, the two strangers suddenly stood before him as if they had popped out of the ground. Quick as lightning he reached for his spear and aimed it at them. They said, "Do not kill us, we are your father and your brother." Now he realized that they were spirits. They asked him to follow them. They were male spirits (*puntidirs*) who wanted to teach him a powerful dance, a Corrobóree. Being afraid, he ran back to where he was camped.

When, shortly after that, he began to dance against his own volition, the two puntidirs returned with a magic pointing bone which they directed at him. By this gesture they sentenced him to death. They exchanged his en-trails and internal organs and introduced a small snake into his body which gave him the powers of a medicine man. As he had been away for a long time, his friends and relatives began to worry and set out to look for him.

When they found him he was unconscious, but soon after regained consciousness.[10]

Although this report gives no clear indication as to why this man suddenly entered an altered state of consciousness and perceived his future helping spirits, we may assume that the loneliness of the hunter was a decisive factor. A typical sign of entering a transpersonal state is that customary actions, such as starting a fire, can no longer be easily performed. This motif is found in myths and fairy tales as well as in reports of shamanic initiation.

However, the fact that people like Slocum, Messner, and Bird, in their loneliness, encountered phantom human companions does not make them shamans. Only death, only the exchange of the internal organs—in other words, a genuine mythical transformation of mind and body—could turn the Australian aborigine into a medicine man. As the following examples show, the shaman's contact with his spirit companions goes beyond a mere encounter because he establishes a permanent relationship with them. He enters into a covenant, as it were, and remains connected to them for the rest of his life. There is a crucial difference between people who have a single encounter with spirit creatures—as experienced in our culture in extreme states of stress or as a result of sensory deprivation— and a future shaman who enters into a more intimate relationship with such beings and does not treat them as figments of the imagination. On the contrary, by his firm belief in the existence of spirits he strengthens their reality and effectiveness.

We downgrade such phenomena to mere hallucinations whereas the Australian Warramunga tribesman, because of his more constructive attitude, acquires valuable helpers which make him an important person within his community. We do not (yet) know how to use such transpersonal phenomena for our own good, whereas tribal cultures provide fertile soil for them.

We have seen that loneliness and isolation can bring about a disintegration of the ego structures and cultural values acquired in the course of our socialization. In much the same way, the endless repetition of an activity, and its monotonous rhythm, destroy our differentiated and multilayered sense of ego. Our normal consciousness is based on a multiplicity of stimuli and therefore is undermined by monotony, repetition, and an environment lacking in reference points. Once the stream of accustomed stimuli is reduced, our consciousness produces its own scenarios or opens itself to a new dimension of experience. In this dimension we become aware of the existence of another "person" which is the reverse side of our ordinary nature. As our next example shows, it requires no extreme efforts to discover this other self.

The Greenland Eskimo monotonously grinds a small stone against a large rock to put himself into a trance. Reidar Christiansen describes how a neophyte spent the whole of the first day of his search for helping spirits rubbing a small stone against a rock. He continued to do so the following day, without stopping, regardless of his fatigue and hunger. Toward the evening of the second day he saw a swift commotion on a nearby lake, and a bear—he knew it was a spirit in disguise—emerged from it, seized him by the neck, and dragged him into the water. He became unconscious and, on awakening, found himself back on the shore with another spirit, a dwarf. After that he started on his homeward journey, completely naked, but on the way his skins came flying toward him one by one.

However, he still needed a spirit in the shape of a seal that could help him cure sick people. So he again took up the stone polishing and continued until the cliff grew soft, and there appeared in it the breathing hole of a seal which was friendly and promised to help him. By similar rites he then enlisted other helping spirits, some in animal shape, others like human beings. One human helping spirit, which he met out at sea in a kayak, invited him to visit his home on a tiny island where pleasant green grass grew in a valley. There he stayed for a while, noting that his host spoke a language of his own. In this way he became an Angákoq, and one morning inspiration came to him. He felt his head swelling to the bursting point, mighty thoughts welled up in him, and he had to seize the drum in the presence of all—a great Angákoq had arisen among them.[11]

It takes surprisingly little to turn human consciousness upside down or cause it to disintegrate. The mere rubbing of a small stone against a larger one until a state of physical exhaustion is reached can put us into a trance and confront us with the spiritual entity of which we have need at that moment. The medicine men apprentices of the Patagonian Yamana are made to rub their cheeks for days on end and to imagine they are gradually penetrating three layers of skin—that is to say, three levels of consciousness—until they enter a state of trance. It does not matter a great deal whether we rub two stones against each other or keep rubbing our cheeks—the uninterrupted repetition of an activity to the point of total exhaustion is an important triggering mechanism for seeing such spirits. All these techniques of psychic deconditioning are only necessary during the apprenticeship of a healer and in the initial stages of a shaman's training. As a rule, fully developed shamans use such techniques on rare occasions only, because they can communicate with their helping spirits whenever they want.

As mentioned before, sickness, too, can destroy and break down psychic habit patterns. We would like to illustrate this by the amusing story of a Mexican peasant and his encounter with a gnomelike helping spirit.

The Mexican farmer Gabriel Mir was thirty-two years old when he suffered a whole string of catastrophic misfortunes. His wife and five children died in an epidemic and he himself lay ill for several months, escaping death by a hair'sbreadth. He had very little food, was unable to look after himself, and depended on the occasional help given by his neighbors. Too weak to rise to his feet, he chewed coarse grain and drank the rain water dripping down from the roof of his dwelling. One night a small gnome, no more than four feet tall and dressed in blue, appeared to him. Gabriel took him to be San Antonio, whose picture hung over the altar in his house.

"I come to impose on you," said the gnome. "You have been ill, my son. You have been close to La Gloria."

The gnome pointed to an invisible person whom Gabriel was to heal. Gabriel resisted, saying that he neither could nor would heal anybody. At the same time he felt the pulse in an arm that had been extended toward him out of nowhere. Thereafter, the shining gnome appeared to him every night for a whole week and taught him various methods of healing. Every night he brought a patient with him, whose body could only be perceived partially or in outline. At the end of the week the gnome told Gabriel that from now on he would appear to him less often.

After this week of strange appearances, Gabriel quickly regained his strength and put his house and fields in order. He became aware of things he had never noticed before. The birds in the trees talked to him. At night he saw human heads moving across the ground of the cemetery and conversing with him. He also discovered that butterflies were, in reality, the souls of future babies. Gabriel then began to work as a healer. During his healing rituals he always spoke in the plural, because he and his heavenly protector were effecting the cure together. San Antonio always remained close to Gabriel, prescribed medicinal herbs and even medicines that had to be obtained from the chemist.

One day, while walking in the forest, Gabriel encountered Avelin, a three-foot-tall dwarf with yellow hair and dressed like a Ladino, a white man.

"What are you doing here?" Gabriel asked him.

"Well, I am lonesome. I am Avelin. It occurred to me that someone might get a fright passing through this thicket and I could capture a soul to keep me company. You are Gabriel Mir."

Gabriel, greatly surprised, asked the dwarf how he came to know his name.

"By the great whore, man, I know everyone's name. Say, Gabriel, let's get a bottle of Guaro and have a little fiesta, just between ourselves, eh? What do you say? I feel like enjoying myself."

Gabriel went to get a bottle of Guaro. Together they celebrated noisily in his house. Gabriel hadn't laughed so much for a long time or been in such a good mood.

At quite a late hour, Avelin introduced Gabriel to some of his friends, saying: "Gabriel, old man, I want to present some friends of mine. Don Diego, Doña Maria, his wife, Don Manuel Urrutia, and Justo Juez."

Gabriel could only make out these new visitors as if through a veil and even later remembered them only hazily.

As Avelin said goodbye to him he gave him some advice, saying: "Right, my friend, remember this well. Whenever you need a little help, don't hesitate to call on us. We have to get together more often."[12]

Tribes close to nature, whose existence is based exclusively on hunting and the natural environment, obtain their helping spirits and their spiritual advisors from the plant and animal kingdoms and from elementary phenomena such as lightning, thunder, rainstorms, the sun, the moon, various planets, and also from a great variety of nonmaterial entities.

The favorite protecting spirits of the Thompson Indians in British Columbia are heavenly bodies such as The Pleiades, Venus, or the Milky Way; natural phenomena such as sunset, wind, rainbows, snow, ice, waterfalls; and animals like eagles, coyotes, otters, ducks, swans, and snakes. However, they may also obtain protection from tobacco or smoking a pipe. The energy residing in everything and all living creatures can work as a Protecting Spirit.

Dick Mahwee, a shaman of the Paviotso Indians, obtained his skills and powers from animal spirits. He says:

A man dreams that a deer, eagle, or bear comes after him. The animal tells him that he is to be a doctor. The first time a man dreams this way he does not believe it. Then he dreams that way some more and he gets the things the spirit told him to get (eagle feathers, wild tobacco, stone pipe, rattle made from the ear of a deer or from the deer's dew claws). Then he learns to be a doctor. He learns his songs when the spirit comes and sings to him.[13]

Tsak'rankura, a famous healer of the Southern Californian Chemehueve Indians, has a bat, a mouse, and a being he calls Ocean Woman as
helping spirits. He displays them to others in the form of white balls or
eggs. The Chemehueve obtain their helping spirits—animals, birds,
plants, and natural phenomena—either spontaneously, or they go to a
gypsum cave on Kwi'nava Mountain above the Colorado River. They
sleep in the cave and beseech the spirits to make medicine men out of
them. They encounter the helping spirits in a dream.[14]

The intensely personal and intimate relationship between a shaman and
his helping spirits is illustrated by the next two examples.

When the helping spirits of the Yukat shamaness Küögéjér "devoured"
two of her younger brother's children she complained: "When my cursed
devils come up to me, their claws and fangs dripping with blood, I feel only
great sadness." In her desperation she traveled to visit the spirit of the earth
and thereby succeeded in making her dog-spirits wear muzzles, whereupon their wildness subsided.[15]

Lame Deer relates the story of Godfrey Chips, a young Sioux medicine
man and grandson of the famous holy man Horn Chips:

> Although the power at first was manifested in an elder brother of
> Godfrey, it later passed on to Godfrey, because the elder brother did
> not know how to handle it. The spirits talked to Godfrey for about
> three months, but he did not understand them. His father advised
> him to ask the spirits to put something in his ear so he might under-
> stand them. He did, and the spirits told him to look for a certain herb.
> His father told him to rub it in his ear, and right then and there
> Godfrey understood what the spirits were saying. He was only thir-
> teen at the time. He is our youngest *Yuwipi*. He does not go to
> school, because one can either go to a white school or walk the medi-
> cine man's road, but not both. He has a certificate which says that he
> is living according to the traditional Indian way and that he doesn't
> have to go to school.[16]

A healer's relationship with his helping spirit is often no different
from his relationship with his fellow beings. It frequently resembles a
marriage and displays the whole spectrum of human emotions such as
love, hate, jealousy, distrust, obedience, fear, longing, quarrels, etc.
This is difficult to understand for those who had no imaginary friends

when they were children or never encountered helping spirits in an extreme state of exhaustion.

Having given some examples of the various ways in which such helping spirits are acquired, we would like to penetrate somewhat deeper into the psychological and spiritual background of this phenomenon. Anthropological literature sometimes distinguishes between controlling or protecting spirits on the one hand and helping spirits on the other. Among the Tungus and Yakut, the controlling spirit of the shaman enlists the helping spirits. In a similar way, Western mediums make use of "controls"—personal protecting spirits—to monitor the appearance of other spirits with whom the medium has no personal connection. These "controls" act as a kind of filter between the spirit realm and the world of the living. Protecting spirits guide the medium to the Beyond, establish contact with people who have died and generally could be said to account for the paranormal capabilities of a medium.

Furthermore, the call to become a healer, shaman, or medium is initiated, pursued and/or ultimately enforced by the controlling spirit. In most cases a healer or shaman has just one protecting spirit, but can have a large number of helping spirits which are either anthropomorphic, animals, plants, or of cosmic origin. Any form of life may serve the shaman as a source of power and psychic stabilization. Looking at these examples of how helping spirits are acquired, one is struck by their marked cultural coloring. But we should not be surprised at this, because every human being and every culture has its own vocabulary, its historically conditioned imagination, and makes use of them when trying to understand psychic and metapsychic events.

Helping spirits frequently manifest themselves in a very direct and sudden way. That is why descriptions of shamanic experiences often strike us as vague, disconnected, and inconsistent; there seems to be no gradual change from normal consciousness to the trance state. The above narratives therefore give us the impression that an actual material being has been manifested, which is characterized by so many unrealistic elements that we are unable to consider it to be part of the external world.

Until recently we have tended to dismiss such visions of animals and spirits as psychic barbarism. However, the ever-widening fieldview of psychology increasingly recognizes that visionary and transmaterial experiences are psychically meaningful. Along the road from psychoanalysis to transpersonal psychology, new insights have compelled us to dismantle our arrogance toward the "primitive." As more and more of these "primitive" communities and peoples regain their self-respect and reassert their pride in their culture, our own naive judgments bounce back on us, and we come to realize that our ideas about the barbarism of the primitive were, in fact, a reflection of our own "barbaric" shortsightedness, our psychological reductionism.

There is no objectivity in psychic space, just as there is none in the material realm. In Einstein's universe space and time are functions dependent on the observer. Similarly, a culturally-conditioned psyche will interpret both the outer and inner world subjectively and in accordance with its own frame of reference points. Nevertheless, behind these culturally diversified interpretations of reality a number of common features are beginning to emerge. Future researchers into consciousness should therefore adopt the following theoretical guiding principle: Although there are no objective structures in the personal realm in the sense that several observers will have identical experiences, it is possible to find constant patterns that justify the attempt to draw some kind of map of nonmaterial states of consciousness.

In the transition from shamanism to the various organized religions the animalistic and anthropomorphous helping spirits are gradually replaced by abstract ideas, until in the end we are left with completely depersonalized and deanthropomorphized cosmic and existential principles which—to give them at least some semblance of clarity and vividness—are occasionally cast in figurative form. This historical process of change has often been cited as proof for the primitiveness of a belief in spirits.

What theories, then, offer themselves to provide an explanation for the existence or appearance of such helping spirits? I should like to put forward three possible hypotheses.

1. *Psychodynamic hypothesis:* Helping spirits are a psychodynamic complex arising from the imagination or from a projection of the unconscious. Spirit helpers are externalized personifications of psychological needs. A protecting spirit is an imaginary creature expressing inner needs in anthropomorphic or zoomorphic form. Imaginary friends and invisible companions play an effective role in the household of the psyche. By being made to come alive as advisory beings they serve as a psychic catalyst, strengthen the satisfaction of inner needs, and help the person to select a lifepath that is adequate in respect of his needs and his environment.

According to this theory, which is the one most frequently adopted in anthropological circles, the advice given by a helping spirit corresponds to the expectations and demands of a specific culture. It expresses suppressed desires and helps to bring to the surface that which cannot be verbalized and is felt to be embarrassing or dangerous. There is then no longer any need to identify with the negative actions to which the spirit prompts us, because these actions are felt to be the responsibility of the helping spirit who, moreover, cannot be criticized. In this way the helping spirit makes the general conduct of life easier and helps one to relax and to act in a more easygoing manner. This is the way most anthropologists interpret the phenomenon of helping spirits, but they ignore the possibility that Western psychology might also make use of such a "psychotechnique."

On the other hand, one often hears that modern man, to become whole and healthy, no longer has need of such a method for externalizing psychic complexes. Such a view, however, would seem to echo the kind of arrogance that considers our psyche to be more transparent and more highly developed than that of "primitives." If psychology is to develop a genuinely effective psychotherapy it will have to pay greater attention to the spirit and the world of spirits. Recourse to spirits therefore is both an archaic as well as a future form of psychotherapy—a therapy that is open toward the resources of our consciousness and thereby acquires unsuspected and compelling potency.

2. Transpersonal hypothesis: Transpersonal anthropology considers the acquisition of a helping spirit to be a central means for mobilizing psychic forces. Such an approach sees spirit beings as more than mere psychodynamic complexes of the unconscious. They are, in fact, considered to be characteristic phenomena of a suprapersonal realm of consciousness which reveal themselves only after the dissolution of the ego structure. In this way situations of psychic or physical stress, as well as near-death experiences, can lead to a transpersonal experience. It follows that a protective being is not an agent of the unconscious but a superconscious revelation, qualitatively beyond what we call normal consciousness.

Due to the fact that available research data is as yet rudimentary, transpersonal anthropology is not yet able to arrive at any definite conclusions regarding the actual character of an experience of the Beyond, of spirit beings and, in the last resort, of the nonphysical or quasimaterial dimension as a whole. It wavers between a psychodynamic and a spiritist hypothesis, yet does not consider the belief in spirits to be a useless cultural fantasy, but rather the expression of a breakthrough to a more comprehensive level of psychic reality.

3. Spiritist hypothesis: The spiritist hypothesis has to be included, because the whole of the shamanic universe would be inconceivable without a belief in spirits and in a realm of the dead. Indications for a spiritual survival after death can be found in certain areas of parapsychological research and in contemporary thanatology.

Not only tribal cultures but also the traditional lore of Western peoples as well as occultism, spiritualism as practiced by mediums, and metaphysics provide us with numerous examples of encounters with the dead and spirit entities. Basically, there is no difference between traditional Western experiences and tribal experiences. If ethnology has neither appreciated this nor made any attempt to study it, the reason may well be a fear that any acknowledgment of the underlying basic identity of both these areas of culture might expose anthropological hypotheses about the mental limitations and underdevelopment of tribal man for what they in fact are— scientific abstruseness. There is no point in presenting here a welter of spiritual and parapsychological data. Such data are indeed extensive but would not provide conclusive proof for the existence of a physical parallel world. We must await the results of further research before firmly committing ourselves to either a materialist or a spiritual view of the universe.

11

Sacred Weddings, Spirit Marriages, and Dream Sexuality

I learned to see thoughts as spatially extended creatures which, no sooner than they were born, were clothed with form and life.
—Eileen Garrett[1]

A special relationship to the world of the spirits is that of shamans who enter into a proper marriage or a sexual relationship with certain spirit beings. However, in discussing such cases it is necessary not to overstress the difference between such sexual or marriage partners on the one hand, and helping and protecting spirits on the other. The dependence of the shaman on his helping spirit ranges from absolute obedience to reciprocity. The shaman has an extremely personal connection with the Beyond, and thus sexual and erotic contacts between the levels of existence involved should not be seen as unusual or extraordinary. Basically, such amorous relations with Beings of the Beyond are no different from the psychic reactions associated with love in everyday life. After all, do we not love ideas, cherish memories, long for our homeland, or fall in love with a landscape? Is not every kind of love primarily psychological? Even physical attraction can be said to have its origin in our psychological notions about what is desirable and beautiful.

Psychology recognizes the role subjective projections play in forming sexual relationships, yet sexual love between humans and spirit beings is considered perverse and pathological. At first sight there would seem to be no valid reason for making any distinction between an ordinary marriage and a marriage to a spirit: both are fed by instinctive as well as hormonal energy and by the energy of the mind. The only essential difference is the level of consciousness involved—the shaman communicates with his beloved of the Beyond only when he is in an altered state of consciousness.

To be united with a spirit wife or spirit husband does not merely satisfy a hedonistic need. To a much greater extent we are here confronted by a sort of spiritual division of labor: the spirit beings grant the wishes of the shaman by healing through him, undertaking exploratory flights to obtain visions of the future, observing and reporting on the actions of an enemy and, in extreme cases, causing the death of a competitor. The shaman, for his part, during the illness leading to his initiation had to promise his protecting spirit that he would act as an agent of healing—and this is a promise he must keep if he doesn't want to attract the wrath of his spirit companion.

The celestial partners involved in such relationships are often beguilingly beautiful, even though they may have much in common with earthly creatures. For that reason, sexual contact with a being from another dimension can be more refreshing and intense than might be the case with an earthly partner. On the other hand, sexual intercourse with spirit beings can be somewhat onesided—for instance, when the shaman is literally raped by his spirit partner. Protecting spirits furthermore are able to transform themselves into ugly and terrifying monsters, and frequently do so. In this way, the beautiful spirit wife may suddenly turn into an old witch or a ravenous wild beast. We may assume that such experiences are mechanisms which help the shaman to become aware of the projections of his own consciousness, because it may well be that all he can experience in the Beyond is what his culture or ego lead him to expect.

Many near-death experiences and journeys to the Beyond throw light on the play of human consciousness, and it has been observed that every individual perceives the beings and creatures encountered there within the framework of his own cultural traditions. However, in view of the latest findings in the field of consciousness research, it is no longer possible to argue that the configurations of the Beyond are merely unconscious productions, archetypes, or symbols without any real and practical consequences. The spirit wife is not the daydream of a romantic neurotic. She instructs the shaman, makes him into a person that fulfills an important role within his culture and allows him to display a great number of inexplicable parapsychic phenomena. Over and above that, the spirit partner establishes the urgently sought contact to the world of the dead.

As messengers between the various world realms, the shaman, and his spiritual partner consolidate the traditional cosmology. The contact of humans with other forms of life and alternative levels of existence is an ancient experience of mankind, and its impact will continue to be felt by society, because cooperation with or inspiration by dream and spirit creatures has given rise to many cultural and artistic achievements. Moreover, any human being can gain access to higher levels and forms of consciousness if his sense of identity is dissolved or dismantled as a result of an accident, an NDE, a long fast, prolonged rhythmic dancing, shock, pain, fear, extreme stress, or some other blockage of normal neurological mechanisms.

Split personalities and figurative hallucinations also occur in schizophrenics. The diverse psychiatric theories, however, aim at desanctifying and defunctionalizing such archetypal and transpersonal phenomena by denying them a meaningful psychic role, suppressing them with the use of drugs or eliminating them by the application of purely personalistic or reductionist therapies. Visions of an unearthly being, irrespective of whether they occur in a dream or in a trance state, must be considered one of the highest capabilities of the human mind, and all tribal societies, as well as genuine cultures in both the old world and the new, have always correctly interpreted such visions as a source of creative inspiration. A true psychology—such as we still have to develop—would consider the gift of experiencing spirits, visions, or landscapes of the Beyond an indispensable therapeutic agent and aim at enriching the lamentable onesidedness of our intellectual powers by the therapeutic provision of a spirit of the Beyond or a spirit wife or husband.

Given our present therapeutic attitudes, such an approach may sound absurd and ridiculous, but in the not too distant future it will and must be as commonplace as imagination therapies and dream analysis are today. As yet psychology sees its primary task as accumulating comprehensive knowledge of the psychic "apparatus"; in actual fact, however, we are increasingly being driven back to traditional and archaic sources of insight and knowledge. The first "backward" step consisted in the development of psychophysical techniques of self-control such as biofeedback and Autogenous Training.

The trend continues with ever more people becoming interested in meditation and similar practices and is supported and consolidated by the reviving interest in ethnopsychology, transcultural psychiatry, and the whole spectrum covered by the term "ethnoscience." Modern research into shamanism and the growing attraction of Eastern philosophies will give rise to new criticisms being leveled at present day psychological theories. These criticisms will thus be nourished by the wisdom of the past and of tradition. The journey to an alternative domain of consciousness—

perhaps with the purpose of finding or seeing a spirit wife or husband—is therefore closely connected with a time journey undertaken by the theory of cognition into the historic past, that is to say, with a true return to the *illud tempus* and to ancient knowledge.

Ethnological literature about India mentions a number of strongly standarized initiatory experiences in which spirit marriages play a central role.[2]

These examples illustrate the extent to which personal and psychic expectations are influenced by transpersonal experiences. On the other hand, these reports again and again show a variety of general human characteristics such as resisting or fearing the spirit guide, followed by resignation and consent to a marriage with a spirit husband or a spirit wife. Sometimes the marriage results in spirit children being born in the Beyond. Another standard feature is that initial psychopathological symptoms subside after the person in question has ceased rejecting the advances of their spirit suitors.

The narratives about such sacred weddings appear to be rather simple because shamans tend to describe their path of suffering in a greatly abbreviated way. In any case, they themselves are not sufficiently aware of the mechanisms involved in the transformation of their consciousness or, for that matter, the psychic principles of intercourse with their spirit partners, for their reports to satisfy our scientific and analytical curiosity. The shaman is deeply and unconsciously rooted in his traditional culture and looks upon contact with a spirit being as a relatively normal occurrence. In consequence, he feels no need to search for complicated explanations.

Let us now look at the initiatory experience of a shamaness called Champa, a member of the Saora in the Indian province of Borai. She at first resisted the advances of her spirit suitor with great determination, but then married him out of fear and even gave birth to a spirit child by him which cried whenever she tried to breastfeed it. In the morning the neighbors would ask whose child had been crying. Later, Champa gave birth to a spirit daughter. In addition, she married a human husband who also made her pregnant. Her narrative of how she became a shamaness is as follows:

> My father's mother was a shamaness, so was his sister. After her death, my father's sister's tutelary came to me in a dream, bringing with him another tutelary called Potnadevi. He was a Paik by caste and was dressed in smart Hindu clothes. My aunt's tutelary said, "I have brought this man to marry you, but you must serve me as well." I

was afraid, saying to myself, "This is a Paik; how can I marry him?" and I refused.

Again and again he came to me in dreams, and I always refused. Then one night he took me up in a whirlwind and carried me away to a very high tree where me made me sit on a fragile branch. There he began to sing and as he sang he swung me to and fro. I was terrified of falling from that great height and I hastily agreed to marry him. Then we sat for a time swinging and singing together.

The following night, my tutelary came and taught me how to use the winnowing fan. Many other gods came with him and they said, "We are all very pleased with you; now celebrate your marriage with a feast." When I woke and the memory came to me, I was like a mad-woman and I fell unconscious to the ground. For six months I did nothing and was unwell all the time.[3]

A spirit husband can cause many problems for the earthly marriage of his partner. In such marital triangles, the wife with two spouses naturally has the stronger position. We shall illustrate this by the example of Somra, another member of the Saora, from the town of Taraba, whose wife was a shamaness but also married to a spirit husband. One day, when Somra had an argument with his wife, the spirit husband threatened to take her away for ever if he quarrelled with her again. Here is Somra's de-scription of the episode:

One day I said to her, "Give me some hot rice to eat." All she did was to pour some hot water over stale cold rice and feed me on that. I was very much annoyed and I abused her. Next day I went down with fever. It lasted for two days, and when I thought I was going to die, I had to ask my wife to find out what was the matter with me. Her hus-band, her tutelary, came to her from the Under World and said to me, "If you ever abuse your wife like that again, I shall take her away. I am pleased with her. That's why I married her, and I'd very much prefer to have her with me here. She may be young, but she is also mine. I have one child from her, though you may have had a son from her too, as well as a daughter that I have not had. But from today, never abuse or beat her, or I will come at once and take her away." Since that day I have never quarrelled with my wife. My fever stopped that very evening.[4]

Samiya, a shaman from the Indian town of Sogeda, at the age of fifty-five, shortly before he died, described how he came to have several spirit wives. He had inherited two helping spirits from his mother and married them. Later, two more spirit women wanted to marry him. When he rejected them because of their caste, the two helping spirits he had inherited from his mother beat him with branches from a thorn bush until he agreed to enter into another double wedding. Thereafter he made regular sacrifices to all his spirit wives at the appropriate festivals. He also had a child by one of his spirit wives. Occasionally all his wives would meet and fly with him to the Underworld.[5]

A shamaness from the Indian town of Sondan was seduced by a spirit spouse at the early age of ten after he had given her some wine to drink. During the following years she occasionally became unconscious, but this only lasted for a few minutes. Nevertheless, her parents consulted a healer who diagnosed her condition by saying that a spirit wanted to marry her. Her father said to the spirit:

> "Why do you keep on troubling this girl? She may die if you don't leave her alone." But the tutelary said, "No, I am pleased with your daughter. I have given her a lot of wine to drink and I am going to marry her. Then if anyone feels ill and she sends for me, I will tell her what is the matter, and help her cure the patient. I insist on marrying her. Give me a she-goat and I will come into the house."

Her parents then gave way, the spirit moved into the house, and their daughter was married to him. Soon the young woman gave birth to a child by him in the spirit world, and he would bring it to her at night for her to breastfeed it. He came when everyone was asleep. The people in the village heard the child cry, but her own family slept as if they were dead. Later she married a man in this world, but because she had had a child in the other world she did not think that she could have more children here.[6]

Tarendu, a shaman from the Indian town of Patili, was forced into a multiple marriage to several spirit wives. His father also was a shaman whose helping spirit turned himself into a wild boar to force him into marriage. Here is Tarendu's description of his own trials:

> I too had a lot of trouble before I was married, for several tutelary girls were after me. First a potter woman came to my house. I hid inside and she put a pot on the verandah and went away. When she had gone I came out and smashed the pot. Then a Pano girl came with skins and again I hid inside. She put the skins on the verandah. When she was gone I came out and threw the skins away. Then came two Saora tutelaries, sisters, the elder was crosseyed, the younger lame and fat. When they arrived I was up a sago palm. They called to me,

"Give us some wine, too. We are both going to marry you." I looked at them and said, "Oh no you aren't."

At last came a Paik girl, a lovely girl in fine clothes. She smiled at me from a distance. She said, "I am a Paik girl, and you are only a Saora, but I am going to marry you." I said no, but she caught hold of me and took me to the Under World where she shut me up in a stone house and gave me nothing to eat. I grew thin as a tamarind leaf, and then she took me to the top of a high date palm and shook it until I was so terrified of falling that I promised to marry her after all. Her name was Sirpanti.

But I forgot all about it, and the result was that I went crazy and wandered about the fields like a lunatic until after several months I suddenly remembered what I had promised. At once I arranged for the wedding, sacrificed a goat, dedicated a pot, drew her an icon, and in no time I was well again and began my work as a shaman.[7]

From Japan, too, we have narratives about shamanesses who marry a protective deity.[8] In the town of Yamashiro, almost all shamanesses, surprisingly, are completely blind. Being unable to earn a regular income, they become apprentices of a senior shamaness who teaches them how to summon the gods, the souls of the dead, methods of ceremonial cleansing, etc. It soon transpires which apprentices are gifted. Those that have no talent are sent away. As a rule, the senior shamaness passes on her knowledge to no more than four or five apprentices.

Prior to their initiation the novices live in isolation. They fast, continuously cleanse themselves, put on a white shroud, and eat the food of the dead in ritual fashion. They keep pouring water over themselves and crush rice in a mortar until it turns into a stiff paste. They then fall to the ground as if dead, but regain consciousness when someone touches them. There follows the marriage to the spiritual husband who appeared to them during their initiation.

After the novice has spent a further week by herself in the shrine room of the deity of her clan, she publicly takes up her work as a shamaness and medium. If the deity of a shrine calls her to service she brings the usual household utensils such as a pot for cooking rice, a frying pan and so on with her into the marriage, as an ordinary woman would bring her dowry. Until recently, sexual marriages between a shamaness and a priest of the shrine were customary, the priest delegating for the deity during intercourse.

Suitability for training as a shaman is not confined to particularly sensitive people. In some cases physically abnormal people are also considered suitable. It is believed that blind women, because of their limited capacity for housework and the absence of social obligations, are much more likely to become aware of the propensities of the gods. The inner life of the blind is of necessity more highly developed than is the case with normally sighted people, who are held in thrall by the attractions of the phenomenal world. The training of blind women thus arises quite naturally. Other forms of physical handicap that exclude people from normal everyday life and force them to withdraw from society can equally facilitate insight into alternative states of consciousness.

Just as the Greenland Eskimos put themselves into a trance by monotonously rubbing two stones against each other and finally become unconscious—in which state they make contact with spirits and beings of the Beyond—so the Japanese shamanesses ceaselessly pound rice in a mortar until they, too, lose consciousness and their celestial spouse appears to them. We can see from this that the psychic process of deconditioning is identical, despite a considerable cultural distance. At first, anthropology did not recognize this and so came to regard the shamanic profession as a kind of dumping ground for people who cannot perform a useful social or economic role. The early anthropologists were thus unable to see that psychic and physical abnormalities can dispose a person towards the transpersonal, because such individuals, by virtue of their abnormality, are excluded from normal life within their culture.

After all, what anthropologist has taken the trouble to imitate such "nonsensical" activities as rubbing stones against each other or pounding rice with a pestle and mortar for days on end? Yet only someone who has himself experienced the helplessness and suffering of such a long drawn-out struggle, and has gone right through it, is able to pass judgment on such matters. One would, in fact, discover that such a simple activity—we might almost call it a form of "behavioral therapy"—can free us from the fetters of our habits and bring us into contact with the realms of gods and spirits. Why can contemporary psychology not muster the courage to acknowledge and study these border areas? They are, after all, the very areas from which we receive our deepest insights and our highest potential. Why does Western man avoid and resent pain? Why do we recoil in fear from this "little death" . . . the temporary dissolution of our ego?

Today anthropologists know that such seemingly absurd activities as the continuous pounding of rice are not performed out of superstitious ignorance but could be described as relevant to a "psychology of higher states of consciousness." We have to concede that tribal cultures have psychological insights which, one day, we may once again share.

Marriage to a disembodied partner is also known in Burma, where the refusal to marry such a Nat spirit results in suffering and illness. However, because these Nat shamans are not particularly respected, many people that are approached by a Nat spirit try to delay the marriage for as long as possible by making various excuses. Here are some examples given by Melford Spiro.

U Ka, a male shaman in Mandalay, was first loved by his Nat when he was eighteen, but he did not marry her until he was forty-five. She announced her love by appearing to him in a dream and lying beside him "as a sister." Because of the long delay between her declaration of love and his eventual marriage to her she not only caused him to lose all his money and property, but she killed his wife as well. To protect himself from further harm he married the Nat. It was only after he had agreed to bow to her will that she no longer objected to his having a sexual relationship with a human woman.

The shamaness Daw Pya first encountered her Nat at the age of seventeen when he appeared to her in a dream. As she did not want to be tied to him, she sought advice from a Burmese doctor about how best to avoid it. That same year she married a human husband and subsequently had two children. At the age of thirty-seven she divorced her husband at the insistence of her Nat. During the previous twenty years she had been punished by the Nat in a variety of ways for refusing to marry him. He not only caused her to lose all her property—she had been a cigar merchant—but also to become ill. Her symptoms included long fits or seizures, severe palpitations, vomiting, and an inability to digest solid food. Finally, apprehensive lest she go mad, she married him. Since then her symptoms disappeared and she recovered her property. Although the Nat husband thereafter had no objection to her taking another human husband she stayed away from other men since her marriage to the Nat.

U Maung Maung was twenty-five years old when he attended a Nat festival at which a female Nat fell in love with him. She appeared to him in his dreams as a beautiful woman and asked him to have sexual intercourse with her. Although he had taken a human wife only two months prior to that, he divorced her at the bidding of his Nat spouse. As soon as he had transferred his affections to her he discovered that she had another husband, a Nat, who interfered with the new couple's attempts to have sexual relations although he had consented to their marriage, which suffered greatly as a result.

Daw Kyoun was possessed by her Nat husband at the age of forty when, at a Nat festival, she fell into a trance while dancing. She agreed to marry this Nat but remained married to her human husband as well and indeed has since borne children by him.

Several Nats appeared to sixteen-year-old Daw Ei Khin in a dream. Five or six years later, she was possessed by one of them. Thereafter, as if deranged, she drifted about the village in a trancelike state, barely eating or drinking. Prior to becoming possessed she had been married and borne a child, but her Nat spouse, jealous of her husband, forbade her to resume sexual relations with him. Her human husband had to become a servant of the Nat, doing his (i.e., his wife's) bidding. She does not suffer from sexual deprivation because she has sexual relations in her sleep with her Nat husband.[9]

As all these examples show, the rejection of the love of a spirit does not go unpunished but as a rule results in illness, bad luck, and general misery. The spirit suitor keeps alive this fear of punishment in the person he or she has chosen for marriage, and in many cases this fear is the main reason for agreeing to the marriage in the end. Normally, a future shaman encounters a Nat spirit as a teenager but does not marry that spirit until he is in his thirties, whereafter he is officially confirmed as a shaman.

It is said that a Nat is attracted to a shamaness by his "love for her beautiful soul"—a very apt metaphor for a psychic disposition towards shamanism.

The spirit suitor appearing to a shamaness in a dream or state of obsession is identified by her on the basis of his qualities. This is not always easy, due to the existence of a whole pantheon of different spirits. The wedding itself takes place in a ceremonial chamber. A shamaness who lives with a spirit of the same type as the bride wishes to marry, performs the Nat dance, accompanied by an orchestra, and sings the specific song of the Nat in question. The bride then enters a screened-off area of the room, where two beds—one for the bride and one for the groom—are to be found.

The central function of the marriage ceremony consists in "guiding the butterfly soul of the bride into sleep." The shamaness moves a mirror to and fro in front of the bride's face, at the same time pressing another mirror against her back. Another shamaness attaches strings of cotton to the ankles and wrists of the bride and then places a longer cord diagonally across her shoulders. Finally, she pierces the bride's hair knot with a needle to which a string of cotton is attached. It is believed that the bride's soul has at this point gone to sleep and will soon become the wife of the Nat, who is in love with her butterfly soul and not with her body. This union between two nonmaterial entities constitutes the actual marriage of two beings from different worlds.

The ritual ends with a Nat dance by the bride, during which she goes into a trance. Shamanesses are not only loved by their spirit spouses; during the dance they are also able to transform themselves into their spirit spouse by appropriate dress and gestures. Subsequently, the novice spends seven days alone with her Nat partner, after which she resumes her normal life. She is now known as a Nat dadaw, a Nat's wife.

By marriage to a Nat spirit, unmarried women are afforded an opportunity to live out their sexual fantasies and desires freely and with the approval of a society in which extramarital and premarital sex are taboo. Because marriage to a Nat spirit is accepted by society, even homosexuals and transvestites have the possibility to act out their emotions and attitudes without being judged. This extends to bisexuals who, for instance, might become obsessed by a sister and brother spirit pair.

Most anthropologists see in such succubus/incubus relationships an expression of sexual abnormality. They interpret marriage to a Nat partner either as an escape from the reality of a sexually unsatisfactory conventional marriage or as an attempt to acquire recognition by performing the socially acceptable role of a shaman. The fact that people who enter into marriage with a spirit spouse will turn to dreams and the imagination to justify their behavior is seen by those anthropologists as a pathological compensatory mechanism of the psyche, even when such forms of dream sexuality are harmoniously embedded in the everyday life of the culture in question.

Such a view, however, amounts to putting the cart before the horse. The people concerned are not sick or perverse and do not escape into a world of fantasy. Rather, their "sickness"—their deviating psychic constitution—permits a dissolution of their personal and social identity and affords access to higher transpersonal layers of consciousness and to the world of the spirits. As long as traditional anthropology clings to its upside-down tendency to pathologize transpersonal phenomena, it will, in all probability, remain unable to arrive at an inner understanding of the significance of spiritual marriages.

Whereas the balance of a normal person must first become disturbed by shamanic sickness if that person is to experience another reality, socially abnormal people could be said to have a certain predisposition in this direction. In other words: Shamanic transformation is more accessible to them than it is for someone solidly rooted in the cultural values of his community. Sickness, psychic, physical, and social handicaps as well as sexual deviations result in a disturbed identity, a lack of inner balance, which can shorten and facilitate the path of initiation.

Deviations from the norm, imbalance, disturbance, and derangement have for centuries smoothed the way for transpersonal capabilities. The adjusted individual timidly goes along with the herd and lacks the requisite courage for such a path. It takes great daring to attempt the ascent to a higher dimension of consciousness, and people who make such an attempt have to be prepared to break through routine thought patterns and socially accepted conventions and practices. Just as in the intellectual realm extraordinary achievements are brought about by the unconventional approach of a free and independent thinker, so the psychically abnormal, the physically ill or the sexually deviant more easily attain a higher level of reality, providing they are willing to submit to the rigors of shamanic training.

A Gold shaman (southern group of the Tungus, northeastern Siberia) has given Shternberg a detailed account of how he became a shaman and of his marriage to a spirit wife. He was forty years old and a married man. Up to the age of twenty he had been very healthy, but then began to feel unwell. In the course of time he became quite desperate and could not obtain help from anyone. So he began to shamanize by himself. During his sickness an unusually beautiful woman appeared to him, dressed in the attire of the Gold tribe. Her magnificent hair was decorated with small plaits and hung down to her shoulders. (Other shamans of the Gold tribe described their spirit wives as having a face which is half black and half red.) She told him who she was, saying:

> "I am the Ayami of your ancestors, the shamans. I taught them shamanizing. Now I am going to teach you. The old shamans have died off and there is no one to heal people. You are to become a shaman."
>
> Next she said, "I love you. I have no husband now. You will be my husband and I shall be a wife unto you. I shall give you assistant spirits. You are to heal with their aid, and I shall teach and help you myself. Food will come to us from the people."
>
> I felt dismayed and tried to resist. Then she said, "If you will not obey me, so much the worse for you. I shall kill you."[10]

Every day she came and caressed him; at night they were like husband and wife, but she bore him no children. When she did not appear to him as a beautiful woman she showed herself to him as an old crone, a wolf bitch, or a winged tiger whose back he would fly to distant places. She gave him three spirit helpers—a panther, a bear, and a tiger—who came to him when he called them and appeared to him in dreams. If one or the other of them refused to come, his spirit wife would make them obey. During healing seances, she and the three spirit helpers would penetrate him "as smoke or vapor would." When she was within him she spoke through his mouth. When he was eating the offerings it was not he who ate and drank. It was his spirit wife. In the tradition of the Gold Eskimos, the helping spirits, too, have to be fed, otherwise they will become abusive or complain.

At the time this shaman told his story to Shternberg, he did not yet know whether he would become a great shaman. He said that his spirit wife would decide what abilities he was to have. There were three degrees of shamans:

1. The siurku shaman, who only knows how to heal

2. The nyemanti shaman, who performs a special ceremony over a deceased man's soul a day or two after his death

3. The Kasati, the greatest shaman, who conveys the soul of the deceased to the other world

But in any case his protecting spirit had already shown him how to make his shaman costume, how to paint and decorate the drum, and how to fashion images of spirit helpers.

At the time Shternberg recorded the story of the great Gold shaman Chucke Ominka, Chucke was considered the greatest shaman along the Amur River and still capable of escorting souls to the Land of the Dead. He had been a roaming shaman all his life, visiting various localities to hold ceremonies for the dead. Many villages and communities would wait several years for him, so that a great number of souls, sometimes as many as twenty, had accumulated by the time of his arrival. In such cases it was very difficult to escort all of them at once, because some of them might get lost, so he would have to turn back to round them up again. At the same time he had to feed the three Ayamis that permanently lived in his body, so he was always drunk. Nevertheless, Shternberg assures us that Chucke conducted his ceremonies with a completely clear mind. When Shternberg invited him to record his incantation formulas for raising the spirits on a phonograph, however, he declined in horror because his Ayami might well kill him for doing such a thing.

His father, brother, and sister were also shamans. His career as a shaman began with a sickness, during which an Ayami revealed herself to him in a dream. He soon married this Ayami. She was ravishingly beautiful and looked just like a real woman of the Gold tribe. He later acquired a second Ayami, who provided him with various spirit helpers such as a rabid dog, a rabid fox, a dwarf, a headless man, and a heath-cock. From his father he inherited a helper known as Heavenly Spirit and a spirit called Bolo, who thereafter assisted him in escorting the souls of the dead to the Beyond. In addition, Chucke Ominka married a young and pretty woman of this world. She was only eighteen-years-old at the time, but cared for him lovingly and patiently, which was no easy task in view of his continuous drunkenness. She played her role as a shaman's wife with great dignity and never showed any signs of jealousy toward her husband's spirit wives.[11]

Among the Yakut, spirit wives are known as Abassi. When they appear to the shaman in his sleep, he knows he will soon be called to heal a patient. The Abassi maidens reside in the *Mānarikta challan*, the heaven of the spirits of ecstasy.[12]

The Shortzy Eskimos (an Altai tribe) have a legend about a primordial shaman called Kam Atis. When his wife discovered that, in addition to her, he had a celestial wife, she became enraged with jealousy and insisted that he show his mistress to her. He began to beat the drum to call his spirit wife. His earthly wife, however, was unable to see her rival and so shouted out in anger: "Where is your wife then? It's all a lie. You have no other wife except me!" The shaman had no other choice but to ask her to look into the drum. Instead of glancing at the drum from a respectful distance she stood right in front of it. Within the drum she beheld a light as bright as the sun and a warning voice said to her: "You *were* jealous of your husband . . . ." At that moment the shaman's wife fell dead to the ground. At the burial ceremony, during a drumming seance, the shaman escaped through the smoke hole of the tent. Before that, however, he explained to those present that the shamans that were to follow him would visit him at the place where he was going.[13]

Shortzy shamans have a celestial wife as the main protecting spirit and other helping spirits and spirit animals. Among the Shortzy the encounter of a shaman with a "little girl" is a widespread tradition, although each shaman experiences this little girl in his own way: sometimes as a black maiden with seven breasts or seven plaits and three eyes; at other times as a shining maiden with white hair.

The vocation for shamanism is signaled by the spirits, more specifically the former spirits of a dead shaman of the same clan, who choose the next shaman by returning to Erlik Khan (the god of the celestial world) asking him to grant them a new shaman to be their master. As soon as a suitable candidate has been selected within the clan, he is visited by the shamanic sickness. At this point the celestial wife begins to woo him. If he accepts her she comes to live in his drum. The drum therefore is an external symbol of the shaman's spirit wife. It is made by the oldest relative of the new shaman, and during its making this oldest relative refers to the drum as "maiden" and to the shaman as "bridegroom."

Don Soltero Perez, the only shaman in the small Mexican town of Tecospa, is an old man and a highly respected member of the community. In 1918 his house was struck by lightning, and all the inhabitants were knocked unconscious. Everyone in the house revived quickly except Don Soltero, who recovered very slowly and remained in a daze. Over a period of about six months he continued to lose consciousness once a week. On these occasions his spirit was abducted by the *enanitos*, dwarf-sized rain deities who have existed in the Valley of Mexico since Aztec times. They took him to the caves in which they lived. Whenever the enanitos attacked him, Don Soltero fell to the floor as though he were dead. His limbs became rigid and his teeth began to grind. Soon after, his body became limp.

The enanitos wanted Don Soltero to become a healer and told him they would not allow his spirit to return to his body unless he agreed to their request. They beat him until he consented. However, after his spirit returned to his body, Don Soltero changed his mind, deciding not to become a healer. The enanitos returned again and again. Each time his spirit reentered his body, he felt sore all over from the beatings he received at the hands of the enanitos. After six months Don Soltero entered into a permanent agreement with the enanitos to become a healer. He knew they would kill him if he did not give in to their demands. The enanitos presented him with a staff, three healing stones, and a spirit wife. The staff is invisible to all except Don Soltero and the enanitos. He found the three healing stones in his pocket upon returning to his body; one was shaped like a cannon, the second like a doll, and the third like a duck. During a night thunder storm, when Don Soltero is asleep, these stones may leave his house never to return, but they are replaced by other stones which come to his house by their own power.

Don Soltero's spirit wife is an enanita who lives in a cave with others of her kind. Had Don Soltero refused to marry her, she would no doubt have killed him in revenge. She and Don Soltero have children who live with their mother in the cave. Since he became a healer, Don Soltero has not been allowed to have sexual relations with his human wife. He tried once but immediately had an attack and fell to the floor as though he were dead. During this attack his spirit was forced to go to a cave, where it was beaten by the enanitos. Since then Don Soltero concentrates all his sexual activity on his spirit wife.

Don Soltero is knows as a *curandero de aire*, a healer working with air and wind. He and all others of his kind die twice a year. Their spirits go to a cave of the enanitos where they receive further instruction in healing. The first annual death occurs in October or November, after the end of the big rain fall. All the curanderos "die" at the same time and remain dead for half an hour or an hour while their spirits attend the great assembly of curanderos and enanitos.[14]

Don Soltero's vocation begins with a death experience, which is triggered off by a stroke of lightning and reveals another world to him. His healing powers are regularly renewed and strengthened when he is taken, in a state of unconsciousness, to a cave in the nonterrestrial realm. Once again we are confronted by the whole spectrum of shamanic experience: death, journey to the Beyond, encounter and contact with spirit beings, resistance to marry a being from the Beyond, acceptance of the vocation, development of healing powers, the use of magical objects, regeneration of powers by periodic out-of-body experiences, and soul journeys to the Beyond.

In the Western world also, marriage to a supernatural being is by no means unknown. An example of it is the Christian symbolism connected with the Bride of Christ. Catholic nuns experience themselves as brides of Christ and are, in fact, wedded to him in a formal marriage ceremony. Benedictine nuns, after a similar ceremony, lie in a bridal bed adorned with flowers. On the pillow is a crucifix with which the newlywed virgin spends her wedding night. Medieval mysticism freely uses this symbol of the wedding bed, and sexual themes are not uncommon among many Christian mystics. Mechthild of Magdeburg had a love affair with Jesus and recommended all nuns to surrender to the eighteen-year-old son of God. Many nuns, while in a state of ecstasy, believe themselves to be embraced, kissed, and even made pregnant by Jesus. In some cases mock pregnancies have occurred. Other female mystics have assumed the role of the Virgin Mary and in their imagination became pregnant.

The idea of supernatural conception was very widespread. In several orders the nun received a golden wedding ring and was addressed as the bride of Jesus Christ. The ceremonial reply, "I love Christ, whose bed I share" still reminds us of this tradition. A ritual text calls upon the nuns to embrace their beloved, the redeemer, who descends from heaven into their breast, and to hold him tight until he has granted all their wishes. Virgins who dedicated themselves to God left their dead body to Christ. Plotinus also speaks of "the divine soul becoming pregnant," and Origen of "becoming pregnant by the mystic spirit."

All mystical traditions describe the *unio mystica* as a sexual union, because—as Indian mystics would put it—someone embraced by the primordial self can neither be within nor without. From the love mysticism of the Krishna cult to the ecstatic avatar Ramakrishna, who had an erotically colored relationship to the goddess Kali, the spirit world of India is marked by the possibility of metaphysical eroticism. The concept of the sexual transmaterial union with God is found throughout the history of religion. It is indeed a universal symbol of mankind.

12

The Song of Power:
Joy, Joy, Joy!

Songs are thoughts, sung out with the breath when people are moved by great forces and ordinary speech no longer suffices. Man is moved just like an ice floe sailing here and there out in the current. His thoughts are driven by a flowing force when he feels joy, when he feels fear, when he feels sorrow. Thought can wash over him like a flood, making his breath come in gasps and his heart throb. Something, like an abatement in the weather, will keep him thawed up and then it will happen that we, who always think that we are small, will feel still smaller. And we will fear to use words. But it will happen that the words we need will come of themselves. When the words we want to use shoot up of themselves—we get a new song.

—Orpingalik, A *Netsilingmint Eskimo*[1]

By the image of an ice floe being moved by the current, Orpingalik provides us with a very beautiful metaphor for the dissolution of our rigid thought patterns and of our ego structure. This "flowing force" or, as we might call it, the "experience of flowing" arises in all forms of heightened emotional engagement, extreme fear, unbearable pain, and in moments of ecstatic joy or mystical bliss. It can thus be said that peak experiences as well as acute depressive states can bring us to the point at which we enter this whirling "current" of power.

Orpingalik uses a further impressive image when he says that "something like an abatement in the weather" will cause us to thaw. While cold and ice will cause the pores to contract, thoughts to freeze and feelings to cool, the Eskimos, during the summer, experience a reawakening of all their human sensibilities. Orpingalik expresses this by saying, " . . . and then it will happen that we, who always think that we are small, will feel still smaller." Western man, on the other hand, tends to reject the idea of his own insignificance with great determination. However, this feeling of insignificance and smallness in comparison to universal phenomena is essential for any kind of mystic inspiration or an ecstatic peak experience. Our psyche is so paradoxically constructed that we can rise from the deepest depression with renewed life strength, like a phoenix from the ashes—with a song that tells of the sources and places of power pervading the universe.

When we have made ourselves small, by shedding our socialized ego like an old winter pelt, we can share the joy of creation and come to know "the love of all things," as is spoken of by shaman Avá-Nembiará, quoted below. A characteristic of ecstacy and enlightenment is an indescribable feeling of bliss, of cosmic joy at the unity with the higher self, the helping spirit of nature. The Eskimo shaman Aua, in an altered state of consciousness, encountered a "shore spirit" and thereafter would call this spirit helper by singing:

> Joy, Joy,
> Joy, Joy!
> I see a little shore spirit,
> A little aua,
> I myself am also aua,
> The shore spirit's namesake,
> Joy, Joy!

"These words I would keep on repeating ," he recalls, "until I burst into tears, overwhelmed by a great dread; then I would tremble all over, crying only, 'Ah-a-a-a-a, joy, joy! Now I will go home, joy, joy!"

> Then I sought solitude, and here I soon became very melancholy. I would sometimes fall to weeping, and feel unhappy without knowing why. Then, for no reason, all would suddenly be changed and I felt a great, inexplicable joy, a joy so powerful that I could not restrain it, but had to break into song, a mighty song, with only room for the one word: joy, joy! And I had to use the full strength of my voice. And then, in the midst of such a fit of mysterious and overwhelming delight, I became a shaman, not knowing myself how it came about. But I was a shaman. I could see and hear in a totally different way.[2]

If such an experience is barely comprehensible for one to whom it happens, it is even more so for rational science, because of its tendency to get caught up in metaphors and superficial descriptions. The song of power may well be the true song of life—a direct expression of all joy in existence and of vitality. Ecstacy is our enthusiasm about the mystic unity of all things and beings. It is a feeling of being able to surrender to the waves of our existential "ups and downs" without trying to control them, and free from the fear-ridden egoism of our rational psyche.

There are many ways of singing a song and many reasons for doing so. We can sing a song as we might read a book, just reading the lines, as it were. Or a song might rise spontaneously in our hearts, as a kind of improvisation to praise a blessed moment. Yet again, a song or melody can be born in us, almost half-consciously, as a result of profound concentration. Such is the case with the great composers. We can hear a song in a dream or feel it rise in us quite unexpectedly at a time of leisure and relaxation. It may also happen that we discover a song in ourselves after a complete psychic or physical collapse—a song that reflects our own state and acquaints us with the archetypes of the soul. Finally, we may receive a song from beings in the realm of the dead, from spirit animals, or dead relatives in the course of a journey to the Beyond. These various ways of acquiring songs of power are representative of different levels of consciousness. The song becomes more powerful and effective with the gradual dissolution of our ego.

The same applies to visions which may come to us in a harmless daydream or during a near-death experience. Western science believes that shamanistic phenomena can be explained by psychological categorizing and thereby blinds itself to the reality of a continuum of levels of consciousness of varying degrees of intensity. It assumes that the dream revelations of a patient, or the pathological symptoms of a neurosis, are comparable to the process of shamanic transformation. Such an attitude reduces the shaman to the level of traditional Western ego psychology and judges him by its criteria. While these phenomena show certain similarities, they occur on different levels of consciousness. When this is taken into consideration it will be seen that the shaman towers high above the neurotic patient dealt with by Western psychotherapy.

A song is not simply a string of words to which a melody has been added. Rather, it is the expression of a psychosomatic and spiritual transformation which makes the shaman into a representative of another physical dimension—I say "physical dimension" because, in the last analysis, the shaman is capable of influencing our physical world, albeit in an acausal and nonmaterial way. His transformation has practical consequences. We can seldom say this in the case of psychiatric patients that have been cured.

The Bella Coola shamaness Sikwalxlelix, in her song, submerges herself in the "place of power":

Sky moving
as they sang
spirits sang of salmon

Sky waving
up and down
spirits singing

I was drowning
in the basin
the place of power
for curing

Spirits tossed
eagle down
to the surface
I rose singing

He pulled me out
the one who saves
those struck
by spirit power

I gazed deep
into the face
that gave me power
as a shaman

He stood up
in the center
in the center
of power

Spirit standing
in the place
of petrified
power

Sky moving
as they sang
spirits sang of salmon

Sky waving

up and down
spirits singing[3]

In her "place of power" Sikwalxlelix hears the salmon song of the spirits, who cause the sky to rise and fall in waves like the sea. This place of power is the domain of transpersonal existence. Here man is connected to a source of power which, in the earthly realm of normal consciousness, is manifested as magical expertise and the knowledge to heal. It is a place charged with energy; in fact, energy would seem to be its very nature. Anyone who gets in touch with such a place can salvage something of this energy and bring it to our realm of existence. This "something" transcends the causal mechanics of our world. Sikwalxlelix uses allegory to describe the indescribable. She speaks of a basin (of water). As is well known, water is a symbol of transformation, spiritual purification and, in fact, of the primordial source of insight. The power of the spirit raises Sikwalxlelix from the primordial ground of Being and a song rises to her lips.

Immersion in the spirit realm or the spirit, the true source of shamanic knowledge, results in a heightened sense of reality, because a person thus immersed breaks through the congested channels of perception of our everyday consciousness. And through our "gaze into the face of power" the sacred song of liberation, mentioned by so many shamans, comes into being.

Isaac Tens, a Gitksan Indian shaman, had twenty-three such songs that he acquired in a trance state, during which he entered a house where he met his two uncles—both former shamans—who sang them to him. To him, this "house" was what the basin of water was to Sikwalxlelix and the great ocean or river to Uvavnuk. The symbolism can take many forms, because any place in the universe is suitable for the revelation of the sacred. There may be what we might call archetypal places of initiation, but in the last resort any place, element, or form can be a bearer or vehicle of initiation into the realm of the spirit and of power. Isaac Tens acquired his power in an isolated house on a great plain:

> When getting ready for the songs, I fell into a trance and saw a vast fine territory. In the middle of it a house stood. I stepped into it, and I beheld my uncle Tsigwee who had been a medicine man (halaait). He had died several years before. Then another uncle appeared— Gukswawtu. Both of them had been equally famous in their day. I heard them sing many songs. While they were singing, a Grizzly ran through the door, and went right around. Then he rose into the air

above the clouds, describing a circle, and came back to the house. Each of my uncles took a rattle and placed it into one of my hands. That is why I always use two rattles in my performances. In my vision I beheld many fires burning under the house. As soon as I walked out of the house, my trance ended. From then on, I sang those chants just as I had learned them in my vision.[4]

A song of healing power may also be acquired directly from the realm of the dead, usually from a dead relative or shaman, but also from indefinable, amorphous, or mythical beings who bestow the song of power upon the initiate.

Let us illustrate this by an example from the Paraguayan Avá-Chiripá tribe. A shaman of this tribe, Avá-Nembiará, journeyed in his sleep to the realm of the dead, where his grandfather presented him with a song of healing and revealed to him the secret of the ladder connecting heaven and earth. Avá-Nembiará observed the dances of the spirits from a mountaintop in the Beyond and heard their songs. Later, as a test, he was asked to cure a dead man lying by the roadside. He succeeded in doing this by the use of his newly acquired songs. He was astonished by their unexpected power of healing. His training continued, however, after his journey to the Beyond, because his celestial helpers continued to instruct him in the use of medicinal herbs.[5]

The song of power forms the central focus of the religion of the Papago Indians, but there are several ways of acquiring power. The first consists of taking a scalp in war. This scalp, however, is used by the Papago warrior only as a preparation for his "dreaming" the song of power. War, the killing of enemies and the taking of scalps affect the consciousness of the warrior to such an extent that he subsequently "dreams" a song of power. After their return from the warpath the scalp hunters live for a while in quarantine outside the village. A protector is assigned to each warrior during this period. This wife of the warrior also spends sixteen days in isolation, while he sits throughout motionless in one spot, his arms crossed and his head bowed towards his chest. Fasting and isolation soon cause a song to rise within him, whereafter nothing can prevent him from singing.

The Papago will accept songs of power cast in the simplest possible language, even if such a song differs only by a few words from that of the warrior's father or uncle. His song serves the warrior for the rest of his life as a magical and therapeutic means of healing. On the seventeenth day of the period of isolation a great fire is lit, around which the members of the tribe dance. The warrior is now presented with a basket by his protector, in which he places the scalp, known as "the prisoner." This scalp is thus treated like an imprisoned spirit, and the warrior thereafter has scalp power.

If a warrior is unable to take a scalp, but still wishes to have the possibility of "dreaming" a song, he kills an eagle and then fasts and dreams for a period of four days. In his dreams an eagle comes to him, not as a bird, however, but in its original human form and sings to him. In this way the young warrior is given clear information about the path of his life. One such warrior "dreamt" that he would become a gambler, a socially accepted occupation among the Papago and, true enough, he never lost whenever he gambled thereafter. Another dreamt of becoming a runner, and became one. If a warrior is dissatisfied with his dream, he kills another eagle the following year and waits for a new song. After the four-day fast all former killers of eagles gather to sing a song for their new brother.

The third way of acquiring power is an exhausting four-day pilgrimage to the Gulf of California for the purpose of fetching salt, which the waves of the ocean deposit on the rocks. The pilgrims set out toward the south, which the Papago refer to as the direction of suffering. The deprivations and exertions of the journey, together with the ritual commands to be observed, and the sight of the vast expanse of the ocean are so overwhelming for the Papago, who are a desert people, that they receive supernatural revelations on arrival at their destination. Before the journey begins, a hereditary priest sings sacred chants and performs a ritual to "make the pilgrimage safe." The initiate must perform his pilgrimage four times in consecutive years. In the past it was done on foot. Today the pilgrims ride on horseback. When they rest they lie with their head in the direction of the Pacific Ocean so that its power can draw them on.

During these salt pilgrimages many wise sermons are preached, in which the end of each sentence is marked by the words being pronounced at an unusually high pitch. As the speaker approaches the magical part of his sermon and begins to converse with the gods, the flow of his language is distorted into a sound not unlike that of an old car engine. On the afternoon of the third day, the group of pilgrims arrives at a legendary waterhole at the foot of Mount Pinacate. At first, however, everyone avoids contact with the water and joyfully rushes instead to the top of the mountain. The sight of the ocean from there transposes the pilgrim into a state of bliss, and they reach out for the ocean with their hands so as to take some of its power into themselves and then rub their hands along their bodies. Then they go to drink, and set out for the final twenty-four-hour lap of their journey, during which they do not stop for rest. These last hours are almost like a race; the salt pilgrims ride throughout the night, on and on toward the world ocean.

For a desert people that knows no brimming waterholes and no great rivers filled to their banks, the encounter with the ocean is a sacred experience. Famished and weakened by the stress of the journey, the pilgrims wait for a vision. When they have scraped the salt off the rocks and loaded it onto their horses, they wade into the shallow water and offer a sacrifice of corn flour to the ocean. Now, in rapt suspense, they wait for signs of the divine from the depths of the ocean. Many of them behold a sea coyote gliding on the surface of the water in a curious fashion. Other pilgrims will run along the beach for hours on end and then perhaps discover the power of healing in a cranny between two rocks, or a swarm of cranes will call them up into the sky to have a race with them.

After such visions the neophytes are in a purified and sanctified state. On the journey home they will not touch their body, and each one of them walks alone to avoid physical contact with others. They know they are all charged with power. They must not turn to look at the ocean lest it call them back. Upon their arrival in their village they fast for sixteen days and entreat the gods for further visions and songs. Only then are they considered to be mature warriors that may be fully integrated into the community.

Women also have the possibility of acquiring the song of power, but not by going on a salt pilgrimage or by "dreaming" such a song in some other way. They withdraw for four days during their time of menstruation. Like the eagle killers or the scalp hunters, they construct a simple shelter and avoid all contact with the opposite sex so as not to weaken their magical powers. If they wish to receive a vision or a song they will undertake a fast as well.

The Papago Indians have thus developed an impressive range of ceremonies by which any member of the tribe may strive to obtain a vision or a song of power. Life-and-death battles, the killing of an eagle, the strenuous salt pilgrimage, and even isolation and fasting during menstruation: All these aesthetic practices—providing they make extreme demands on the body and, as a result of additional fasts, consciousness becomes receptive—are considered to be suitable for presenting the initiate with a vision or a song of power. Pilgrimages and isolation during menstruation are universal practices by which aspirants endeavor to make contact with higher powers and to gain access to the hidden resources of human consciousness. The fact, however, that the Papago have incorporated even war and the taking of scalps into their sacred framework is an indication of the high level of their psychic integration.[6]

Psychic development and the regeneration of life are always accompanied by song, dance, rhythm, or the experience of joy. The song of the shaman arises from deep psychic purification and emptying. Emptiness and purity are also the cornerstones of an ancient therapy Western society is beginning to rediscover. A song born of inner harmony is a spontaneous expression of psychic and spiritual clarity.

The "song of power" lies dormant in us. It is awakened by great physical or existential suffering and then spontaneously bursts forth from within us. In the last analysis all transpersonal experience slumbers in us, buried under thick layers of habitual and ego-oriented psychological processes. Heightened concentration and sharpened attention can act like a drill boring toward the center of our personality. In this way successive layers of ego are penetrated until the higher self, or what we might call the transpersonal dimension, is reached. The parings and shavings brought to the surface by this drill are only a small part of this extensive realm of the psyche, but they can give rise to a song or vision which deeply transforms us by making us aware of another reality.

The language of that other reality is poetry, whereas ordinary consciousness speaks in prose which is often hard, unmelodic, mechanical and calculated. The song of power, on the other hand, is lyrical—a spontaneous rhythm freely unfolding without intervention of the will. In the company of his spirits the shaman finds himself in a place of petrified energy, at the very center of power. Here poetry is the only appropriate language, and the song of healing expresses continuous reality, because the place of power is also the place of healing, wholeness, and the holy.

The shaman submerges himself in this sphere where he is healed, and salvages part of this healing wholeness for our world. Having been made a bearer of power by the mere contact with this higher realm of consciousness, he is now able to allow others to partake of it. The song of power expresses a transpersonal experience and can thus develop into a song of healing. It is holy, because it comes from the very core of that which pervades everything. In ordinary language we might say that the peak experience, the trance state, egolessness, or meditative absorption are in themselves health-giving and healing, because they bring the highest potential of consciousness within the reach of human awareness.

The song of power speaks in the language of the transpersonal dimension. Such songs or poems are not *about* something—they *represent* something. Because even metaphorical language is inadequate for the description of a true state of altered consciousness, only a melody and the vibrations of musical sound can convey to us something of the flavor of unconditioned consciousness. Attempts to understand the meaning of transpersonal song by the methods of traditional science are of necessity paradoxical, for when we are in the centre of power and feel the song rise within us, we are in no way inclined to talk about it. Although there has always been a connection between the intellect and intuition, they are like the front and reverse sides of a coin, so that their eyes can never meet.

According to Abraham Maslow peak experiences and states of ecstasy are a biological need of man. This is also true of song, no matter whether profane or sacred. A song expresses our longing to attain an integrated level of experience; it wants to reach out, beyond the limitations of the material world, and bring all things into harmony. A simple song is just as capable of doing that as the healing song of the shaman. The ordinary song remains personal, whereas the song of power penetrates the unfathomable. If all the participants at a spiritual gathering sing together, they thereby bridge their individualities and weld themselves into a group. The shaman, by his song, establishes a connection between the material world and the realm of the spirit. He places a ladder against the sky, climbs the cosmic tree, hauls himself to heaven along the cosmic rope, or transcends the separation of the spheres in mystical flight.

Transpersonal experience cleanses. Spiritual dismemberment, life-threatening sickness, or pervasive pain make it possible for our consciousness to arrive at important psychic insights which culminate in an expanded view of the world. Thus humankind, with every pore of its being cleansed, is hallowed and resurrected.

We can see this happening in the case of the well-known Eskimo shamaness Uvavnuk. During a vision, a celestial ball of fire enters her body and customary reality is suddenly transformed into pulsating vitality. Freed from their material ballast, all her feelings unfold spontaneously and unhindered. In such a state the joy of life pervades us, and every fiber of our muscles and nerves joins in a single shout of ecstasy, a great song of liberation. Such songs are a spontaneous response to the newly forming psychophysical constitution; the "song of the heart" is an unprompted psychic process. It announces our entry into a personal paradise, our arrival at a state of balance between the conscious and the superconscious. Knud

Rasmussen heard the story of Uvavnuk's initiation from a shaman called Aua.

> One evening she had gone out to pass water. It was a dark winter evening, and suddenly a shining ball of fire showed in the sky. It came down to earth, directly toward the place where Uvavnuk sat. She wanted to run away, but before she could do so she was struck by the ball of fire. She became aware all at once that everything in her began to glow. She lost consciousness and from that moment on was a great summoner of the spirits. The spirit of the fire ball had taken up residence within her, and it was said that this spirit consisted of two parts. One part was like a bear, the other human; the head was human, but it had fangs like a bear.
>
> Uvavnuk came running into the house, half unconscious, and sang a song which since then has become her magic formula whenever she has to help others. As soon as she began to sing, she became delirious with joy and all the others in the house also were beyond themselves with joy, because their minds were being cleansed of all that burdened them. They lifted up their arms and cast away everything connected with suspicion and malice. All these things one could blow away like a speck of dust from the palm of the hand with this song:
>
> > The great sea has set me in motion,
> > Set me adrift,
> > Moving me as the weed moves in a river
> >
> > The arch of sky and mightiness of storms
> > Have moved the spirit within me,
> > Till I am carried away
> > Trembling with joy.[7]

The idea that a song can become a spell of magic, a powerful formula for healing, a last refuge when life is threatened by sickness or danger, no longer seems so wayward when we see singing as an expression of an inner loosening of the fetters of rational thought. Suffering extinguishes habitual memory structures, dismantles the subdivisions of our unconscious and, on the rubble of our personalistic view of the world, opens our eyes so that we may become aware of unsuspected vastnesses and holistic connections and relationships. The freed consciousness then rises from the ruins of our smallminded ego view and transcends three-dimensional limitations and mechanical one-sidedness. That which once existed separate and only for itself is now perceived as being connected with all other things—the world is governed by acausal contacts, mysterious synchronicities and the laws of paradox.

Just as Sikwalxlelix sees heaven move up and down like waves to the rhythm of the spirit's song, so Uvavnuk is moved by the air currents in the vault of heaven. Her feelings and heaven, in fact, are one and vibrate with the sound of creation. To describe her experience Uvavnuk, too, uses the image of a mighty ocean or river, in which she allows herself to float like algae; passive, surrendering, swimming in the stream of power. Poetry and melody reflect a higher consciousness freed from conditions and value judgments. The only remaining emotion is one of joy.

Uvavnuk's initiation began with an experience of light. She felt illumined inside herself by a ball of fire. But such an illumination or enlightenment is not without its dangers. The spirit emerging from the ball of fire has a human head but the fangs of a beast of prey. This spirit tears the veil from the eyes of the initiate. It represents both enlightenment and the destruction of old habit structures: it gives and takes at the same time. Uvavnuk glows with ecstatic joy, her innermost psyche awakens, and is carried away by the wonder of pure being. Whether such an illumination can be compared to the samadhi of the Hindu or the kensho experienced by Zen monks must remain uncertain, because we do not know enough about the inner experience of Eskimos. One thing, however, is certain: Euphoria and bliss are clear indications of the experience of transcendence.

We have seen that the apprentice, in the case of many shamanic initiations, spontaneously breaks into song after his transpersonal experience. According to the findings of modern research, people who had near-death experiences heard what they described as music of the spheres, sounds of indescribable beauty that pervaded the whole atmosphere. In fact, the atmosphere itself appeared to *be* pure sound. It would seem, then, that in an expanded realm of consciousness all the structures of existence manifest as, and are themselves, musical sound. The experience of the environment as a vibration of sound, like other synaesthetic experiences, is a well-known phenomenon of altered states of consciousness. The reason why the sound of celestial beauty is frequently encountered in the transpersonal realm might well be that our deconditioned consciousness is a synaesthetic world, in which the divisions between form, color, sound, smell, and taste are not as rigid and impenetrable as they are in our world.

What we are trying to say is this: After a journey to Heaven or an initiatory death, something of the Beyond continues to cling to the shaman or medium. They bring back this "something" to our world and thereby become microcosmic symbols of that higher dimension. The shaman's song is capable of reuniting him with this higher realm of consciousness and, at the same time, gives him the power to heal and prophesy. He embodies the cosmos and is an incarnation of the celestial world, a representative of higher powers which act through him, because he was once part of them; he has "been there." Furthermore, the repetition of his song is a way of recalling and reliving this experience. It is an echo of the music of the spheres at the human level.

This, however, is only a partial explanation. Song and music undeniably are the most ancient means of bringing man into harmony with himself, his environment, and nature. Psychologists are increasingly recognizing the healing power of rhythm and melody and use them therapeutically. And if a song or melody reaching us from without is capable of healing, why should not the wisdom of our body, in an endeavor to heal, produce its own song from within? Perhaps the shaman's song of initiation and transformation is the quintessence of his efforts to find the way to higher levels of consciousness, a sign of the resolution of an extended inner struggle to overcome the self, to gain transpersonal insight. If, as we have seen, the song of power is a song of joy, this surely must be the joy at being reunited with our higher nature.

Inspired song, the song of power, is a worldwide phenomenon of the process of psychic deconditioning. Moreover, song and chant play an important role in the context of the sacred. The shaman frequently makes use of chants and ceremonies to put his listeners into a receptive state. They hear his song and are no longer caught up in mundane problems and preoccupations. The creation of new songs and the feelings of cheer and happiness that spread when we sing together are important harbingers of sacred intoxication.

The alteration of ordinary consciousness, with all its rational reservations and its "ifs" and "buts," does not occur all of a sudden. It requires careful preparation, so that song and ceremony offer themselves as eminently appropriate bearers of the sacred. With many shamans, music and song have become second nature. They use their songs to accompany ceremonies and to prepare the participants for the arrival of the spirits. Apart from that, the shaman himself has need of the enthusiasm and expectant tension among the participants in order to put himself into a trance. However, we should not forget that a basic difference exists between his personal song of power and his public ritual songs.

The former Siberian shaman Kokuiev—interviewed by Vilmos Diószegi—was forced by an extended illness to become a shaman. For more than three years songs streamed from within him until, consumed by his sufferings, he finally agreed to follow the shaman's path. Diószegi assures us that Kokuiev became a totally different person. His whole experience of life expanded, and he perceived his world to have a new structure. This is not surprising if we consider the shaman to be a mediator between two different realms or dimensions of consciousness. In the following we reproduce Kokuiev's narrative about his illness and transformation, in the course of which a spontaneous song, streaming forth from within, became his song of healing and at the same time led to his recovery:

> I also became ill when I was about to become a shaman. First my head began to ache, then my hands. Around the full moon my head was splitting with pain. I had been ailing for about three years. In the meantime the spirits came to visit me. While I slept, my tongue was chanting. It chanted like the shamans do. But I did not know anything about it. When I awoke, my mother and father and my sister told me, "You were chanting shaman songs." After such occasions I always felt better for a few days. After three or four months the sickness overpowered me. My head was aching all the time, and when I slept my tongue was chanting shaman songs again. It went on like this, alternating every three or four months, for three years. One keeps suffering and suffering. When you want to rest or sleep, your tongue would be chanting. One does not know anything about it, because really the spirit is chanting. But not all spirits chant equally well. Some chant beautifully, some chant hideously. The great spirit chants best. I was twenty-seven years old when I heard him chant. The little one, the little spirit used to come to me. He had flown into my mouth and then I used to recite shaman songs. When I had no more strength left to suffer, finally I agreed to become a shaman. And when I became a shaman, I changed entirely. Because being a shaman turns one into quite a different person.[8]

Not every sickness is a call to shamanism and not every spontaneous song is a song of power. If the experience of suffering is to lead to a profound change of personality, certain personal and psychic dispositions towards this must be present. The shaman's sickness does not occur by accident. Its true cause lies in the psyche of the shaman himself. And through this sickness part of the struggle that takes place within the person is externalized. Although we can take the temperature of a feverish patient with a thermometer, this tells us nothing about the specific biochemical processes that are its cause. Similarly, the symptoms of a shaman's sickness are only a sign of changes taking place at a deeper psychological level. The actual nature of these changes is often a mystery to the prospective shaman.

Franz Boas describes the illness of a young woman of the Kwakiutl Indians, which did not lead to a shamanic transformation. The girl had been feverish and could not stop coughing. As time went on, her body wasted away until she was only skin and bones, and her relatives feared that she was close to death. So they placed her into a small hut and left her there undisturbed, except that her father visited her every day to ask whether a dream had spoken to her. When she was so weak that she could no longer raise her hands and appeared to be on the point of death, a song suddenly came from her lips. This song circled her small hut four times and then returned to its mysterious place of origin. The following night the song was heard again. This continued for four days, and in this way she received four sacred songs which cured her illness, but did not give her any power to heal others.[9] It is therefore important to distinguish between songs of personal healing and liberation and songs that turn the person concerned into a shaman or healer.

Husko, a shamaness of the Japanese Ainu, for example, at about fifteen years of age started to feel every day at midafternoon a strong desire to sing out loud about anything which came into her mind. At the same time it seemed to her that a strong wind was eddying inside her body. Her elders told her that she was feeling the desire to perform shamanistic rites. Her first actual performance of a rite did not come, however, until she was thirty-eight years old, when her daughter drowned in a lake. At the sight of her daughter's dead body caught in a fishnet, she lost consciousness and was carried back to her home. Here she regained consciousness, but her body started to shake vigorously. Those present gave her the necessary equipment with which she performed her first rite. Not until her son died several years later, however, did she perform the rites regularly.[10] Two great shocks were thus required to force Husko to penetrate deeper into her psyche, despite her basic disposition toward shamanism. Only through suffering do we learn to appreciate our world and make an effort to uncover the hidden causes of illness and pain. What else are wisdom and insight if not the result of the gradual abandonment, at various levels, of the illusion of an individual self?

It is, of course, not only the content of the song that effects the healing.

Its rhythm, too, transports the shaman back to the place of his initiation—a place that does not correspond to any actual or even hallucinatory topography. Rather, the song is a sign of a capacity for consciousness and experience more embracing than discursive or rational thought. This capacity produces insights and healing processes which go beyond the mechanical principles of cause and effect. Through the rhythm and words of his song the shaman establishes an empathy with the sacredness of the present, as a result of which his supersensory ability to heal and predict is spontaneously released. That is why song and chant are traditional means of magic and ancient psychology—a primordial method to raise consciousness to a higher level of perception.

To round off our picture we would like to mention that sound and music, according to many esoteric traditions, have a profound psychophysical effect. We know today that certain tonal frequencies can kill or physically damage a human being and that some animal species kill their natural enemies by emitting high pitched notes, just as a Japanese Samurai will use a scream, pitched at a certain level, to paralyze his opponent. In Indian philosophy, certain tonal correspondences are ascribed to the chakras, and the whole universe is seen as a manifestation of graded vibrations or tonal sequences. Many yogins believe that chanting such sequences can give access to occult powers. Throughout India the ancient mantra *OM* is considered to be the primordial sound of creation, and the Buddha, too, has spoken about an inner sound and inner hearing.

Modern science speaks of matter coming into being as a result of densified vibrations of light and sound.[11] This has led to renewed interest in the creative power of sound and tones, the knowledge of which is part of many ancient spiritual traditions. The Sikhs speak of Naam, the Christians of the Word (*Logos*), the Hindus of Nada Brahma, and the theosophists of the Voice of Silence. It remains to be seen what contemporary science will call it.

13

Sacred Drugs:
Where the World Is Born

I can look down to the very beginning. I can go to where the world is born. —Maria Sabina, when eating the sacred mushroom[1]

With me, as with every other person of whom I have heard, the keynote of the experience is the tremendously exciting sense of an intense metaphysical illumination. Truth lies open to the view in depth beneath depth of almost blinding evidence. The mind sees all the logical relations of being with an apparent subtlety and instantaneity to which its normal consciousness offers no parallel; only as sobriety returns, the feeling of insight fades, and one is left staring vacantly at a few disjointed words and phrases, as one stares at a cadaverous-looking snowpeak from which the sunset glow has just fled, or at the black cinder left by an extinguished brand.[2]

In these unmistakable words William James, the famous psychologist and researcher into consciousness, describes an experience he had when he took laughing gas (nitrous oxide).

The normal waking consciousness James considers to be so sobering is described as false or a lie by the Latin American Jîvaro, according to whom the birth of the real world can be experienced only during intoxication with psychedelic substances. For that reason the Jîvaro even give a foretaste of this reality to their children a few days after their birth, but also when they have been disobedient. By this, they want to show them another world that is more embracing than the one on which they base their normal everyday behavior, and at the same time demonstrate to them that their knowledge is puny compared to that of the grownups. For the same reason they feed Ayahuasca *(Banisderiopsis caapi)* to their hunting dogs, because contact with the supernatural sharpens the hunting instinct.[3]

Mankind has made use of hallucinogenic plants from the earliest of times. The comprehensive herbal knowledge of many traditional peoples, as well as their knowledge concerning the correct application of herbs, has never ceased to astonish people living in a modern Western culture. How did these "primitives" acquire their knowledge? We hear that it was by accident, by trial and error. Traditional ethnology, as a matter of principle, rejects the possibility that a shaman, in a state of altered consciousness, can receive intuitive knowledge or have a vision concerning a plant with powerful healing properties and where to find it. But no matter how, healing plants were discovered: The shaman, during his initiation and rituals, frequently receives pointers to the appropriate herb, root, or cactus.

Just as physical and spiritual exercises are capable of breaking through the filter of normal consciousness, so psychoactive drugs bring about a lowering of our threshold for absorbing information so that properties of the environment, of which ordinarily we would remain unconscious, can be taken in and a heightened receptivity and vividness of feeling perception arises. The excitation/inhibition mechanism of our perceptive capacity is altered. There is an explosive expansion of reality in the consciousness of the beholder. The curtain in front of a larger stage of life is drawn aside—and we experience a vision.

Shamanic initiates of many cultures will cleanse their mind and body before beginning their psychedelic training. The novices of the Colombian Siona-Tukano spend a whole month in total isolation to cause their memory of the ordinary world to fade, because irritating and distractive thoughts connected with everyday events are an obstacle to the proper learning of higher things. At the same time the hallucinatory Ayahuasca extract is drunk at fixed intervals: The initiate will take it for three days in a row, followed by a rest day, and this rhythm may continue for two weeks or even up to two months. During this period he passes through various psychic phases, the first of which is merely marked by a sort of intoxication. Soon, however, the fear of death sets in, marking the beginning of the actual trial. Those who give up at that point will gain nothing, but whoever learns to overcome or face his fear will encounter the Jaguar Mother, who sheds tears at the fate of the initiate, because she feels that he is going to die. But this is only a further test of the initiate's steadfastness. When, at last, the novice begins to suckle at the breast of the Jaguar Mother he reverts, as it were, to a state of infancy. Frequently, fully trained shamans even transform themselves into small jaguars and feel themselves to be children of the Jaguar Mother.

The return to childish innocence, purity, and an unscarred mind is the most common prerequisite for further progress. Only after such a return can the "visions of knowledge" begin. When the fear that expresses itself as ego-oriented doubt in the existence of another reality has been overcome, the aspirant enters the subliminal realm of the "true world." To do so, however, he must have left his physical body, because now he sees everything with his soul body, which the Siona see as a parrot.

During his training, the pupil also learns to play on a small reed flute, which is no ordinary flute. It has "fallen from heaven," where the Yajé people live. Throughout this training the knowledge that finally makes him a shaman continues to grow within him.[4]

The Amazonian Yebámasa divide the drug experience into three stages. At first everything appears in brighter colors than usual and multicolored lines flicker through the air. During the second stage things appear that do not exist at all in everyday reality. Finally appear the mythical heroes, the gods and demons, with whom the initiate travels through the universe to fathom its secrets.[5]

Florian Deltgen, one of the few anthropologists who have themselves experimented with psychedelic drugs—in this case with Cají (*Banisteriopsis* spp.)—had the experience of being split into three such egos: a body ego, a soul ego consisting of his feelings, and the spiritual ego which was in charge of all three. He perceived things for the most part with his spiritual ego, his actual consciousness. He says that he "saw" directly with his brain, not with his eyes, and that what he saw was in itself pure spirit and had, in fact, remarked so to himself. At the same time he felt that he understood those mystics who speak of a "marriage of the soul with God."[6]

The Yebámasa distinguish among five classes of spiritual men or Kumú. The fifth and highest level corresponds to that of a shaman (Payé). Every male member of the tribe endeavors to reach one of these levels. Whoever fails in this loses the respect of the tribal group. The drug itself will not produce a Payé unless there is a predisposition toward becoming a Kumú. The taking of the drug (Cají) is, as it were, a test which reveals the spiritual "talent." The drug is capable of drawing out latent spiritual qualities, but does not itself produce them. The disposition toward becoming a Kumú is innate.

The five levels of spiritual master are as follows:

1. The Maśari Masí—a ritual singer, who has knowledge of dances and songs

2. The Nangúri Masí—the speaker, who knows the traditional lore and leads the recitation of mythical texts, particularly myths of creation

3. The Baséri Masí—a healer with limited abilities, who cures certain illnesses by sucking a wound and blowing tobacco smoke onto it. He also has knowledge of herbs, can see into the future, and has the power of influencing others. In addition, he practices black magic

4. The Masíní Masí—a more complete healer than the Baséri Masí

5. The Jé-Yái—a shaman and priest, who protects the tribal group, prepares the psychedelic drink and possesses all the knowledge of spiritual masters on the four lower levels

As can be seen, purely aesthetic experiences are not enough to make someone into a shaman. It is necessary for visions of the mythical past to occur, particularly visions of Jéhino, the supreme being, or Rómikumu, the goddess and first shamaness who created the world, or of Váihino, the mythical anaconda.

After a festival, at which the men drink Cají and then dance and sing, they will relate to each other their visions and interpret them. There are no external signs to indicate whether or not the dancers are under the influence of the psychedelic substance, because it is said that a man should not allow himself to be ruled by Cají. In fact, it is necessary that he keep a tight rein on it. Otherwise demons will enter his consciousness and he becomes a slave of Cají.

The medicine men of the Carib Pujai (Dutch Guiana) are known as masters of the spirit, spirit conjurers, or simply "Grandfathers." The latter term is applied to them by the villagers, because they are leaders and examples for everyone. In a trance state the Pujai does not see material things, only nonterrestrial beings, who appear as if in a dream but are essentially different from the figures one sees in dreams. Experiencing the other world is referred to as "ascending." The body is in a state of unconsciousness, in which the spirit of the novice must learn to ascend to the celestial realm.

The Pujai Maliwiaju gave a description of his initiation to Philipe

Penard. A hut was built for him and the other shamanic candidates, and a new field of tobacco was planted, the leaves of which were needed to prepare the tobacco juice. Then a bench was constructed on which the aspirants had to sit. This bench was mounted on a swivel so that it could be rotated rapidly, with the aspirants seated on it, in order to induce a trance state. (The well-known researchers Robert Masters and Jean Houston have developed a similar device, which they call an Altered States of Consciousness Induction Device, and found that a person being subjected to vertical or horizontal movements would, after about twenty minutes, experience an altered state of consciousness marked by highly realistic fantasies.) Every aspirant would construct for himself a rattle and a magic staff and be assigned a young untouched girl, who would paint his body red at night and prepare the tobacco brew.

A three-day period of instruction, during which the initiates danced and sang at night, was followed by three rest days, when they received further instruction from the master. Throughout the period of initiation the aspirants had to fast, drink tobacco water, chew tobacco leaves, and smoke long cigars which had a strong narcotic effect. Tobacco intoxication, fasting, rhythmic dancing, and continuous singing, interrupted only by further teaching about the various kinds of spirit, bring the initiate to an altered state of consciousness. During the fifth night they are not allowed to drink anything at all, and the master takes them "above," to the tobacco mother, the great tobacco tree. For the ascent to heaven, the master mounts various horizontal ropes, some lower, some higher, on which the pupils dance during the night, their feet on the lower rope, their hands clinging to the higher one. Dancing and balancing over these ropes they ascend, toward midnight, to the "crossroads of life and death."[7]

Maliwiaju also spoke of his personal journey to the realm of the spirits. He said that heaven was radiating a wondrous light. As he set out for the celestial realm, he encountered a friendly spirit who assured him that he would be taken up to heaven any moment. In the company of another spirit he ascended a spiral staircase and, in this way, reached the first level of heaven, where he visited the villages and towns of many spirit peoples. Maliwiaju went on to describe in detail the various kinds of spirit and their abode. He finally came to a celestial river where he and his companion could go no further. A beautiful virgin emerged from the river and invited them to go with her into the depth of the water. But Maliwiaju preferred to roam further with his spirit guide. In the end he crossed the river and soon found himself at the "crossroads of life and death," where his guide instructed him about life after death.

He woke up after this experience, because his master had placed a net filled with ants onto his forehead and belly, and the bites of the ants had brought him back to the earthly realm. Now all the aspirants related their journeys to heaven. There was only one who said he had just been unconscious and had not gone to heaven.

The swiveling bench already mentioned is another method used by the Carib to bring about an out-of-body experience. The initiate, already intoxicated with tobacco juice, sits on the bench, which is suspended by a rope and rotated by a number of assistants, who then let go of it, allowing it to unwind with great speed. The aspirant chants, "The turning bench of Pujai Alanapali will bring me to the wall of heaven. I shall see the village of Tukajana (the spirit) from within."

Apart from the tobacco juice, the juice of the Takini tree is used to make aspirants experience a journey to heaven, but the use of this substance is, as a rule, followed by extreme feverish fantasies, paralysis, and uncontrollable shivering. The drug derived from the Takini tree is governed by both good and evil spirits, and the pupil, through his contact with them, acquires knowledge about fighting illnesses and their negative effects.[8]

The Venezuelan and Colombian Guajiro also use tobacco as a catalyst to induce psychic experiences. When, during their initiatory sickness, shamans (Piache) are no longer able to bear their torments, the spirits frequently instruct them to eat manilla (a paste made from fermented tobacco) or to drink tobacco juice. Such was the case with the shamaness Graziela:

> I was sick when the spirits came. I went to a doctor, but he could not help me. The spirits told me that they would heal me if I ate manilla. The spirits did not all come at the same time. One year one spirit came, the following year another. Every time I became ill, I was feverish. My sister was the first to tell me that I would become a Piache.[9]

It would seem that the use of tobacco brings about a sort of psychedelic clarification of the psychic condition of the initiates, because many of them feel cured after using it. The references in the dreams of the initiates to the use of tobacco can thus be understood as a form of self-healing. The drug reveals the true causes and symptoms of the sickness. After such a psychedelic vision, the Piache is said to possess "knowledge."

The shamaness Petronilda felt that the spirits had taken root in her and were speaking through her. But as her narrative shows, it is in fact the tobacco that speaks through her and brings clarity, knowledge, and visions:

> When I dream, the spirits come. Sometimes they look like small Guajiro boys, at other times like Arcjuna (Europeans), but they are always small and sit on my shoulders. The spirits are not like people, they are what is inside people. They speak through the thoughts of the Piache. I chew tobacco, and more spirits descend. I don't see them, they come out of my head. The tobacco speaks through my thoughts.[10]

It is said that the spirits have need of the tobacco and that is why each Piache must continually chew it. The shamaness Juanita says, "The tobacco juice makes you feel drunk. But a Piache will not lose control over herself like someone who is drunk."[11]

To break through the barriers of their natural environment and advance to the other world, known as Ahpikondiá, the Latin American Desana (a subgroup of the Tukano) take Yajé and also Vihó (Piptademia), a psychoactive powder, which they suck in through the nose.[12] In his vision, the Payé wanders along the Milky Way and must be able to see it as a long road with mountains, lakes, and houses. Aspirants unable to react in the prescribed manner will see only stones and clouds during their trance state. They lose control, undress themselves, and urinate and defecate in public. A really experienced Payé, however, is in control of himself. He rises aloft to the Milky Way and consorts with the beings living there. He later returns into his body which lies, quietly sleeping, in a hammock.

The Tukano, too, reach a visionary state, known as Ventúri, by the use of Vihó and then enter the "blue zone" where they meet Vihó-mahsë, the Lord of Snuff, who can bring good or ill and grants permission for the aspirant to enter the "blue zone." There is another spirit being called Vaí-mahsë, the Keeper of the Game, who must be called upon before embarking on a hunt. If he gives permission for some animals to be killed, the hunter must swear to compensate him by killing some humans, whose souls then return as animals to Vaí-mahsë and replenish his herd.

The interpretation of visions is a basic feature of the Tukano religion. At these "vision sessions" only men are present. The women sit in the back of the house and goad them to tell their visions. According to Tukano mythology, Man originally entered this world on a Snake Canoe. And now the men, by taking Yajé, travel back to their place of origin. For that reason, the pot in which the Yajé is prepared is known as the "snake canoe." Soon after taking the drug, the first signs of entering an altered state of consciousness appear in the men.

The Kumú (shaman), step by step, interprets their visions which run through several phases. During the first phase, a strong gust of air is experienced as if a violent wind were trying to bear the men away. The Kumú explains that this is the ascent to the Milky Way. To leave this world, the Tukano must establish contact with this strong wind. Only in this way can they reach Ahpikondiá, where everything is bathed in a yellow light. The second phase begins with their arrival in Ahpikondiá, which is inhabited by luminous beings of various colors, who continuously vary their size. The Kumú explains to the visionaries that these figures are the daughters of the sun. In this manner the visionary is guided through the various stages of his vision and comes to meet all the primordial and mythical beings.

The younger participants do not have very clear or impressive visions. They only see hazy lights and suffer from headaches. The women laugh and sing, "Drink, drink! This is why we were born. Drink, drink! Because this is your task. By drinking, they will know all of the traditions of their fathers. By drinking, they will be brave. We will help them!"[13] The Tukano consider the drinking of Yajé to be equivalent with a return into the cosmic uterus, the primordial source of all things. And the Desana say that "to take Yajé is to die."[14] By their encounter with these supernatural beings they witness the universal origin with their own eyes and experience it through their own body. In this way, the religious tradition is established firmly within each individual. Everyone has seen the Snake Canoe and how the first man leapt from it. The Kumú, with his chant, directs the visions of the men and assists them through his interpretations.

From this psychedelic drug experience, during which each of them personally reexperienced the origin of the world and of mankind, the visionaries return to the normal world with strengthened confidence in their culture and its mythical traditions. We have here an example of socialization by the use of psychoactive plants which, by strengthening the feeling for the glory of being, help to consolidate the cultural identity and the individual autonomy.

To the Tukano, the pot in which the Yajé brew is prepared is a symbol of the uterus. A member of the Tukano tribe has described the experience of taking Ayahuasca as "spiritual coitus." In the Tukano culture, spiritual and sexual experience are closely connected. The men go on time journeys back to the embryonic phase, to the maternal belly, and even further to the origin of the universe, in order to encounter the deities of the tribe. Under the influence of the drug, the origin of being and of mankind are reexperienced as a creation of the divine cultural heroes.[15]

The Tukano consider Yajé to be divine spermatozoa and see narcotic ecstasy as an orgasm, which they compare to drowning, because to them man also "drowns" during sexual union.[16] Some Indians pointed out that during sexual intercourse they had the same visions as under the influence of Yajé. When one drinks Yajé one dies. The flow of time is, as it were, reversed: One regresses to the embryonic phase and in this way returns to and reexperiences the beginnings of mankind and the origin of the universe.

Like many other tribes the Tukano, too, subdivide the drug experience into several phases. They basically distinguish among three marked stages.[17]

1. In the first stage, after some violent bodily reactions such as vomiting, diarrhea, and profuse perspiration, the person will feel like flying upward through the air toward the Milky Way, and will perceive, with half closed or completely closed eyes, an increasing number of luminous sensations. After a series of brilliant yellow flashes, dancing dots will appear, soon to be replaced by a multitude of small luminous images that seem to float in space and now begin to change their shapes and colors in kaleidoscopic fashion. These luminous sensations perceived by the person are called *gahpí ohori*, "Yajé images." The Indians explain that all these images and luminescent motifs appear in the field of vision and completely engulf the person who sits watching the everchanging patterns of these dancing "stars and flowers." The first stage, then, is said to be a pleasant experience.

2. The onset of the second stage is marked by the gradual disappearance of symmetric light patterns and by the slow formation of larger images of irregular shapes. As the ecstatic flight takes the person beyond the Milky Way, dreamlike scenes overwhelm the beholder. Three-dimensional forms, like rolling clouds, begin to fill the visual field and slowly turn into multicolored, recognizable shapes of people, animals, and monsters. People say that they can see the Sun Father and his daughter, the Snake Canoe of the Creation Myth, the Master of Animals, Thunder Person, jaguar spirits and other supernatural beings and that these appear to reenact the Creation. Thus the beholder is present at the construction

of the first maloca (communal dwelling place), the execution of the first dance, or the introduction of the musical instruments. But there also appear monstrous animals and menacing shadows in weird shapes. The game animals crowd the scene and—speaking a language that can be understood by humans—clamor for justice and accuse the hunters of killing too many of them. During this second stage many acoustical sensations are said to be experienced. It is believed that the individual "dies" when he drinks the potion and that his spirit now returns to the uterine realm of the Beyond, only to be reborn there and to return to his ordinary existence on this earth when the trance is over.

It is furthermore said that the visionary returns to the womb in the shape of a phallus. Since all this is only brought about by the drinking of Yajé, he is said to enter as a phallus into the vagina—which is painted on the lower part of the Yajé pot as a representation of the female body—and thereby into the realm of birth. For this reason, the Yajé pot is also referred to as "place of origin," "uterus," or "place of death."

3. At the third stage, the moving, swirling colors and shapes begin to settle and turn into wide open scenes of placid clouds bathed in a soft, greenish light. There is a coming and going of waves of music, and the person is lost in dreamlike contemplation.

Spiritual training among the Tukano takes place under the direction of an experienced Payé at an isolated spot in the forest and can last up to a year. The pupils live during this time in a temporary shelter that contains only the barest commodities. Women are not allowed to visit the spot. During the daytime the men go hunting, fishing, or gathering, and in the evening they will dance and sing, smoke tobacco, and take narcotic drugs, mainly snuff and different Yajé potions.

During the narcotic trance, power objects "fall out of the sky" and suddenly materialize before the apprentice. These objects may be rocks, known as "thunder stones," or quartz crystals.

The master of drugs, the Vihó-mahsë (snuff ruler), is present both during the visions and while the pupil fashions his shamanic objects. As a result of the reduced food intake, lack of sleep and the visionary seances taking place every evening, the pupil finally ascends to the Milky Way, the home of Vihó-mahsë. Later, as a fully trained Payé, it will be his task, assisted by Vihó-mahsë, to negotiate with the Keeper of the Game, Vai-mahsë, about matters concerned with the acquisition of food, medicinal herbs or hunting animals, or to request the help of other supernatural beings in the struggle for survival.[18]

Reichel-Dolmatoff has pointed out the neurochemical basis of the shapes and color patterns appearing during visions.[19] With reference to the myriad of galvanic light patterns discovered by Purkinje in 1819 (he called them phosphenes), which occur during sensory deprivation, in hypnagogic states, under emotional stress, as a result of exhaustion, and through pressure on the eyes or a knock on the head, Reichel-Dolmatoff argues that the light experiences of, and decorative motifs seen by, the Tukano have their origin in an excitation of brain cells which is also noticeable on the retina of the eyes. By the systematic electrical stimulation of the cerebral cortex, a large number of light patterns have since then been caused, observed, and catalogued. These light patterns correspond to a large extent to those observed by the Tukano. Geometrical patterns, however, mainly appear during the initial phase of intoxication, and figurative phosphenes such as flowers, animals, and landscapes appear in a later stage.

As many examples show, a psychedelic experience begins, as a rule, by seeing purely neurological patterns and personal motifs and ends with visions of cosmic archetypes and transpersonal symbols. The phosphenes, therefore, only belong to a lower (physical) stage of the visionary experience. Consequently, the theory that human symbols are no more than matrices of excitation (engrams) within the brain, or that mystical experiences are patterns of phosphenes, is neither worthy of serious consideration nor can it be empirically substantiated.

It will sooner or later in all probability be shown that mystical and parapsychic experiences, as they are assimilated by the brain, are subject to a filtering process and therefore adapt to neuroanatomical structures. This in itself, however, is still a long way from providing an adequate explanation for the occurrence of visions. No matter whether visions are at some future point found to be a higher form of the unconscious or a manifestation separate from and beyond our physiology: It is highly unlikely that we shall ever completely track down the inner nature and origin of mystical visions.

Another physiological explanation postulates that certain opiates which are a natural part of the brain chemistry, such as amphetamines and cocaine, could account for visionary hallucinations. Such explanations are calculated to shrug off the fruitful cathartic and therapeutic power of visions and any theories that stress their transpersonal, transphysical, and cosmic aspects. Modern holistic researchers, on the other hand, tend to see the brain as a filtering mechanism that allows only a small part of a larger reality to penetrate to the level of conscious awareness. They put forward the theory that psychoactive drugs reduce the filtering efficiency of the brain and the "doors of perception" are pushed open[20] so these drugs can contribute to a more objective perception of the world.

Research into altered states of consciousness is based on the understanding that our perception of the world arises from habitual structures which very quickly can be destroyed or disrupted by changes in the biochemical and neurological balance. It appears, for instance, that the disruption of brain cell secretion, which is regulated by a substance called serotonin, triggers a loosening of inhibitions and a process of deconditioning. When this happens, things lose their familiar appearance and a new world appears before us. We look at the wonder of existence like a wide-eyed child, everything fascinates us, the mundane comes alive, and the familiar becomes mysterious. We are born anew. We return to the embryonal, prenatal, primordial realm. This is not a case of pathological hallucinatory self-deception. On the contrary: The world of daily routine is washed away and replaced by a glorious display of colors and forms.

Serotonin dampens the brain's reaction to incoming stimuli and is released whenever it appears necessary to prevent or weaken excessive stimulation. In this way it promotes habit formation and protects us from a surfeit of information. Psychedelics evidently delay habitual reactions by inhibiting the production of serotonin, but this can also happen as a result of fasting, exhaustion, meditation, concentration, and extreme temperatures, causing the brain to react to familiar stimuli as if they were something completely new.[21] That is why the chewing of peyote is experienced by the Mexican Huichol as a return to the naivete and freshness of childhood. During their pilgrimage to Wirikuta, the sacred land of the peyote cactus, the Mara'akame (shaman) tells the peyoteros to chew the cactus well, so they will "see their lives." The Huichol believe that in Wirikuta you lose your soul—a process we might describe as loss of ego, ecstasy, or mystical union. In Wirikuta the pilgrims chew peyote; as they do so time assumes a mythical duration, history is abandoned, and eternity is reached.[22]

As a general rule, the psychedelic state is characterized by the loosening of ego limitations, the collapse of the dichotomy between "I" and "other," a heightened emotional response, and a lowering of the threshold towards stimuli from the unconscious, the superconscious, and the external environment. Due to the increased fluidity and flexibility of perception, intellectual and psychic problems are seen in a larger context. Our visual imagination, our capacity for fantasy and concentration as well as our empathy with external processes, objects, and human beings are enhanced.[23] Our thought processes and our capacity for differentiation and feeling as well as our sensory responsiveness and the richness of our experience are raised above the known limits of normal consciousness, so that our heightened perception of ourselves and the environment leads to a more precise knowledge of reality and a more objective understanding of human interrelations.

A drug experience therefore is not confined to its psychotherapeutic effects, but has equally valuable philosophical and moral implications. The expansion of conscious perception should thus be seen as both the most ancient form of psychotherapy and the most radical and complete method of healing known to us. It does not limit itself to dealing with particular facets of behavior, as is customary in modern psychology. Its aim is to make us see individual existence in relative terms and to expand our being toward other beings and forms. Communication between species, contacts with suprapersonal beings and personified anthropomorphous configurations of the higher self, as well as with cosmic entities and archetypal formations, leads to a holistic experience of the world—an experience that fulfills our inner human needs to a much greater extent than contemporary psychological theories that restrict their view of us to the lowest possible common denominator of biopsychic capacity.

Michael Harner describes the expansion of psychic capacity resulting from consuming Ayahuasca as follows:

1. The soul is felt to separate from the physical body and to make a trip, often with the sensation of flight.

2. Visions of jaguars and snakes and, to a much lesser extent, other predatory animals.

3. A sense of contact with the supernatural, whether with demons or, in the case of missionized Indians, also with God and heaven and hell.

4. Visions of distant persons, "cities," and landscapes, typically interpreted by the Indians as visions of distant reality, i.e., as clairvoyance.

5. The sensation of seeing the detailed enactment of recent un-

solved crimes, particularly homicide and theft, i.e., the experience of believing that one is capable of divination.[24]

Furthermore, Harner quotes, among others, the experience of Manuel Villavicencio, who himself took Ayahuasca and reported the following: "As for myself I can say for a fact that when I've taken Ayahuasca I've experienced dizziness, then an aerial journey in which I recall perceiving the most gorgeous views, great cities, lofty towers, beautiful parks, and other extremely attractive objects."[25] The Cashunahua Indians take Ayahuasca with the specific aim of obtaining information about distant places and people. Some of them, for example, have described in adequate and correct detail, scenes that occurred in Pucallpa, a large city they had never visited, on the Ucayali River. The ethnologist Kensinger was told by six of altogether nine people who participated at an Ayahuasca ceremony, that they had seen the death of his grandfather. He was informed two days later by radio of his grandfather's death.[26] Many ethnologists have had similar experiences which can be found in their writings, usually hidden away in travel narratives and monographs.

Altered states of consciousness seem to awaken a heightened experience of unity in us and, according to William James, extinguish the differentiations of our world which are in reality of a graduated nature.

After his experience with nitrous oxide James wrote:

> . . . and that truth was that every opposition, among whatsoever things, vanishes in a higher unity in which it is based; that all contradictions, so called, are but differences; that all differences are of degree; that all degrees are of a common kind; that unbroken continuity is the essence of being and that we are literally in the midst of *an infinite*, to perceive the existence of which is the utmost we can attain.[27]

All the phenomena of shamanic consciousness we have discussed show that beneath our apparently well-founded everyday reality there lies a realm of undifferentiated unity, in which our ego loses its sense of separateness and everywhere encounters unexpected correspondences, synchronicities, and paradoxes. The shaman's sense of "I" does not, however, dissolve completely. It is true that he experiences an unlimited field of awareness but, unlike Asian mystics, he does not aim at the dissolution of all forms of consciousness.

Merely consuming a psychoactive drug will not bring us a mystical experience. The adherents of the Native American Church of Peyote say that without an appropriate ritual and preparatory physical and psychic purification, it is useless to chew the peyote cactus. Moreover, someone chewing peyote with a view to being rewarded by a mystical experience must be humble, honest, aware of his personal weaknesses, and capable of complete concentration if he is to have any chance of success. They also say that without introspection, prayer, and a confession of one's transgressions it is impossible to obtain an authentic revelation.[28]

Yet it is not inner purity alone that brings about a harmony with the powers of the psychedelic cactus, liana, or mushroom. Self-sacrifice, trust, and particularly love are also indispensable. Maria Sabina, A Mesoamerican Mazatec curandera (healer) who has become fairly well-known in the West, speaks to her mushrooms, referring to them lovingly as "*niños santos*" (sacred children), and says to them, "I will drink your blood. Your heart I shall take into me, because my conscience is as pure and as clean as yours. Let me see the truth."[29] Only someone who, like Maria Sabina, is happily capable of seeing mushrooms as living entities and at the same time has a mythological concept that allows him to understand his relationship with them, has a chance of partaking of the wisdom of the mushrooms. Maria Sabina says:

> One has to show respect for the mushrooms. I felt within myself that they were related to me. They were like my parents, they were my blood. It is true that I am born with my destiny, and destiny of being an orphan. I am a daughter of the niños santos.[30]

Who of us could claim to be of the same blood as a plant, or call a mushroom his parent? The gateway to the ultimate effects of sacred drugs is opened by self-sacrifice, total surrender, and innermost faith.

14

The Acquisition of Power by Inheritance, Transmission, and Change of Sex

I do not want to give this (the shamanic power) to you; I want you to live normally, not to suffer.
—The Chemehueve Shaman Tsakara to his six children[1]

You become a pejuta wiĉaśa, *a medicine man and healer, because a dream tells you to do this. No one man dreams all the medicines. You doctor where you know you have the power. You don't inherit it; you work for it, fast for it, try to dream it up, but it doesn't always come. It is true that some families produce a string of good medicine men, and it helps to have a holy man among your relatives who teaches you and tries to pass his power on to you. It works sometimes, but not always. Medicine men aren't horses. You don't breed them. You can give a boy a car for a present and teach him how to drive, but if there's no gas in the tank the learning and the car won't do him any good. Sometimes the power skips a generation and reappears in a grandchild.*

A medicine man, when he's old, tries to pass his vision and his knowledge to his son. There's a power line there, but sometimes no juice is coming through. If in spite of all the learning and trying and begging for a vision a man doesn't obtain this power, he'll know it.
—Lame Deer[2]

In our discussion on the bequeathing of shamanic knowledge it is not our intention to specifically refer to the findings of modern genetic research, although we could no doubt claim that even in this case biological hereditary factors come into play, because the physiological disposition toward heightened sensitivity can be passed on from one generation to the next in the same way as any other characteristic. Future research into shamanism will have to take a closer look at the genetic basis of shamanic powers. For this it will be necessary to study the psychobiological and psychophysiological factors and processes involved in bringing about altered states of consciousness. Only after the parameters of mediumistic phenomena and of the paranormal psyche have been clearly determined will it be possible to examine inherited characteristics.

Perhaps the future exploration of the genetic structure will make it possible to establish that there is a genetic disposition toward the transpersonal. We still lack conclusive data regarding the psychological and physiological determination of transpersonal states. One of the reasons for this is that, until recently, such data has not attracted the interest of ethnologists.

Many cultures believe that the shaman is born with his gifts and that his abilities cannot be learned. Nevertheless, it seems to be very difficult to tell at birth whether a child is destined to become a shaman. The Iglulik shaman Angutingmarik told Knud Rasmussen:

> As to myself, I believe I am a better shaman than others among my countrymen. I will venture to say that I hardly ever make a mistake in the things I investigate and in what I predict. And I therefore consider myself a more perfect, a more fully trained shaman than those of my countrymen who often make mistakes. My art is a power which can be inherited, and if I have a son, he shall be a shaman also, for I know that he will from birth be gifted with my own special powers.[3]

According to the Maliseet-Passamaquoddy Indians a shaman may be born with superior powers, particularly if he is the younger of twins and born with a cowl (Dutch folk tradition also considers this to be an indication of the gift of clairvoyance), or if he is the seventh son. This latter belief, however, may be a modern phenomenon of European origin, where the seventh son of a seventh son is thought to be especially powerful.[4]

The Indonesian Wahaerama and Tanabaru say shamanic power is inherited but must in addition be formally transferred by a ritual. The father bestows his head cloth—the shaman's mark of office—to his son by breathing upon it, touching his forehead and navel with it and saying, "Now you must pass from me to my son." The "you" refers to the creative power (Alahatala) of which the head cloth is a symbol. During this ceremony the healing power leaves the father. At the same time the son inherits the seat beside the central post of the house because Alahatala, the creator, descends through this central post.[5]

The shamans of the Tungus are connected to the spirit of their clan. If the master of that spirit dies, a new shaman has to be found. The Yakut shaman is "called" by his shamanic ancestors. It is said that the shaman is "käp tounar"—destined to sing—because the songs of the shaman tell of his sufferings as a result of being called.[6]

Manchurian tribal communities also speak of shamanic powers being inherited within the clan. Shirokogorov, who visited one of their villages in 1915, describes how the grandfather and father of a family—both of them shamans—died and left behind their spirits. Someone from the clan had to accept these spirits which had been part of this clan for generations. The spirits chose the grandchild (respectively, the daughter) of the two dead shamans. The remaining members of the clan were upset, because they did not want to have a shamaness within the clan. The woman fled into the forest and climbed to the top of a tree, where she remained despite all attempts of the men following her to drag her down. She later disappeared altogether and did not return to the village until eight days had passed. On her return she had to be initiated as a shamaness.[7]

These examples show that it is necessary to distinguish between two ways in which shamanic powers are passed on: hereditarily in this world or from the Beyond. Frequently the spirits of former shamans or of dead people transmit their knowledge from the Beyond through dreams, visions, and signs. When shamanic powers are passed on in this world, for instance from a father to his son, the former may lose these powers altogether. But this is not always the case.

The Siberian Buryat believe in shamanic power being passed on hereditarily from the Beyond. The spirit of the ancestor (Uxta) calls upon the relative to become a shaman. As we have seen, such a "call" often causes the chosen relative to lose consciousness; he may also have convulsions and visions or become nervous and shy of people. The Uxta is either a dead ancestor or a spirit that has been passed on for generations from one member of the clan to another.[8]

The medicine men (Xon) of the Patagonian Selk'nam transfer their power to the novice by rubbing his body in circular movements with open hands. The Selk'nam speak of an immaterial power (Wáiyuwen) which a shaman can pass on to his apprentice. At the onset of the process of transformation, the apprentice's inside is said to become soft like down. He develops extrasensory skills, in that he is able to see over long distances as well as into human beings. He can also tell with great accuracy the dwelling places of other Xon, because he can see the brightness they radiate. The whole transformation lasts from two to four years. It is said that at shamanic rituals the soul and Wáiyuwen are united, and the same may well apply in the case of the actual transmission of power.[9]

Among the Point Hope Eskimos, anyone can acquire such powers by making an appropriate payment. In addition, however, the candidate must be willing to be beaten unconscious during the actual initiation. After that he is instructed by an experienced shaman. A certain minimum of personal psychic experiences would still appear to be a prerequisite, so that the payment should rather be seen as a general recompense for the actual training.[10]

Among many tribes it is possible to sell one's shamanic powers and helping spirits, or shamans may make presents to each other of power objects, or generously give a helping spirit to a friend. On the other hand, it is also possible to steal the helping spirits of a hostile shaman.

Bull Lodge, a medicine man of the Gros Ventres Indians, had a vision shortly before his death that he would die within eight days. On the eve of the day on which he was to die he made all necessary preparations and transmitted his power to his daughter Garter Snake Woman. Then he died.

Garter Snake Woman says that during the transmission of power a small crystal-clear marble appeared in her hand. This Bull Lodge placed into his mouth and then blew into his daughter's mouth, making her feel as if something were slithering down her throat. Here is how Garter Snake Woman describes what happened:

> My father lit his pipe and began to smoke. After taking several puffs, he laid it down and began to sing one of the Chief Medicine Pipe songs. It was the song that is sung while the Feathered Pipe is being unwrapped. He sang it four times, and while he was singing he placed his hands on his sides above the hip bones. After singing, he shook his body from the waist up and coughed lightly. He repeated this act four times.
>
> When he coughed the fourth time, I felt as though something had touched my hands. He asked me if I had felt anything on my hands, and I said yes. My eyes were closed, but he told me to look into my hand, and when I did I saw a round object there. It was the size of an

ordinary marble and it was crystal clear. Inside it I saw the image of a baby. The whole body was red. My father then sang again, and after he had sung four times he again asked me what I saw in my hand. I told him I saw the body of a baby inside of the object, and that it was red. He asked me if I knew what the object was, and I said no.

The object was a hailstone, he said. He took it from my hand and, holding it in his own, he began to sing again. He sang the song four times, after which he put the stone in his mouth. He told me to open my mouth, and he blew gently into it three times. When he blew into my mouth the fourth time, I felt something going down my throat. I felt it going down until it reached the pit of my stomach, then I didn't feel it any more. "Now you can go and sit down," he said.[11]

In conclusion, I describe a transmission of power among the Comanche. Sanapia, a medicine woman, had been training for four years to collect medicinal herbs and to diagnose and heal illnesses, when the high point of her initiation approached. Her mother, also a shamaness, transmitted the power to her in four stages. During the first stage, her mother dribbled it into the mouth and hands of Sanapia, who was holding glowing embers without experiencing any heat or pain. On the contrary, her fingers felt cool. This coolness was a sign that the power was concentrated in her hands. (Many fire walkers have stated that their feet feel cool as they walk across the glowing embers.) Then two eagle feathers were drawn through her mouth four times. At the fourth time, one of the feathers disappeared without trace. It had penetrated into Sanapia's mouth and remained there for the rest of her life. Sanapia was of the opinion that she had not sucked in the feather itself, but only its symbolic power.

Her mother also imposed taboos: Sanapia was not allowed to eat any more fowl or let anyone pass behind her back while she was eating. This was because the eagle, whose power she had acquired, will not tolerate any creature behind it as it eats. At the second transfer of power, an egg rose vertically into the air from her mother's hand and it—or rather the essence of it—then entered Sanapia's stomach. She was not allowed thereafter to eat eggs. When she later developed a strong appetite for eggs and had an Eagle Doctor remove the egg from her body, she lost the magic power connected with it. Soon after that she began to feel sick whenever she thought of eggs—a kind of punishment for rejecting the power transmitted to her.

At the third transmission she received a song of power, which is so powerful that she will only use it when all other methods fail. With this song she can summon the helping spirits of her mother and her uncle. Connected with this is the taboo that she must never ask anyone directly for anything. She gets around this by speaking in a very awkward and roundabout way. She must also always be alone when performing a healing ceremony, because her power might otherwise harm those present. However, other Eagle Healers or people whose powers match hers may assist her if necessary.

Sanapia became a medicine woman by a strongly ritualized transfer of power. She felt a new energy penetrating her body. She says the power itself is inexhaustible but belongs to another realm of existence from that of man, animals, and spirits, so that a kind of bearer or bridge was necessary for it to be communicated. If a human being came into direct contact with the source of the power it would kill him.[12]

In some tribal communities the acquisition of power and initiation as a shaman is accompanied by a change of sex. Among the Siberian Chuckchee there are womenlike men and menlike women, that is to say women who have changed into men and vice versa. They will even marry a member of the same sex, and if a manlike woman wants to have children, she enters into an "exchange marriage," into which the desired child is born.[13]

Bogoras, who witnessed several such sexual transformations, says that women change into men at the command of the spirits. They take a keen interest in men's affairs, carry out tasks normally performed by men, take a female lover or even marry a woman. The Chuckchee call a shaman who changes into a woman a "soft man," because he has changed to a weaker sex.

Closer analysis shows that there are various gradations of sexual transformation. The most complete of these is when a young man is told by a spirit to change into a woman and he then not only starts wearing women's clothes but also casts aside the rifle and the lance, the lasso of the reindeer herdsman and the harpoon of the seal hunter and takes to the needle and the skin scraper. He displays all the characteristics of a woman and even speaks like one. Because his fighting spirit has ebbed away and he is physically weaker, he no longer wrestles and runs with the other men but becomes shy and likes looking after children. He will take a male lover, even marry him with the usual rites and customs and have sexual intercourse with him. His new husband then goes out hunting and the "soft man" devotes himself to domestic chores. Such transformed men are, of course, a subject of scorn but no one dares to talk publicly about such matters, because these men are even more feared and respected than ordinary shamans.[14]

Among the Saint Lawrence Island Eskimos, not every sexual transient becomes a shaman, but transients are referred to by a special name: the soft womanly man is known as an Anasik and his counterpart, the mannish woman, as an Uktesik. In recent times, however, the custom to accord a culturally deviant sexuality a recognized place within the tribal community has died out among both the Saint Lawrence Island Eskimos and many other tribes.[15]

Because of their psychophysical deviation from the norm, homosexuals and transvestites or hermaphrodites—like the Navajo medicine man Hosteen Klah, who succeeded in combining masculine and feminine characteristics in perfect synthesis[16]—develop a heightened sensitivity for their environment, themselves, and their inner strength and energies. This sensitivity could be described as a fruitful basis for shamanic intuition. If this is indeed so, it would explain why "sexually abnormal" shamans or medicine men are found in many cultures. As a rule, the psychically conspicuous, the most sensitive, the loners, are the ones chosen for shamanic training.

15

The Rejection of Power

In many descriptions of shamanic initiation, the initiate resists the wishes of the spirits and refuses to take the path of the shaman, even if his life is put at risk as a result of such a refusal. In the case of people who have already passed through long periods of suffering, sickness, and possibly, near-death experiences, a refusal to submit to the powers of the Beyond usually results in further torment, neverending sickness, and perhaps even madness or death.

It would seem that breakthroughs to a new psychic dimension, to another level of experiencing the world, can only be reversed with great difficulty. Once we are caught in the whirlpool of power, our physical and psychic suffering can only be overcome by our willingness to submit consciously and consistently to the continuation of our further mental deconditioning. It may well be that some present-day psychotics are people who have had glimpses of transpersonal reams but do not know how to go further nor how to return. Perhaps they have become trapped between normality and the transpersonal, in the no-man's-land of the psyche, half healed and half sick, belonging to neither world.

Let us look at the case of Mukulka Borgoyakhov, who lived in the Siberian village of Pitrahti. His brother was a shaman, and after his brother's death the spirits chose Mukulka to follow in his steps, saying, "Let him be a shaman in his brother's place." But he refused to obey. He defied them. When all their efforts came to nothing, they pushed him out of his yurt and said, "If you behave like this, we shall turn loose the spirits of all the dead shamans on you!" With this threat they were able to compel him, and they thrust upon him all the necessary tools of the shaman. Nevertheless, he renounced them all, although he sometimes did practice shamanism, but only if at least twelve or fifteen spirits were after him.[1]

On the other hand, the actual call to shamanism may be delayed and even cancelled. Ruth Underhill quote the following narrative by a Papago Indian woman:

> When I was a young girl, I was always running about on the desert, looking at things. My heart was not cool. I thought I saw Coyote, when there was no Coyote there. Then I saw a spider on the central post of the house, and he stopped and looked at me, just ready to speak. I made a song, a song about Coyote.
>
> They had a shaman to sing over me to find out what was the matter, and in the morning he said: "She could be a shaman."
>
> "That cannot be," said my father. "We have one shaman in the house, and that is enough."
>
> Already the divining crystals were growing inside me, but the shaman sucked them out. He leaned over me and sucked them out of my breast, one by one. They were as long as the joint of my little finger, white and moving, like worms.
>
> The shaman said: "Look! I have taken them out before they got big." Then he made a hole in a giant cactus and put them inside.[2]

The Yamana Indian woman Melly Lawrence refused contact with her protecting spirit (Aóna-xéola or Yefácel) and was brought to the edge of death as a result of it. She might well have died if another shamaness had not intervened. Here is her narrative:

> Once, as I was walking through the forest with my small daughter, I heard a strangely loud sound, like "pax," coming from the trunk of a tree. I looked back, and there in the rotting trunk I saw a tiny Aóna-xéola, waving to me in a friendly way. I didn't think it was a case of *asikáku* (spiritual seeing) but took it to be an ordinary soul (késpix). I dragged myself on, feeling as if I had become unconscious. There was tremendous fear in all my limbs and (on reaching home) I threw myself on my sleeping place in a state of complete exhaustion. I had a dream, and again the Aóna-xéola stood before me. It smiled in a very friendly way and showered me with all kinds of presents—skins and small baskets, ornamental cords and yékus (arrowheads). It even left me a special song. After waking up in a daze, that song continued to resound in me for a long time.
>
> I was weak and sick for many days, feeling lifeless and without strength. A Yékamuskipa (shamaness) said to me: "How is it you are so very weak now? Only recently I saw you strong and healthy." I gave no explanation, but offered her a cup of tea. She touched the cup and, shrinking back in horror, said: "Why are you offering me

this disgusting animal?" I stopped short and said: "But I offered you a cup of tea." Greatly agitated, the woman said: "No, that is a disgusting animal." You see, the Aóna-xéola had not released me after my dream but was following me wherever I went. Slowly, I became convinced that I would have to practice as a shamaness, because that was what that spirit wanted me to do. But I was unable to come to a decision.

The shamaness that was with me held the cup of tea in her hands and, as she did so, instantly became aware of what had happened to me. "You must become a Yékamus!" she said of me. She could see that the Aóna-xéola had placed over my shoulders a coat made of skins which was fastened by a leather strap around my neck. This coat felt so heavy that I often fell to the ground. Full of fear for me, the woman ran back to her hut and soon fell asleep. In a dream she saw how the coat of skins was tightening around my throat more and more, so that I would be strangled within a few days. Early in the morning the woman was still full of fear and began chanting her song. She called me to her and asked: "Did you have an asikáku over there in the forest and do you, since then, feel as if someone were strangling you, so that you often fall down due to lack of breath?" I said: "Yes, it is like that."

Then she made me lower myself to the ground before her. She kept reaching toward the coat of skins with both her hands and toward all the presents the Aóna-xéola had showered upon me. With energetic movements she cast all these things aside until finally I was free of them; she also took the song and asikáku from me. Only then did I feel relief and I have had no complaints since. To this day I am thankful to that Yékamuskipa, because she saved me from near death.[3]

In many cases, however, the rejection of power does not end so lightly but the person concerned, as a warning, continues to suffer a physical ailment or is mentally disturbed. Reidar Christiansen quotes a Mackenzie Eskimo who knew of such a case. The man, K., had one day on the ice seen the head and shoulders of a strange being emerge like a seal out of the sea. He saw it repeatedly and was advised by his more experienced neighbors to follow the unknown creature in order to become a great Angekok. He had no wish, however, to abandon his ordinary way of life. He kept seeing the creature, and one day asked it: "If I take you as my assistant spirit, will I then be able to walk upon the water?" The creature assured him that he would, and that he would likewise be able to summon reindeer and seals at will. He still hesitated.

The following year he met the unknown creature again and asked whether he would have the power, in the presence of the whole tribe, to fly through space and bring down the snow from the clouds. This, the strange creature said, was beyond his powers, but perhaps the help of other spirits might be enlisted. As K. still refused, the stranger said that as a punishment K. would never again be able to eat solid food. K. fainted, and when he regained consciousness he saw the strange creature dive into the sea and return, holding a human jawbone in its hand. From then on K.'s jawbone was missing, there was only some sort of wound, and he had to subsist only on liquid food.[4]

In the above examples the call to shamanism was not wholly successful, either because the candidates were healed prematurely or the spirit, or power, was removed from their bodies, because they considered a life without sacred tasks to be less burdensome and more agreeable. Others managed to fight resolutely and successfully against visitations, trials, and encroachments from the Beyond. Shamans often describe the call of the spirits in a way that suggests that an external power, which is stronger than they, is influencing their psyche and their state of mind.

The resistance offered by shamans and mediums, and to a certain degree also by psychotics, is the resistance of a "normal" consciousness against a supranormal awareness. Sickness and suffering as a process of psychic purification cannot be understood with reference to narrow and limited biological structures of insight and perception. It can be said in the same way that resistance against the acquisition of new and unfamiliar powers is an expression of the ignorance of ordinary consciousness, which does not want to be catapulted out of its entrenched habit patterns. The passage to a higher level of perception entails the death of the ego, and in the ensuing struggle, the physical body is often brought to the very edge of death. Mind and body naturally fight against death, even when it is followed by rebirth. In any case, at the time of actual struggle, people are unaware of such a possibility.

There are also social reasons for rejecting transformation into a shaman. In many societies and cultures, as in Korea for instance, shamans are not particularly respected. In addition, they often live in isolation and are not permitted to accumulate wealth. The practice of shamanism cannot always be reconciled with the satisfaction of everyday human needs. For that reason, certain moral, ethical, economic, and sexual factors can contribute to, or result in, a rejection of the sacred. Because of his responsibilities toward the spiritual, the dangers connected with handling objects of power and consorting with spirits and sorcerers, and risks resulting from violating certain rules and taboos, the shaman must at all times exercise great circumspection and self-control.

The training itself calls for great concentration of all mental and intellectual faculties, so that only someone gifted and sensitive above average can successfully undergo it. We have only to remind ourselves of the long fasts, the sexual prohibitions and nutritional taboos, the need to learn the traditional tribal lore as well as complicated rituals and myths. The inability to meet these enormous challenges often results in a premature curtailment of the shaman's career. A further obstacle are the high fees levied in certain tribes for shamanic training or admission to the circle of healers and medicine men. If the novice is unable to pay for the necessary ceremonies and sacrifices, the rise to full shamanship is made impossible for him, or he may have to content himself with a smaller ceremony which bestows a lower grade of initiation which results in a correspondingly reduced recognition on the part of the tribal community.

16

The Loss of Power

*I was broken by the Cross, the christening by the priest lay
heavy on me.*   —The Lapp Sorcerer Päivio.[1]

After the Eskimo shaman Aua had become a Christian, he had to send
all his helping spirits back to his sister on Baffin Island.[2] Tanklins,
a medicine man of the Australian Kurnai, lost his shamanic skills as a result
of excessive drinking. When his crystals disappeared, he also lost his powers and never regained them.[3]

In 1906 in the Mackenzie Delta, the Arctic explorer Steffansson met a
shaman called Alualuk who told him about half a dozen helping spirits
with which he was able to cure illnesses and even reawaken the dead.
When Steffansson met him again some time later, Alualuk had became a
Christian and sent all his helping spirits away. He admitted that he was now
as helpless against the powers of the Beyond as any ordinary mortal and
that he felt unwell and weak without his spirits, who had formerly supported him whenever he needed them. He often felt lonely without the
spirits, because he missed their friendship and company. The spirits, too,
were sad and lonely because they had to be without him. He pitied them.
Some spirits, however, were angry or even offended. That is why they tried
to get their own back on him at every opportunity. He had to be always on
the alert, pray regularly, and follow the Christian commandments, so that
the Church and Jesus Christ would protect him against the attacks of his
former helpers.[4]

The wife of the Siberian shaman Kyzlasov told of a shaman called
Kopkoyev, who had a similar experience. Many had to give up shamanism
after the power of the Soviets became consolidated. Kyzlasov, too, had

gone to the shaman ancestor, offering him some gifts and returning all the spirits, turning his back on shamanism.[5]

The Gitksan shaman Isaac Tens also lost all his powers when he converted to Christianity. He said:

> Now I use a different method in treating my patients. I employ nothing but prayers which I have learned at the Church. I pray like the minister—The Lord's Prayer. It has been translated into Gitksan by the Reverend Mr. Price of Kitwanga. I have entirely given up the practice of the *halaait*. My two children became sick—Philip (Piyawsu) and Mary (Tsigumnoeq). The folk around here agitated me and urged me to use the *halaait* over them. They blamed me for my refusal and declared that they would consider me responsible for their deaths. So I tried to revive one of my old charms—the Sun or the Moon *(hlorhs)*. But my body was altogether different from what it used to be. I was sure that I had lost my powers as a *Swanassu* (shaman).[6]

Christin, an Eskimo, similarly lost all his helping spirits after he converted to Christianity:

> Later on, I had a great many helping spirits among the fire people, and they were often of great assistance to me, especially when I was overtaken by a storm or by foul weather. When I made up my mind to journey to the West Coast to be baptized, they appeared to me and urged me not to do so. But I did what I willed all the same. Since then they have not shown themselves to me, because I betrayed them by my baptism.[7]

After it had come to the attention of the legendary Lapp sorcerer Päivio that sorcerers are destroyed by Christianity, he visited the King of Sweden to request that Lappland be christianized. But he had an ulterior motive, thinking to himself that if everyone were christened there would be no sorcerers except himself. He would indeed be powerful. When the minister came to visit Päivio's family in Kittila and christened his children, they lost their magic powers so that Päivio no longer had any competitors within the clan.[8] According to another version, however, Päivio, too, lost his magic powers through being christened.

Rosa, a shamaness (Piache) of the Latin American Guajiro, lost her helping spirits through contact with the world of the white people (Civilisados). She says:

I believe my spirits are no longer there. Once I became very ill. I went to Maracaibo to the doctor and was given many injections, and the doctor had to look after me a great deal. This greatly annoyed my spirits. They suffered because of the injections, and the treatment made them ill. The male spirit, especially, felt very miserable because the spirits will only accept tobacco as nourishment.[9]

However, conversion to another religion or contact with Western civilization are not the only ways in which a shaman may lose his magic. The careless or incompetent use of power, as well as moral weakness and the refusal to obey the "rules of the game" frequently result in its loss. Access to the sacred and the revelation of magic powers may promise extraordinary skills and capabilities, but this enlargement of the psychic field of activity is counterbalanced by oppressive taboos and restrictive rules of behavior, diet, etc.

The Kwakiutl shaman Síwít, for example, after receiving his call to shamanism, was to stay away from his wife for four months. Once, during a healing, he suddenly put his rattle down and terminated the ceremony, because he believed that he had allowed his wife to come to him too soon. On another occasion, he put aside his rattle and refused all food thereafter. When asked why he did this, he replied that he had been told never again to use his rattle. He became emaciated and ultimately starved himself to death.[10]

If a shaman of the Chemehueve is unfortunate enough to forget a "dream," he is chased with a firebrand or suspended over a fire lit under him. The fear of dying in the flames is meant to jolt his memory. If he has truly lost his healing powers he is accused of practicing black magic. He might still have dreams after that, but can no longer practice as a healer. It is rare, however, for a shaman to lose his skills, except in old age when he passes them on to someone else. Once that is done, he will soon die, because it is believed that he no longer has anything to live for.[11]

Mun-yir-yir, a medicine man in Northwestern Arnham Land, lost his spirits in a curious manner. He had acquired them at a water hole. As he bent down to drink, his later protectors—two boys and a girl (all three of them water spirits)—dragged him down into the deep, but then brought him back to the surface to prevent him from drowning. He hit them with his stone axe after he recovered consciousness. They in the meantime had turned into opossums. After he caught them he healed them by blowing his breath on them. Back in his camp, the three spirits attracted his attention with popping sounds, by hitting their arms against their sides. They sat on his shoulders and granted him the gift of healing. After that, he would heal by blowing on or sucking the site of an illness.

But the spirits imposed several taboos, which in the end led to the loss of his powers. He was not allowed to eat dog meat, sleep close by the fire, or let his body be touched by salt water.

One day he was out on the ocean in his canoe and another canoe accidentally ran into his, causing it to turn over. He and his helping spirits went into the water. After that he was no longer very successful in healing the sick. When he wanted to look inside them, he could only see darkness. He had lost his "doctor children."[12]

The Paviotso medicine man Joe Green (Pyramid Lake, Nevada) received his power in the form of dreams from his dead father. He inherited the Power of the Otter when an otter appeared to him in a dream and told him to skin it and then cut it into broad strips, lengthwise from head to tail, and fix eagle feathers to the holes at the neck of the skin. At his healing ceremonies he was to spread the otter skin on the earth in front of him. The otter taught him a special song for each ceremony. For some reason Joe Green thought the otter skin was too long and cut off the head. He became sick as a result of this. When the otter appeared to him for the last time it jumped into Pyramid Lake and then ran off across the desert. Although he was later healed by another shaman, he had lost his Otter Power.[13]

Rivalry and battles between shamans can also lead to a loss of power. We shall illustrate this by a final example. Eligio, a pupil of the famous Huichol shaman Don José (who also taught the Western shaman Prem Das) told how an "outside" Mara'akame (shaman) robbed him of his visionary powers.

> When I was a little boy I was able to see in the special way, and I remember well. . . . My father once took me to a Huichol *rancho* near our home. I was sitting next to a grain bin listening to a small mara'akame sing, and I could see colorful visions of all that he was singing about. Then something bad happened. Another mara'akame attending the ceremony was staring intently at me, and I began to feel drunk. The visions vanished, and I have never seen in such a way since. . . . You have to understand there is a jealousy between *mara'akate*. If you can see through the *nieríka* (Entry to the Beyond), sing well, or heal, they may try to psychically cover over your ability. All mara'akate have power to do such things and sometimes misuse the powers in this way. . . .

Eligio shook his head and then added: "I would have been a sha-man years ago if that had not occurred. It is really sad that so many shamans turn to sorcery."[14]

We have seen that many shamans lose belief in their gods and spirits through mere contact with our overpowering and stifling civilization. Or they may get so involved in our culture that they become dependent on it and forget their own cultural values or even consider them inferior.

If they surrender their traditional frame of reference, helping spirits and powerful animal familiars also become redundant as the belief in their ef-fectiveness fades away. We have seen, also, that those adopting a new faith are often punished by the powers they once ruled and may become men-tally disturbed or physically handicapped. Perhaps this is the explanation for the mental illness and physical diseases some explorers have found among shamans.

The effects of an attempt to return to normality are just as inexplicable and unexplored as is the way in which mediumship and paranormal states come into being. The spiritual path cannot be abandoned unpunished. Whoever sets foot on it will, in one way or another, remain under obliga-tion. Evidently, the return to a lower level of experience results in a rup-ture or shock. Once processes of thinking and feeling have become expanded, they cannot be restricted without causing problems, which manifest themselves as physical or mental illness.

Just as the sudden and unprepared submergence of three-dimensional thought into a mediumistic sphere cannot be smoothly absorbed and may leave psychic confusion and even psychosis in its wake, so the withdrawal from this kind of spiritual experience is often accompanied by drastic dis-turbances. In short: Once we have opened the doors of perception and ex-perienced a more diverse and varied world, they cannot be closed again; otherwise the impressions streaming through these doors will congest, swamp everything, and drown us in an *uncontrolled* mystical vision.

The more anonymous paranormal energy with which shamans work may also be lost. This can happen when power objects are wrongly or care-lessly used; when instructions, commands, or taboos are disobeyed; when dreams are ignored, visions wrongly interpreted, healing powers incor-rectly employed, ritual procedures handled negligently, or if the sacred path as a whole is not kept free from earthly desires and impurities. Who-ever loses sight of, treats disrespectfully, neglects, or temporarily forgets his inner powers and nonterrestrial sources of energy becomes ill, is plagued by misfortune, or dies. This is not difficult to understand when we remind ourselves that every illness is ultimately the result of acting or living in a way incompatible with our physical and psychic needs.

It follows that the more we open ourselves to our own nature, the more dangerous it will be to offend against it. For that reason, the shaman's path runs along a razor's edge between a world of supernormal health and fatal sickness. The shaman must continuously keep his balance and never allow himself to be distracted by tempting desires, greed, envy, hatred, or false hopes. He must always follow his vision and his inner counsel. If he strays even one step from this inner truth, his positive powers will turn into their opposite—sickness, catastrophe, poverty, and all kinds of misfortune which no longer can be considered as accidental. No wonder so many people refuse to embark upon such a precarious path. If powers once acquired are not nurtured and the possessor of these powers does not live in harmony with his inner and outer nature, they will turn against him in all their intensity.

PART THREE

Transformative Symbols of Consciousness

Somewhere there must be primordial forms whose images are ideas. If we could see them, we would understand the nature of existence and the connection between mind and matter.

—Gustave Flaubert

It was not my rational consciousness that brought me to an understanding of the fundamental laws of the universe.

—Albert Einstein

17

In the Bowels of the Earth

At the center of many Christian churches that were constructed on ancient sacred Celtic sites, a crypt or grotto is found that opens into a subterranean spring. This place—close to earth and water—is the central point of the House of God, its innermost sanctum.

The original spring, primordial water, sacred water holes, caves, or crypts are eternal symbols of transformation. Water is an agent of purification, healing, and rebirth—a means for the repolarization of profane into sacred reality. It is not surprising that shamanic initiations and the call to healing often occur or are experienced in a cave, a grotto with a spring, or at a water hole—in a wider sense also at a lake, pond, or near the ocean—in which the initiate immerses himself. Caves, after all, are places of safety and refuge and, ultimately, of mystery—in fact, an expression of the self. Here the shaman, surrounded by bare walls and isolated from the hurly-burly and self-seeking strivings of the world, encounters his innermost, higher self. He establishes a connection with the telluric currents of the earth via the subterranean spring, the veins and arteries of our planet, and allows these energies to flow through him.

Samarbahadur, a Nepalese Sunuwar shaman and a direct descendant of Gamdar, known as the first *puimbo* (shaman), met some small elflike beings in the jungle when he was thirteen. They led him to a grotto and taught him various mantras. He became unconscious, and three days later was found by his parents and neighbors, who had organized a search party. Since he had a high temperature, his father called upon Bakshi, the most eminent shaman in the locality, who cured him and later accepted him as his student. Samarbahadur was taught formulae that would allow him to attract helping spirits and ward off and immobilize evil spirits. He was also taught the rituals of officiating as a shaman at ceremonies. He subsequently sought out and was taught by other shamans. After serving for nine years as a Gurkha soldier, he wandered about in the company of *sadhus* (renunciates) and ascetics. At the age of thirty-five he returned to Sabra, his home village. Yogins traveling through the region near his village frequently make a detour to see him.[1]

Among the North American Walapai, the initiate, accompanied by his relatives, must also go to a cave. There he builds a fire and, during the night, tries to establish contact with the spirits in his dreams, hoping to increase his powers in this way. He spends only the night in the cave—during the day he is outside with his relatives, who are not allowed to enter the cave. After his encounters with the spirits, he behaves like crazy man or a drunk, running aimlessly about the desert. During the preparation for his initiation he may sip only an occasional spoonful of water. This rigorous regime helps to increase his mental concentration.[2]

A medicine man of the Australian Unambal may dream that his soul returns to the watering-place from which it originally rose when it was reborn. But the soul does not stay by the side of the watering hole. It travels down into the bowels of the earth where, in a brightly lit cave, it comes upon a pair of copulating Ungud snakes—a symbol of the primordial creative powers. The mating of the snakes produces embryonic spores, Ungud parts (*Jallalas*), many of which enter into the medicine man and thereby enrich and strengthen his soul.

According to other reports, the medicine man acquires medicine crystals in this cave, from which shine forth the colors of the rainbow (because Ungud is symbolically connected to the rainbow). These crystals (*alumburru*) enter the body of the medicine man through his navel, his penis, or the dell above his clavicles. He then experiences a radiant light within himself.

Instead of the crystals he may receive two eggs, which continue to grow inside him. On his return to his tribe he is ill and feverish. He is advised to drink large quantities of water (Ungud power) to regain his strength. As his power grows, the luminosity within him increases, he learns to recognize hidden diseases and ultimately can live forever in the Dreamtime (Lalai) for which he has yearned so long.[3]

Tanklins, a medicine man (*mulla-mullung*) of the Australian Kurnai tribe, also acquired his powers through dreaming. He had the same dream three times. He flew through the air, in the company of his father and several medicine men, to a steep rock face in which there was a cleft. His father blindfolded him and led him through the cleft in the rock face into the inside of the mountain. He found himself in a place filled with light as bright as day. Several men were assembled there and he was shown many shining objects. His father taught him how to make these shining objects disappear into one's leg and extract them again to point them at people who have hostile intentions.[4]

William Beynon has recorded the story of Qamkawl (Only-One), a great halaait of the Canadian Tsimsyan: Among the Gyilodzau (a Skeen River subtribe of the Tsimsyan) were three men who felt that they were to become halaaits. Some distance from the village there was a pit from which people heard strange noises and sometimes crying and singing. It seemed to be the abode of a supernatural being. The three men went to this pit, and one of them said to the others, "Tie the rope around my waist and lower me down. I shall see what there is at the bottom. This must be the abode of the supernatural being." The two men fastened the rope around his body and lowered him down. He had not gone down very far when he shouted out, "Pull me up! Pull me up or I shall perish." When the two men had pulled him up, he told them, "As you were lowering me, a great cloud of insects attacked me, almost suffocating me."

Then the next man tried to go down. They fastened the rope around him and began to lower him, but he was soon shouting, "Pull me up, pull me up!" When they had done so, they saw that his body was all red from the bites of the insects. He was almost unconscious. A long time lapsed before he recovered. Then the last of the three men ventured down. He went right down without being attacked like the others. When he landed at the bottom of the deep pit he found it very dark. Then a great sound, as of thunder, almost deafened him.

A door opened from which a very bright man stepped. He came straight to him and asked, "Where are you from, and what do you want?" "Oh! Supernatural One, I have come to get halaait power, to cure my people." The bright man said, "Come with me, I will take you to my father. He may help you." The visitor followed the shining man, who led him into a large house where he was permitted to sit beside a great chief, with many rattles that looked as if they were alive. As he sat there, another door opened through which a young man entered. He had a rattle in each hand and came to where the visitor sat. The young man's apron was fringed with deer hooves that gave a rattling sound with every movement he made.

While he stood there, one more door opened, and boards came out as if alive and spread out in front of the fire. The people in the house began to sing, following the tune sung by the young man with the rattles. Then a live drum ran out and began to beat itself with one of the beaters. Everything seemed to be alive. The great chief rose and rubbed the visitor's eyes whereupon he could be no longer see. Then he felt that the rope was still fastened to him; so he called out, and his companions pulled him up. When he was back at the surface he could see again.

On their return to the village, the first two men became unconscious and both vomited blood. But the man who had been lowered all the way down into the pit never lost consciousness. When the two men vomited blood, this was a sign that they were now under the halaait influence. After the three men recovered, they went about doing some healing of the sick. After about a year, the man who had been taken down into the pit disappeared. One night, the people heard a great crash at the back of the house. They ran out and found his body face down in the mud. They took him for dead and carried him into the house. Soon after, he began to sing and then said, "I was called back to the house where I went last year and have acquired greater power than any other halaait. Now I have received powers which enable me to restore to life those who are dead. I have been given a halaait name: Qamkawl—Only-One. And the two companions who came with me shall be my aides." His fame began to travel to all the corners of the world. Many times he restored life to those who were dead and foretold great events. Soon he was growing wealthy and powerful.

Many years later, when Only-One was aged, a messenger went to him and told him, "The Master wants you." Only-One got up and made preparations for a long journey. He told his two companions, "I am going to give you powers that I now possess. You in turn shall always have my help. I am going on a long journey and may never return, but you shall be able to continue my work among the people." Then he went down to his canoe, and without any effort the canoe drove away up to the pit where he had first acquired his halaait powers, and he vanished. He never returned to his people, but they knew he was not dead. He had gone to the abode of the great halaait over which he now is the chief and gives out powers to other halaaits.[5]

According to this account the supernatural resides deep in the bowels of the earth. A pit or hole leads down to the home of the shining being who seems to be a combination of the Ruler of the Game (he wears an apron adorned with deer hooves), the Ruler of the Earth, and the Giver of Life. During the ritual of initiation, which is accompanied by songs, the power itself is manifested, moving drumsticks, and finally enters the initiate. Just as everything around him seems to be alive in itself, he, too, is filled with life. Being imbued with the pure essence of life, he must now learn to "see." He becomes blind, loses the limited vision of ordinary eyes, so he may come to see both physically and spiritually.

Having descended to the center of the earth, into darkness, he is illumined. Having been blinded, he comes to see. This is the paradoxical upside-down world of the shaman. There is light in the bowels of the earth and outside, where we are confined to our unillumined ordinary consciousness, there is darkness. Only those who close their eyes or are blinded may see the hidden subtle realm and the causes of events. The journey into the earth once again points to the paradoxical ways of the shaman, who must enter another level of existence—in this case, the underworld—to become transformed and thereafter live more consciously and holistically.

Hermits in their caves, monks in their cells, and people who subject themselves voluntarily to sensory deprivation in a laboratory all pursue the same aim: The elimination of the manifold world of the senses in order to attain greater concentration and inner vision. Outer calm brings inner calm, absence of external stimuli leads to a state of inner emptiness. Without this emptiness there can be no mental equilibrium and, thus, no access to cosmic harmony and life-giving energy. Whoever reaches the heart of being by penetrating to the very center of the earth, partakes of the Whole. Even if one is unable to maintain the resultant awareness of the all-embracing unity of all things, one continues to share the essence of all being by surrogates of wholeness—a crystal, a mantra, or a spirit being that becomes a helper.

In conclusion, let us look at what happened to Charlie Gabe, a Flathead Indian who set out in search of a protecting spirit when he was fourteen years old. He went to seek a "guardian" on top of a mountain, but fasted for four days before he started his ascent, during which a number of strange things happened, such as encountering white muskrats which ordinarily do not leave the banks of low-country rivers. On the summit of the mountain he found a great hole. Looking over its brink, he could see Little People preparing for a dance. He descended the pit but on arrival at the bottom was neither welcomed nor rebuffed. However, when all the preparations were over, the chief of the Little People invited him to the festival. They danced all night and during the day they rested.

They kept this up for four days. The boy knew that he had been on the mountain long enough but wanted to catch a Little Person to take down to the home camp. Three times he tried in vain, but succeeded on the fourth attempt. He took the dwarf down to his lodge, where the captive said to him, "After the fourth attempt you have finally captured me. Well, for this you must keep me and feed me for four years, after which you must take me back to my people and free me. When this time comes I will tell you something good."

The boy kept the dwarf and provided him with the best he could find. After four years, he carried the dwarf up the hill in accordance with his obligation. Upon reaching the summit, he deposited him by the opening of the crater. Then the dwarf said, "I have been your guest. From now on, when you are in trouble or need anything, think hard about me. I will come to your aid, for you need not suffer danger anymore. Furthermore, I will give you my power whenever you want to help anyone else."[6]

Many other reports tell how the inhabitants of the subterranean world dance and rejoice in great exultation, as was witnessed by Only-One and Charlie Gabe. Totally pervaded by the energy of life, their sole aim is to move in harmony with the eternal rhythm of universal power. The dance of beings inhabiting the underworld or the celestial realm is a timeless transpersonal symbol for the exuberant joy and bliss of those that find themselves at the center of cosmic vitality. Charlie Gabe received some of this energy after he skillfully caught one of its bearers and provided for him for four years at great personal sacrifice. Skill, perseverance, and selflessness are clearly indispensable on the path of initiation.

18

Experiences of Light and Balls of Fire

In *Paradiso*, which forms the third part of his *Divine Comedy*, Dante describes the Eternal Light as an everflowing radiance in which he saw the "scattered leaves of all the universe," with substance and accidents fused into a single flame.

Many artists, writers, saints, and visionaries have tried to describe mystical experience, but not a single one of them felt that he had succeeded even approximately. Walt Whitman in his *Prayer of Columbus* speaks of "light rare, untellable lighting the very light—beyond all signs, descriptions, languages." Radiant light is also a central theme in the Greek Orthodox and Roman Catholic churches, in Eastern spirituality and, of course, shamanic experiences of transformation.

According to the Upanishads, the Atman expresses itself as "inner light." In the Tibetan *Book of the Dead*, a light appears to the soul after death, in which it is bathed. Dionysos describes the other world as "blinding with an excess of light."

Light-experiences also occur in Autogenic Training, under hypnosis, during psychotherapy (after the abreaction of traumatic memories), as well as after shock and primary experiences, and of course when one is confronted by one's higher self. Therefore, emanations of light may quite generally be understood as an expression of the breakthrough to another level of existence, the transition from ego to the true Self. Phenomena of light are characteristic of all mystical experience and quite simply part of the process of transpersonal change. The landscapes and beings of the Beyond encountered in near-death experiences are also bathed in radiant heavenly light. In the transpersonal realm, objects seem to have their own luminosity, so that people who have had such experiences are often unable to say precisely where the light came from; it seems to be pervading every-thing and to be all around, like air.

Encounters with bearers of light, shining figures, radiant deities, or spir-its are yet another form of light-experience. Baiami, the Creator god of the Australian Wiradjeri, enters the circle of shamanic apprentices as a human being and sends forth beams of light from his eyes. Only-One, the great halaait, encounters the life-giving spirit in the form of a "bright man" who bestows healing powers. The Mexican shaman Gabriel Mir was initiated by a luminous dwarf.

A third form of light-phenomena occurs in out-of-body experiences during or after the passage through a tunnel or similar entrance. The Be-yond seems to be completely flooded with light, which illumines—one might even say enlightens—purifies, and regenerates. In their descrip-tions of OBES, people frequently mention a transforming intensity of light which heals and causes them to experience existence as wondrous, sa-cred and pervaded by a mysterious regenerative power. When this hap-pens, people feel blissfully happy afterward; they have lost their fear of death, have knowledge about an inner source of energy, and long to re-turn to the experience.

Let us recall the Unambal medicine man who, in his spirit body, de-scended into a brightly lit subterranean cave where he witnessed the coup-ling of Ungud snakes. Their fertility passed into him and he returned to the surface experiencing an inner radiance. Elsie Parrish, the Pomo sha-maness, encountered a white light in the Beyond and was guided by it wherever she went. The soul of the Siberian shaman Markov flew over a dark country until a celestial landscape, bathed in light, was revealed to him. The eyes of the shaman escorting him glowed like fire throughout their journey, pointing his way. Markov, moreover, was told the reason for the darkness upon our earth: The Middle World had greatly fallen prey to sin. Here again we have the theme that a lower level of consciousness is the cause of the suffering experienced in this world. Life in light and life in darkness, inner illumination and inner blindness—these most ancient symbols of spiritual development are here juxtaposed.[1]

All manifestations of light bring about changes in us. They acquaint us with a world of the spirit, with spiritual reality. Among the Eskimos the en-trails, internal organs, eyes, and the brain of the initiate are removed from the body and then reinserted in a special way, to make him understand the essence of being. A light begins to shine within him, and the Siberian Eski-mos say that shamans are bathed in light. In Northern Alaska, the shamanic teacher cuts a large breathing hole through the ice. At this hole his pupil is attacked by swarms of worms which totally devour him. He becomes luminous within and this inner light then attracts the spirits.[2]

It would therefore seem that the radiance of the shaman reaches out to the realm of the dead. He himself is raised to that realm by his enlightenment and then displays characteristics of that other world, such as his body of light, while still alive on earth. Among the Copper Eskimos the spirits of the air—themselves luminous shadows—behold the shaman as a shining body. They feel drawn to him, want to live within him and give him their own strength, sight and knowledge. They enter his body through the navel and then settle in his chest.

The Eskimos say that, compared to shining shamans, ordinary people are like houses with extinguished lamps: They are dark inside and do not attract the attention of the spirits.[3] The shamanic pupil arrives at his illumination (*qaumanEq*) through meditation in solitude. He experiences a light inside his head, within the brain, and can then see through darkness, even with closed eyes, and perceive things and coming events which are hidden from others. He can look into the future and into the secrets of others.

The first time a young shaman experiences this light it is as if the house in which he sits suddenly rises; he sees far ahead of him, through mountains, as if the earth were one great plain, and his eyes can reach to the end of the earth. Nothing is hidden from him any longer. He can also discover stolen souls that are kept concealed in far, strange lands or have been taken to the land of the dead.[4]

Rasmussen quotes an Eskimo shaman who experienced such an illumination:

> Every real shaman has to feel an illumination in his body, in the inside of his head or in his brain, something that gleams like fire, that gives him the power to see with closed eyes into the darkness, into the hidden things or into the future or into the secrets of another man. I felt that I was in possession of this marvelous ability.[5]

The Iglulik shamaness Uvavnuk one dark winter night beheld a glowing ball of fire in the sky. It raced toward her and entered into her. At that moment she was filled with a shining light and lost consciousness. Just before that she glimpsed the shape of a spirit. It had two bodies which chased her through the air. One part was like a bear, the other like a human. The head was human but had the fangs of a bear. When she regained consciousness she ran back to her hut and began to sing, senseless with joy. The other people in the house were also beyond themselves with joy, because their minds were being cleansed of all that burdened them. Uvavnuk was exceptional in that all her capabilities disappeared as soon as she emerged from a trance. Outside the trance state, she behaved like an ordinary human being, but would become all-knowing whenever the fireball spirit entered into her. Shortly before her death, she held a great séance and called upon the celestial powers to provide plenty of food for her people so they would not suffer. She produced large quantities of game from within the earth, and the people of her village had a great surplus of whale, walrus, seal, and caribou for about a year.[6]

We have seen that illumination does not only manifest subjectively, within the shaman; his radiance is often perceived by others as well. It is said, for instance, that a bright flame hovered above the Eskimo shaman Kritdlarssuark as he led his companions on a train of dog sleighs in search of a distant people.[7]

Another variant of revelation by light and by an encounter with relatives in the Beyond was related to the anthropologist Ruth Bunzel by a Zuni Indian:

> When I was sick of the measles I was very sick. On the third day I didn't know anything. Maybe I fainted, or maybe I really died and came back. I never believed that could happen, but it really did, because when I came back the room was going round and round and there was a little light coming through the window, although there was a bright light in the room. While I was dead I dreamed I was going toward the West. . . . I was so happy to see my grandfather. Since then I've never worried about dying, even when I was very sick, because I saw all these dead people and saw that they were still living the way we do.[8]

Light-experiences are very common when a person comes close to death. Tribal societies commonly believe that the inner light is not perceived by the physical body, but by the soul-body in an altered state of consciousness. Sometimes the soul itself is considered to be the body of light.

From this it could be argued that our true existential center is an emanation of light. For that reason, the Desana compare the soul of a shaman (Payé) with a fire whose light penetrates obscurity and makes things visible. It is imagined as a flame that comes out of the "little web" and emits a light, according to the degree of power. It is further said that both the light of the Payé and that of lightning are of the same color—yellow—and that this light also represents the energizing and fertilizing radiation of the sun. Of a shaman who is not very active, the Desana say that "his soul is not seen, it does not burn, it does not shine."[9]

The shining soul of the Payé, then, by its penetrating inner light, dispels all darkness. This supernatural luminosity is also said to be visible when the shaman sings or describes his psychedelic experiences. On the other hand, a Payé who, after taking Ayahuasca, is unable to describe his visions clearly is said to have no luminosity. The power of the Payé comes directly from the sun. When he recites myths or genealogical passages he "sheds light." By his profound and deeply rooted identification with myth and tradition, he is brought to an altered state of consciousness; he submerges himself in the mythical environment and reflects, as it were, the nonterrestrial light of the mystic realm of existence.[10] Without this inner illumination, the Payé would never be able to perceive the inner essence of another human being.

The medicine man of the Patagonian Selk'nam also must develop an inner light to be able to read the thoughts of his fellow tribesmen, but this light can only be perceived by other medicine men. Among the Australian Unambal, the mystical experience of light is brought about by alumburro (crystals) that are introduced into the body during initiation. This inner light enables the medicine man to live uninterruptedly in Lalai, the Dreamtime. The insertion or absorption of these crystals unites the medicine man with the Ungud snake, the primordial creative principle. The inner luminosity so caused enables him to see in a new way, with his spiritual eyes.[11] He perceives another world beyond our conventional one.

It remains unclear how this combination of luminosity and transformed sight results in intuitive and paranormal visions, but it would be short-sighted to suppose that these phenomena are merely symbolic. We may not yet know how or why. Nevertheless, illumination *does* lead to an expansion of psychic capabilities. In all mystical traditions, the transformation of consciousness is signaled by the entry into another dimension of perception after an experience of light.

Being an expression of the celestial, lightning—like crystal—can also bring about spiritual illumination. The Korean shamaness Oh Un-sook, for instance, dreamt of thunder and lightning. Soon after, she encountered a pillar of light three times and three men appeared to her from heaven. Inner luminosity is often preceded by a visible physical phenomenon of light, such as a ball of fire, lightning, pillars of fire, a figure of light, or simply a light beam. In most cases, however, the inner light can only be perceived when a higher level of consciousness has been reached, if the subject is in a trance, or if mind and body are sufficiently exhausted and unbalanced to become open to new insights.

Let us return to the ball of fire, because it does not always represent mystical illumination, as was the case with the Eskimo shamaness Uvavnuk. Such balls of fire often have a negative origin because sorcerers may battle with each other by sending out balls of fire, or they may use them to kill their victims. The Mexican Tzeltal distinguish between red, yellow, and green balls of fire.[12] On the island of Dobu (New Guinea), sorceresses fly through the air with trails of fire behind them and then attack alien souls.[13] The shamans of the Alaskan Eskimos may metamorphose into a ball of fire and fly through space, spreading death and destruction.[14] A Penobscot Indian told the American anthropologist Frank Speck:

> I was hunting up in the country by the waters of the Saint John River. One night, a tremendous ball of fire appeared rushing through the air, moving upstream. It had a large head and behind it was a snake-like body. I could even see scars on the cheek of the creature. Pretty soon another appeared. I thought they were "fire creatures," *eskuda'hit*, but my father said they must be *medeoli'nuwak* (shamans).[15]

Lapp shamans are able to travel through a firmament of fire, and for that reason are also known as "Fire Lapps." When two of these shamans have a quarrel, they will sit opposite each other and chant until they turn into light. Then they meet in the sky as blazing lights and noisily battle each other. The aurora borealis (Northern Lights) is often interpreted in this way. A shaman whose light begins to fade soon becomes ill, and shamans whose light is completely extinguished during such a battle must die soon after.[16]

The Australian Wiradjeri believe that evil sorcerers race across the country in the form of dangerous fires when they are out to catch victims. Jack King told the ethnologist R. M. Berndt how he and his stepfather "King" Dick saw such a flying fire when they were camping in the open. His father rose and turned it away by chanting, otherwise it would have tried to cast a spell on them. The fire had crackled and spit and appeared to singe everything. It was about fifteen meters across. Now and then it might disappear, but only to turn up in another place. Dick had followed the fire and kept it away from the camp toward which it had been traveling. During his pursuit he had encountered the "clever man" Bobby Boney who took over the chase, so that Dick was able to return to camp. But all that happened only in the mind.[17]

The English police inspector James H. Neal has reported an incredible incident that happened in Keta, which is a center for medicine men and the capital of the African Ewe people. Neal was investigating a theft from a state-owned undertaking. One night he was roused by a lot of noise: The birds were chattering in great excitement, dogs were barking, and chickens were fluttering in panic across the yard. He got up to see what was happening and saw a great ball of fire hovering on the horizon and rising in the sky in a sort of rocking motion. The ball of fire was three times as big as the moon and spat out colored scraps of light. The next night it was there again, causing the animals to wake and become excited. Neal and his fellow inspectors, who also witnessed the spectacle, were greatly mystified.

The mystery was solved when the thief gave himself up voluntarily after the ball of fire had appeared over Keta on two successive nights. The thief had been unwilling to share his loot with two of his friends who were medicine men (ju-ju people). They caused an artificial sun to rise in the sky in revenge, and it is commonly believed that if such a sun has appeared three times, a person on whom a spell has been cast will die a painful death. So the thief gave himself up in terror.[18]

Flying balls of fire are said to be especially common in Hawaii. There is hardly anyone who does not claim to have seen Akualele, "flying spirits" or "flying gods." These Akualele race horizontally across the sky, close above the roofs of houses. If they enter a house, sickness or death will soon occur there. The Akualele are of different sizes, similar to shooting stars, and can themselves give off sparks. These balls of fire are produced by black magic (Hoomanamana). It is said that they appear for years at places where owners of Unihipili used to live. Unihipili are the bones of dead relatives or friends, reanimated by prayers and sacrifices and afterwards used for healing purposes, but also to practice black magic.[19]

All these examples show that inner illumination, arising unexpectedly and without warning after an initiate has performed certain spiritual practices over long periods, is one of the most ancient mystical experiences of mankind. Light is considered to be the highest manifestation of spiritual vision. Not only are the celestial realms filled with brilliant light, the soul itself is said to be a body of light. But in order to see this world of the spirits, the séances and ceremonies by which they are summoned are conducted in darkness throughout the world, because the spirits are said to be extremely sensitive to the "hard" light of our world.

Light-phenomena can take a great variety of forms. In the traditional sweat lodges, American Indian initiates may see blue, red, orange, or green tongues of fire, all according to the state of mind of those present at the ceremony. We also have a whole spectrum of Christian light-phenomena: the haloes of saints, emanations of light by relics, and apparitions of the Virgin Mary that send out brilliant rays of light. Furthermore, the bodies of many mystics are said to emanate light. Ignatius of Loyola was surrounded by a glowing light during prayer, and Saint Columba was allegedly permanently cloaked in radiant light. Similar associations account for Jesus Christ being referred to as the "Light of the World." In Eastern cultures, too, such phenomena are not unusual. It is said, for example, that the Indian avatar Ramakrishna shone like gold, even as a child, and had to be wrapped in a cloak so as not to attract attention.

Figures of light and mystical phenomena of light cannot simply be written off as hallucinations or the result of an overexcitation of the nervous system. Spiritual experiences of light occur after the collapse of the ego structure, after rigorous spiritual practices, intense concentration, and meditation. They are supreme phenomena of deconditioning.

19

Ascending the World Tree

In many Siberian communities the World Tree plays an important part in shamanic initiation. Among the Gold Eskimos, the ascent to heaven is the high point of an initiation ceremony. The shaman father (teacher) climbs a birch tree, circling its trunk nine times.

This climb is symbolic of the soul's ascent to heaven. Each circling of the trunk represents the passing from one realm to the next, and those present at the ceremony are given detailed information by the shaman concerning the nature of each realm. The shaman then descends in the same fashion, circling the trunk in reverse direction. Then the new shaman and others previously initiated climb the tree in succession.

In a variant of this ceremony (in the Balagansk region) the shamanic candidate is carried on a felt mat along a row of birch trees nine times, from east to west. Then he climbs each of these birches, circling the trunk nine times, and calls the spirits from the top of each tree. His teacher simultaneously circles that tree on the ground.[1]

The World Tree—the *axis mundi* connecting heaven, earth, and the underworld—is seen as an opening or channel to other realms of being. Along it, gods and beings of the Beyond descend to earth and the souls of mortals rise to heaven. This cosmic axle holds the universe in balance and at the same time is its center. The World Tree is a symbol of cosmic experience. However, because of the limitations of language and conceptual thought, this symbol conveys only a vague idea of all this—a two-dimensional picture of a multidimensional continuum. The *axis mundi* can only be known intuitively and mystically; it defies rational description. Even poetic language, with all its subtle intimations, cannot help us here. All archetypes, the World Tree included, are merely allegories of a higher mode of perception, externalizations of a transpersonal reality. The experience of passing from one level of existence to another, of entering other psychic dimensions, is therefore described either as a descent into the underworld or as an ascent, along the Tree of Life, to heaven. If we want to describe or speak about processes of psychic transformation—and this even extends to emotional and mental experiences in general—we are forced to make use of metaphors derived from our material world. In all cultures the Unconscious makes use of such images as trees, ropes, etc. to convey to the ordinary mind the idea of overcoming cosmological levels.

World Trees, World Mountains, or World Pillars are symbols that enable spirits to come to our world, shamans to reach other cosmic realms, or the dead to encounter the supreme deity, as the Indonesian Dayak believe. Among the Eskimos and the natives of Central Indonesia and in other cultures the center post of the house is considered to be the World Axis along which the spirits descend. Others believe that souls, shamans, or healers ascend to the realm of the spirits along ladders, ropes, or cords.

The shamanic gurus of the Nepalese Bhujel, as they sing and drum, have a vision of a particular pine tree in the forest and direct other members of the clan to find it. In the forest, this tree is stripped of all branches except for a tuft at the top, and then taken back to the center of the village where it is erected upright in a hole. During a further ceremony, the guru transmits his ecstasy to his pupil, who proceeds to climb the tree. The guru then shouts "Ho!" nine times and the pupil, with each shout, slides part way down the tree trunk until he touches the ground.[2]

Among the Magar, the shaman also climbs a tree. He is blindfolded during his ascent. This is to indicate that the journey to the realm between heaven and earth is purely visionary. He brings back knowledge and prophesies from the Intermediate Realm.[3]

After his initiation in a luminous cave, the Australian Kurnai medicine man Tanklins was placed into the crown of a tree by the village elders. Thus he became a mulla-mullung. He later found himself lying under the tree with shining objects of magic in his hands.[4]

The narratives of two Siberian shamans, Kizlasov and Sunchugasev, show the significance of the Cosmic Tree even more clearly. First Sunchugasev:

> On the way to the ancestral shaman, the shamans arrive at the "wealthy birch tree" in the neighborhood of their own mountain and their own water. They rest at its foot and examine its *tamgas*, or brands, placed upon it by the shamans because, as a rule, all the shamans, descendants of the ancestral shaman, place their own mark-

ings upon this golden-leaved birch tree of richly intertwined branches. The ones who get their power through the spirit of the mountain, or through a sickness, have no such symbols. If a member of a family is about to become a shaman, the tamga of the dead shaman of the same clan revives. It becomes clearly visible on the trunk of the birch again. At such times they usually say (that) someone of the clan will soon become a shaman.

Then Kizlasov took up the subject:

When the shaman goes to the chief shaman, that is, to the family ancestor, he has to cross the *ham saraschan harazi* mountain along the way. On the top of that mountain there is a pine tree; its trunk resembles a six-sided log. The shamans carve their symbols into it, between the edges. Whoever places his marking, his tamga, upon it, then becomes a real shaman. It happens sometimes that when a certain marking "falls down," it disappears from the tree. Then its owner dies. After resting at the foot of this tree, the journey is continued.[5]

The "wealthy tree" on the mountain is beyond doubt the World Tree—the cosmic axis. The shaman, by carving his signs and symbols into the bark of the tree, becomes united with its principal elements, that is to say, with heaven and earth. He also partakes of the fertility of creation, because the tree is also a symbol of life and of initiation. By carving his name into the tree and vividly calling to mind the names of the shamanic ancestors, the newly initiated shaman shares the sacredness of the tree and acquires additional spiritual power. Henceforth, he—like the tree—will be at the center of the world, i.e., the zenith of his psychic power.

The Buryat and the Central Asian Altai erect a young birch tree and carve nine notches into the lower end of its trunk, where there are no branches. These notches serve the shaman as steps during his ascent. Whereas the Buryat and Altai believe that the World Tree penetrates all three realms—heaven, earth, and the underworld—the people of the Siberian Gold tribe have a separate World Tree for each realm.[6]

The Tungus of the Lower Tunguska believe in a World Tree known as Tuuru, which grows in heaven. On this tree are nests which contain eggs—the souls of shamans. The closer such a nest is to heaven the stronger will be the shaman emerging from it. Shamans that come from nests halfway up or near the bottom of the tree will have only average or small powers. The eggs are hatched by a great bird that appears to the shaman three times: at birth, during the dismemberment of his body, and at his death.[7]

All creation arises within and from a central point, which in symbolic language is known as the Navel of the World, the Sacred Egg, the Hidden Seed, the Root of Roots, the World Pillar, the World Tree, or the World Mountain. The latter may also be represented by a pyramid, ziggurat or stupa. All these are symbols for the center of the world. It might be said that the existence of so many World Trees and equally numerous tree cults is somewhat illogical because it implies an equal number of world centers. Such an argument, however, is based on a misunderstanding that arises from confusing the visionary experience of the Center with an actual geographical center. The Siberian shaman knows, of course, that the tree he climbs during his initiation is not an actual World Tree but a spiritual symbol. On the other hand, there are tribal cultures who believe in a holographically structured universe in which every place, every tree—and in fact every human being—is considered to be the center of the world. This belief gives rise to a universe sacred from every aspect, a universe in which each detail represents and incorporates the whole so that everything is related to everything. The cult of the World Tree thus reveals a cosmos of mystic union. The world resembles a "primordial sphere" containing innumerable centers in which the Sacred is omnipresent.

The World Tree is also the Tree of Life and represents fertility, regeneration of life and immortality. Whoever climbs it ascends to real life, and the higher he climbs the more comprehensive will be his experience of cosmic unity and of the interconnectedness of all life. The vision of the World Tree grants us new life because by experiencing the cosmos comprehensively we are able to break through the limitations of ordinary consciousness. We experience the creative energies of Being, the secret of fertility and growth.

Regenerated by our vision of the Creative and vitalized by our experience of other realms of existence, we descend from this World Tree in a state of ecstasy and bliss, as if reborn. Our view of existence has been expanded, as has our compassion toward and empathy with the world. Having beheld the hierarchies of the heavens, we have become visionaries, seers, and shamans.

20

Portals to Heaven and the Underworld

According to their myths of creations, many American tribal people, particularly the Pueblo Indians and the tribes of the Great Plains, came into this world from the innermost caverns of the earth through a hole in the earth's surface. Not only do whole tribes—and life altogether—enter their earthly existence through a small orifice; individual shamans obtain their power—or access to a higher dimension—by passing through a narrow channel to another realm of being.

The medicine men of the Australian Kurnai, accompanied by their helping spirits (*Mrart*), climb to heaven along a kind of rope or staircase, where a spirit of the dead creates a hole for them through which they can slip into heaven.[1]

A medicine man of the Australian Barkinyi cuts a circular piece of skin from the belly of his dead wife. He chews a small piece of it after drying it, whereupon her spirit (*gumatch*) appears to him. It lifts him up and carries him to heaven. There he comes to a hole or window that is guarded by another gumatch. He requests permission to enter the realm in which he, too, will one day dwell as a spirit. On the other side of this entrance he meets spirits of the dead, who teach him many things but soon after urge him to return to earth.[2]

The Tsimshian of the Canadian northwest coast often have holes in their totem poles, which serve as ceremonial routes of access to the house of Haidzermerh, the Creator. The shaman begins his soul journey at this "hole through the sky." The Mexican Huichol speak in this context of Nierika, and Latin American Indians, after taking the psychedelic Ayahuasca brew, say that the "horizon opens like a door."[3] One Siberian shaman related: "As I looked around, I noticed a hole in the earth. . . . The hole became larger and larger. We [shaman and spirit ally] descended through it and arrived at a river. . . ." And with this vision of the river of the dead began his journey into the Beyond.[4]

The opening or hole is the entrance to the world of the spirit. It is not only humans that use it as a passage. Spirits, too, need such a place of entry. That is why there is a hole in the wall of the house of the Indonesian Tobelorese. A palm leaf is placed into this hole, with a stick through it that establishes the connection between inside and outside. This construction is referred to as the "path of the spirits."[5]

We want to discuss here in somewhat greater detail a legend of the Californian Chumash Indians, in which Axiwalic, a wizard who is critically ill, slips through a hole into the other world while he is trying to heal himself. Until then all his attempts to do so had failed. He therefore decided to go and die at a place far away from people. He was walking one night by the side of the ocean on his way to such an isolated place when a light appeared from a nearby cliff. This light flew around for a while, disappeared again and shortly after reappeared, dancing above the cliffs. Axiwalic decided to catch it, come what may.

The small flickering light resisted desperately, calling out, "Let me go." After considerable argument and a violent tug-of-war, it submitted to the will of Axiwalic and guided him to a narrow orifice that led into a tunnel. After they had passed through this tunnel and entered a house , the little light disappeared and Axiwalic found himself in the company of various animals—a deer, a beaver, and birds. Soon yet more arrived: coyotes, bears, and wild cats. All these animals defecated on Axiwalic, and when he was covered all over in feces, the old deer asked him what he wanted. Axiwalic replied that he was sick and wanted to be healed. Thereupon the animals held a great celebration, at the end of which they bathed Axiwalic, who soon felt better. He then returned home, having reached the earth's surface through a spring.

When he reappeared at his village, all the people were overjoyed. "He that we thought dead has returned to us cured," they said. He told them everything that had happened and was amazed when they said that he had been gone for three years, for he thought he had been gone only three days![6]

The healing experience of Axiwalic contains a great number of transpersonal themes. Here light, as a manifestation of another realm of existence, takes the place of the spirit creatures that usually escort the seeker or show him the way. After passing through the tunnel connecting our world with the Beyond, Axiwalic arrives at the house of the animals—an image of regeneration, the creation of life and the highest symbol of the Self. We should not be surprised at the animals defecating on him, for whoever wishes to be purified and experience the sacred must first be aware of the "dirt" of the profane that clings to him. Just as a farmer will spread manure on his fields to produce a richer harvest, so the animals—living symbols of the natural life—defecate all over Axiwalic and then celebrate a great festival of resurrection, which ends in a bath of purification—that classic symbol of initiation, of the transition from an old to a new self.

Axiwalic, healed and reborn, returns to our world through the "spring of life." He is astonished at having been away for three whole years because to him it had felt like only three days. The world of expanded consciousness is subject to a different time scale and, in the last analysis, time there is timeless—the time of the divine.

The various time scales of different worlds are a theme of many fairy tales, myths, and journeys to the Beyond. As far as the transformation of consciousness is concerned, we have as yet no space/time theory of relativity. The impressive and adventurous odyssey of Axiwalic shows the great experiences of healing that await us when we pass through the heavenly portal into the "house" of our higher Self.

21

Rulers of Nature
and Givers of Life

What is the source of man's creative energy, of the richness of our earth? For tribal people, life is vital energy that comes directly from the Creator of Being or from subordinate Givers of Life, Rulers of Nature, and lesser deities—not, as science would have us believe, a banal sequence of behavioral patterns and movements. Many shamans receive their powers from these sources of life and only after that are assisted in various ways by spirit helpers or objects of power.

Vaî-mahsë, the Ruler of the Animals among the Tukano Indians, dwells either in the earth or in water. If a Tukano tribesman enters the realm of Vaî-mahsë, this is tantamount to sexual union with him. The Ruler of the Animals occasionally holds festivals at which all the animals dance and drink Yajé, just like humans. Through attending such a festival, the shaman (Payé) experiences a great increase in his power. Furthermore, the game stock increases after such festivals. Joining the dance festival of the animals transforms the human spectator into a Giver of Life who partakes of creative vitality and who thus becomes a shaman. Tukano shamans therefore may also be described as people with heightened life energy and with the power to heal and to sanctify.

To be able to visit the Ruler of the Animals, however, the shamanic aspirant has need of the intervention of Vihó-mahsë, the Lord of Snuff, who is in charge of psychoactive tobacco substances. If a shaman wishes to learn where game can be found or when best to carry out a large-scale fishing expedition, he must sniff Vihó (*Virola* spp.) in order to be able to consult the Lord of Snuff while psychedelically intoxicated. Vihó-mahsë lives in the Milky Way and keeps mankind under continuous observation. The shaman travels to him, into the land of fertility and health.

As we have seen, shamans are intimately connected with the well-being of our planet. The Payé is himself a ruler of life, if only on a small scale. He is able to let the vital energy of more powerful Givers of Life pass through himself on to his people. He has a profound empathy with natural processes and a deep understanding of the relation between man and nature. This indeed is indicated by his name. *Payé* means to cohabit. The Tukano shaman thus represents fertility as can be seen from the whitish quartz crystal (the Sun Penis) that he wears around his neck. He collects quartz crystals, which the people believe to be drops of semen created by lightning. His rattle is a staff in the shape of a phallus, from which—according to the Tukano myth of creation—the sperm of the Sun Father dripped down upon the earth.

The Payé is thus equipped with a number of fertility and life symbols—a phallus, crystallized sperm, the power of the sun and the Milky Way. He "cohabits" with nature, he rests, as it were, in the bosom of nature, fuses with her manifestations and represents vital life principles by his supernatural abilities which, in the last analysis, *are* the innate forces of nature.

In many cultures, the incarnation of life is represented by a snake. As the example of Loti, a healer from the Fiji Islands, shows, snakes are believed to be possessors of Mana, the life force. It is Loti's task to wrest this mana from the seasnake. Here we have a combination of two themes: dangerous obstacle and sacred power. Among the Australian aborigines, the adept is swallowed by the Rainbow Snake and in this way partakes of its power.

In many myths it is the task of the hero to wrest higher knowledge from the claws of frightening monsters. This calls for determination and courage, but also for a certain psychic predisposition. In Western fairy tales, the hero is usually described as brave, strong, and physically robust. This is a somewhat materialist interpretation because the hero/initiate requires, above all, a predisposition toward the parapsychic and transpersonal. Are not the snake or dragon an expression of our own fear of the dangers we have projected into the world? This fear is very different from ordinary cowardice: it is the fear of self-dissolution, of the destruction of the inner structure of our solid conceptual world.

The primordial mythological creatures and dangers, as well as the obstacles encountered by the soul on its journey to the Beyond, are our fear of the loss of ego. Whoever overcomes his fear and faces the unknown with equanimity will find that there is nothing *to* fear. He will be aware of being torn to pieces by the demons, swallowed by the snake, or of his bones being crushed by the bear, but he observes all this calmly, almost as if it did not concern him. His transformation comes about of its own accord without any contribution on his part. The initiate follows these events from behind a veil as it were. In none of these narratives about initiation do we find a conscious impulse toward carefully considered action—things run very smoothly, as if by themselves, as if predetermined from the very beginning.

Loti, the Fijian shaman, was asleep when the ancestor of the village appeared to him as a woman, told him to go to the cliff by the shore and jump down into the bay where he would find an ancient Fijian canoe. He jumped and landed on the canoe, which carried him out to sea. Suddenly a seasnake appeared, and around its neck, hanging by a gold chain, was the mana-box.

Loti could hear the voice of the village ancestor telling him to take the box, but he was very afraid and started using a long pole to lift the mana-box off the snake's neck. He tried this twice, but without success. The voice of the ancestor then told him to return to the village. It said, "The mana is not for you today." The next day the ancestor appeared again, saying, "You have one more chance. Leap into the canoe and take the mana-box." This time Loti did not hesitate. He slipped the mana-box off the seasnake's neck, thereby acquiring great healing powers.[1]

We could describe numerous further encounters with the rulers and lords of various natural phenomena and animals, but the examples given should suffice to demonstrate the general principles involved in encounters with the supernatural. Modern people, of course, do not believe that the visible forms of nature have such subtle manifestations.

Biology has examined cellular and molecular structures and found nothing that cannot be explained rationally, either now or in the near future. Tribal communities and peasant cultures, on the other hand, see the whole world not only as pervaded by life—modern man has yet to rediscover this after a long phase of environmental pollution and destruction—but as something that is ruled by immaterial beings who, as it were, form the essence—the actual moving principle—of the various natural phenomena. The form and behavior of these beings reflect cultural traditions of the tribal communities concerned.

The shaman receives his powers from Rulers and Nature and Givers of Life and thereby becomes an intermediary between nature and the tribal culture, between the living, the dead, and the nonhuman spirit creatures. He ascends to supernature, to the supernatural, because he now shares the power of the spirits. A biologist may develop a deep understanding of, loving empathy with, and profound admiration for the little miracles of the plant and animal kingdoms, but the shaman goes beyond that: by extreme concentration he enters living nature so fully that he becomes able to see what lies behind its external forms. He beholds the matrix or, as Plato would say, the Ideas of Being and may then describe his experience in the language of the transpersonal or, symbolically, as a participation in the dances of animals and dwarves.

Perhaps modern science will one day—albeit in its own language—describe the matrices of energy, the bioenergetic processes or, as Rupert Sheldrake puts it, the morphogenetic fields that form the framework of our visible material world. And then perhaps we will be brought to realize that the shaman, once again, is way ahead of us. He describes a world we cannot accept because both his framework of symbols and the idea of psychic communication and union with all living things are alien to us.

22

Crystal Came Whirling,
Crystal Came Raining

Ha-a, ha a, ha a, ha, ha-a nae, ha a a nee
I was taken far away to the quartz mountain
I was taken far away to the quartz mountain
quartz came rolling quartz came raining
I was take far away to the quartz mountain

Ha-a, ha a, ha a, ha, ha-a nae, ha a a nee
I was covered with crystals on the quartz mountain
I was covered with crystals on the quartz mountain
I danced the Matem dance my joints were crystal
I was covered with crystals on the quartz mountain

Ha-a, ha a, ha a, ha, ha-a nae, ha a a nee
I became a bird a Matem on the quartz mountain
I became a bird a Matem on the quartz mountain
a cloud came and took me to the edge of the world
I became a bird a Matem on the quartz mountain
Ha-a, ha a, ha a, ha, ha-a nai, ha a a nee[1]

This Song of the Matem Dancers is chanted by an actor during the great Winter Ceremony of the Kwakiutl Indians. It is a song of initiation, and it clearly demonstrates the significance of crystals on such occasions. Here crystals combine with the symbol of the Sacred Mountain, the quartz mountain, where the shaman receives crystals, the transparency of which reflects the clarity of his own psyche. He is literally showered with them and performs the dance of the mythological Matem Bird, turns into a bird himself, and leaves his body to fly to the "edge of the world"—to a new dimension of being.

Crystallomancy and crystal gazing are ancient practices. Shining, mirrorlike, smooth, and reflecting objects of all kinds have, in fact, been used for purposes of divination. We know of the magic mirror of classical antiquity, and there are records to show that basins filled with water, polished stones, and gems—even fingernails coated with oil—were used for prophecy. The pioneer of scientific hypnosis, James Braid, used crystals for fixing the gaze and his predecessor, Franz Anton Mesmer, used a mirror for his "animal magnetism" therapy.

Crystal gazing is also mentioned by Agrippa von Nettesheim, Paracelsus, John Dee, and Cagliostro. Crystals, and stones in general, partake of the sacredness of heaven: they have been thrown down to earth by the Supreme Being or were fragments from the thrones of the gods. Because of their uniqueness, rarity, unusual shape, and transparency, crystals attract attention, and we tend to ascribe special qualities to them. Even in our culture there has always been a love of glittering gems. And, on the principle that like attracts like, the absorption of crystals into the body is said to promote inner light, transparency, illumination, the power of concentration, and the ascent to heaven.

Crystals are of particular significance among the Australian aborigines. All Australian tribes employ quartz crystals in their ritualistic practices. They consider them to be emanations of the mythical Rainbow Snake—and thus directly connected with cosmic creativity—or a symbol of the heavenly god. Either belief stresses the celestial origin. The medicine man receives his crystals from the Rainbow Snake, or they come from deep water or the bowels of the earth. Among the Unambal, such crystals are known as Alumburru. They enter the body of the medicine man through his navel, penis, or the dell above his clavicles and fill him with radiant light.[2]

Once crystals enter the body, they become pliable and—according to the medicine men of the northern Kimberley region—create tremendous luminosity within. Here we have an association of the mystical experience of light with the transparency of crystals. The Mulla-mullung experiences an agreeable warmth, a taste of sweetness, as the crystal penetrates into his body. At the same time, he begins to see things that cannot be perceived by ordinary humans. For the Yualayi shaman, crystals are living spirits that he can remove from the body and reinsert.

Some tribes use shells, which are said to have the same effect. After their contact with Westerners, natives also began to use shards of glass, bits of porcelain, coins, metal buttons, glass marbles—in fact, any kind of shining object. They gave up doing so when they realized that such artifacts did not produce the desired effect.

Generally, however, that which shines is a symbol and substitute for the Rainbow Snake. And so the microcosmic shine of a small crystal or metal button is equated with the celestial luminosity of the universal creator and with the origin of life, because for a mind disposed toward myth there is no essential difference between the microcosm and the macrocosm. It is merely a matter of degree.[3]

Crystals have an eminent function in healing in practically all cultures. The Arizona Hopi believe that there are various spirito-physiological centers along the spinal column, comparable to the chakras in Hinduism, and they gaze through crystals to perceive these centers more clearly.[4] Similarly, the Tarahumare shamans of the Mexican Hechizero make use of crystals for diagnosing internal illnesses, and the Latin American Tukano, in much the same way, use crystals during healing as a kind of magnifying glass to enhance their power of vision. They then extract the illness from the body by means of these crystals.[5]

The Keresan Pueblo along the Rio Grande employ crystals for identifying objects that have been introduced into the patient's body by a witch's spell. Apart from that, crystals are used for clairvoyance[6] or—as is the case among the Californian Yuki—bloodletting.[7]

The shamans of the Papago Indians have "shining stones" which are brighter than the headlights of a car or flares. By the use of these stones they can discover the site of an illness or unmask an evil shaman in hiding. Most Papago healers have four of these precious stones. They are said to carry them in their heart, so that their saliva is charged with energy as they spray it all over the patient. One Papago has described how he acquired his crystals:

> The eagle told me to go at sunset to a certain place and look for crystals. So I did, and in a little hollow I saw four of them lying all together. I held out my hand, and they jumped into it. Then I held my hand before my mouth, and one by one they jumped down my throat.[8]

Among the Australian Oruncha, the shamanic candidate undergoes a very wearying and painful initiation. He is taken to an isolated spot by two medicine men and there he must stand, relaxed but unmoving, his hands folded behind his back, no matter what happens to him. A third man holds the novice in a tight grip from behind, as the other two produce crystals from their bodies and with them gash his legs and other parts of his body up to his chest, to press the crystals into him. There is considerable loss of blood as the precious stones slowly enter the candidate's flesh. Crystals may also be projected into his body from a distance, and sometimes they are pressed against the scalp or pushed deeply into the flesh under the fingernails.

The initiate must then press these gashes together to prevent the crystals from falling out. This procedure is repeated three times a day. He is also given water to drink in which crystals have been dissolved. At the end of the three-day ceremony of initiation, his tongue is perforated and his body decorated with images of spirits and of the sacred Alcheringa beings as well as with white lines, which represent the crystals that have entered him.[9]

The Kwakiutl shaman Lebi'd, who traveled to the Beyond and there received the power of healing from Nau'alakume, his spirit helper in the shape of a wolf, also owned crystals which resided within him. After his initiation, the spirits took him to "the very edge of this world" and also healed him by their crystals and their magic powers. Nau'alakume gave Lebi'd the crystals whereby he became a shaman, a healer.

After his return from the Land of the Dead, Lebi'd sang:

> I was seized
> and taken far
> to the very edge
> of this world
> by the spirit
> the magic power
> the crystal
> ha wo ho
>
> Only then
> was I healed
> it was thrown
> deep in me
> the life-bringer
> of the Wolves
> the crystal
> ha wo ho
>
> I am a life-bringer
> I come to heal
> with the ways

of the Wolves
with the crystal
I will heal
ha wo ho

I have come
with living waters
these healing ways
of the Wolves
the living waters
the spirit crystal
ha wo ho[10]

23

The Rhythm of Life

The heavens ascended and blood dripped from its edges, and the drops of blood splashed into the ocean. This was what Fanny Flounder, a Yurok Indian woman from Espeu in Canada, saw in a dream. Suddenly there was a woman standing by her side who reached right into heaven, broke off some of the bleeding icicles hanging down from there, and placed them into Fanny's mouth.

This is how she received her magic powers from the Bringer of Life. Later, as she was dancing, the face of a goshawk appeared to her. He, too, placed something into her mouth, and then she fainted. Thereafter she knew that a healing ceremony would be successful whenever this spirit helper appeared to her on her way to it. At these ceremonies, Fanny would enter a deep trance and afterward be unable to remember the songs she sang.

Among the Yurok, the spirit protector places "pains" into the initiate, which then have to be "cooked"—that is to say, tamed—by prolonged dancing and singing. Fanny danced for five days inside the sweat lodge, and only after she had vomited up "something" was she able to dance with all her strength and with true abandon.

Transcendental experiences can produce pain and suffering which, in turn, trigger biopsychic changes and help the subject to arrive at new insights. The path of the mystic is always one of suffering—not only because of the ascetic practices involved but, above all, because of the inevitable pain that the disentangling of the personal ego entails. Yet these pains have to be "tamed," and this requires rigorous training and persistent practice; that is to say, concentration and meditation.

The Yurok path is one of dancing. By dancing, the initiate learns to digest new experiences.

Another Yurok shamaness dreamt how her husband, a Chilula Indian, gave her the flesh of a deer to eat. She fell ill the next morning. She then fasted for ten days and every night went into the sweat lodge to dance. One night she danced until she became unconscious. Not until the tenth day did she succeed in controlling her "pains" and—as with Fanny Flounder—something that looked like the liver of a salmon came up through her mouth. She slept in the sweat lodge closely guarded by several men, to ensure that she did not harm herself while in a trance or perform any unintentional actions. A monster appeared to her one night in a dream. One of its legs was straight, the other bent, and it had only one eye. She jumped up in horror and ran down to the river, but her guards pursued her and brought her back to the sweat lodge.

After that, she danced through three nights and received her fourth largest "pains." Her training lasted two years altogether, and she applied herself to it diligently, because she wanted to become a good medicine woman. If she danced for a long time, she was able to track down illnesses in other people, but she could never cure every patient or illness.[1]

All shamanic experiences of initiation involve a deautomization of ordinary consciousness. A shamanic technique may be anything that disrupts and confuses the normal stream of thoughts, the habitual experience of emotions and ordinary physiological processes, and then produces a new rhythmic pattern. Such techniques are universally employed by all esoteric and spiritual schools, secret societies, orders of healers, and so on.

Dancing is one way of restructuring our consciousness and thereby entering another world. In our culture, unfortunately, dance has to a large extend become profaned, and its connection with alternative states of consciousness is at best only rudimentary. Dance involves the whole body, causing it to sway rhythmically to a chant, to the sound of the drums. We have only begun to study the extent to which musical rhythm is capable of affecting brainwaves and, in doing so, producing an altered state of consciousness.

Incessant dancing, in any case, interrupts the stream of discursive thought which continuously produces ideas, memories, and sensations. Monotonous rhythms or dance movements synchronize or harmonize the confused and disorganized thought fragments and associations. In this way, consciousness settles. It becomes like an empty screen on which can be reflected objects of perception and unconscious and intuitive elements of experience that are ordinarily suppressed, distorted, fudged, or blocked by our ceaseless and chaotic stream of thoughts. Dancing is one of the oldest and most effective ways to produce this kind of clarity, this cleansing of the consciousness. Looked at in this way, the trance dance of the Yurok can be understood as a deliberate method of training which—in combination with fasting—safely guides the shamanic apprentice toward the realm of visions.

A Californian Shasta woman, who was destined to become a shamaness, heard a voice speaking to her in tones of great intensity. When she turned around, she saw a man with a drawn bow and arrow. He commanded her to sing or else be shot through the heart by his arrow. She tried to obey his command, but under the stress of the experience became unconscious. Her family gathered around her. They had known for some time that she had dreams of a special kind. At first the woman lay rigid, hardly breathing, but after a few hours she began to moan gently and roll about on the ground, trembling violently. Her moaning gradually became more and more clearly the spirit's song. Soon after, she called out the name of the spirit and, as soon as she did so, blood oozed from her mouth.

When she regained consciousness, she performed her first shamanic dance, holding herself by a rope that was swung from the ceiling. She danced for three nights and on the third night received the power of the spirit into her body. She was dancing at the time, and as she felt the moment approach, she called out, "He will shoot me, he will shoot me." Her friends stood close to her, because she was reeling uncontrollably and they had to seize her to prevent her from falling. From this time on she had in her body a visible materialization of her spirit's power. It was an object like an icicle, which she would exhibit during her dances, producing it from one part of her body and returning it to another.[2]

Dance also plays a central role in shamanic training among the Californian Yuki. One Yuki shaman, after such a dance, dreamt about the Creator, whom he encountered in heaven, where he also saw many colors and flowers. The next morning he was bleeding from his mouth and nose and became very frightened. He later told how the Creator, when he first saw him, had been singing a song which he (the initiate) was to sing ever thereafter. The Creator had been connected to his head by something like a cord and then sang another song and told him to use that one as well.[3] Then his brother began to sing with him, and everyone was convinced there would soon be a new healer.

People entering an altered state of consciousness are pervaded by something which, for the moment, we would like to refer to as the "rhythm of life"—a kind of cosmic vitality that so far has not been an object of scientific investigation but which, according to many myths and religions, is to be found at the very source of all life-processes. The ideas and beliefs of most tribal cultures are based on a great number of extremely varied energies and forces that are barely recognized or acknowledged by the scientific view of the world. A shaman who feels the power of the Creator flowing through him remains incomprehensible to us.

The shaman usually receives this creative power through a particular medium—lightning, an object of power, a vision, helping spirits, crystals, light-phenomena, but also through songs and dancing. Again and again, we encounter the theme of the "Dance" of the animals, gnomes, or spirits, to which the initiate is invited, either in the underworld or in heaven. The initiate therefore dances not only on earth—in our reality—thereby entering a state of trance—his dance is also performed in an altered state of consciousness or in another world. At these festivities in the Beyond he is taught the songs he brings back to earth, the songs which express his shamanic power and by which he transports himself back to what he experienced during his initiation.

The festival the shaman attends in the underworld—and the dances and songs performed at such festivals—is of a different order of being than ordinary dances and songs. Here, life itself is experienced as an endless celebration, an eternal dance and rhythm, continuously pulsating sound. To the initiate, life is a vibrating, harmoniously synchronized melody. The shaman works with this feeling of sharing the rhythm of the cosmic dance of fields of energy that are the source, the matrix of all matter. Essentially, it is this process of sharing that makes the shaman what he is.

Dance, song, and movement—like fasting, suffering, isolation, and sickness—are ancient ways of effecting physical and psychic changes and of opening oneself to the experience of new realms of existence by a process of deconditioning. Although these methods are as old as mankind itself, they continue to be effective and applicable. In our civilization, however, song and dance play a fairly modest role and are no longer practiced with ecstasy and total abandon. We use them for relaxation, to generate good cheer, but they lack the intensity and concentration the shaman has to bring to them if he wishes to explore the world of the Beyond.

The shaman's song of power, and the ecstatic, trance-inducing dance demonstrate the true power of rhythm and sound. They are gateways to a dimension with which our civilization has lost touch. One thing is certain: Song and dance are no mere symbols, but an expression of an inner psychophysical attitude that leads to a change in consciousness and brings us nearer to the pulse of life and thus to ourselves.

24

Walk in Balance,
Walk in Beauty

But then, a sensitive is not always walking about with his head in the clouds. The meaning of mediumship is balance—balance between two worlds—and you are the balance wheel in the middle.

—Ena Twigg, *an English medium*[1]

What I am trying to say is hard to tell and hard to understand . . . unless, unless . . . you have been yourself at the edge of the Deep Canyon and have come back unharmed. Maybe it all depends on something within yourself—whether you are trying to see the Watersnake or the sacred Cornflower, whether you go out to meet death or to seek Life. It is like this: as long as you stay within the realm of the great Cloudbeings, you may indeed walk at the very edge of the Deep Canyon and not be harmed. You will be protected by the rainbow and by the Great Ones. You will have no reason to worry and no reason to be sad. You may fight the witches, and if you can meet them with a heart which does not tremble, the fight will make you stronger. It will help you attain your goal in life. It will give you strength to help others, to be loved and liked, and to seek Life.[2]

Balance, both inner and outer, gathers together the supernatural powers of the shaman. A diffused and unbalanced state of mind would turn these powers against the shaman himself. The Huichol shaman Ramón Medina Silva demonstrated his equilibrium in a wild mountain region cut through by waterfalls and ravines up to three hundred meters deep. He felt this to be appropriate terrain for a shaman and prepared to leap across one of the waterfalls. He succeeded in doing this, and afterwards said, "The mara'akame [shaman] must have superb equilibrium. Otherwise, he will not reach his destination and will fall this way or that. One crosses over. It is very narrow, and without balance one is eaten by those animals waiting below."[3]

Here we encounter again—in the form of rocky ravines and a waterfall—the ancient theme of overcoming obstacles. The way is barred, and only those whose psychic and physical powers are in perfect balance will safely reach the other side. This state of psychic equilibrium is not just a transpersonal symbol. It is a characteristic of personality marking the nature of an enlightened, transpersonally realized human being—"transpersonal" because only by crossing over the personal dimension of the ego can equanimity and inner harmony come into being.

As long as our "I" is continuously caught up in projects to ensure its survival and reinforcement, as well as in all kinds of longings and desires, we remain a jungle of contradictory motivations and our inner turmoil will never allow us to come to rest. Only those who transcend their ego-bound motivations can observe their personal drama from a higher perspective and are then able to assess the motives and tendencies of their psyche in an objective way and thus also harmonize them.

The leap across the waterfall requires physical balance, concentration, courage, self-confidence, and egolessness; if any one of these qualities is lacking or inadequate, such a leap can result in death. This is not the harmless long jump of an athlete aimed at victory and bolstering the ego—it is an act of daring, to obtain certainty concerning the harmony of inner forces. It is a real life-or-death trial, requiring immaculate equilibrium.

The art of the shaman consists in healing, which he effects by guiding the patient to the sphere of the Sacred and letting him experience his human nature as a totality, a whole. In this way, the energies of the patient are deliberately reweighted and brought into harmony with each other. However, in order to afford the patient such insight into his higher self, the shaman must not only be able to discern the patient's state of imbalance, he must have eliminated imbalance in himself. He must be able to walk in balance, which is another way of saying that he must walk with inner beauty. And, in the last analysis, this inner beauty enables him to leap across ravines.[4]

The anthropologist Barbara Myerhoff witnessed Ramón's crossing of the waterfall. She writes: "At the edge of the fall, Ramón removed his sandals and . . . proceeded to leap across the waterfall, from rock to rock, frequently pausing, his body bent forward, his arms outspread, head thrown back entirely birdlike, poised motionlessly on one foot. He disappeared, re-emerged, leaped about and finally achieved the other side."[5]

Myerhoff mentions another example of shamanic balance. The Luiseño shaman Domenico—a famous Indian healer whose patients included people of many nationalities, even white Americans—would often climb to the top of the gable of his little hut and stand there, on one leg, for long periods of time. At first Myerhoff suspected that he did this to look out for his patients who usually arrived on the weekend. It became clear to her, however, that this was an exercise in equilibrium.[6]

The Siberian Tofa shaman Bolchoyev told Vilmos Diószegi how his grandfather had been able to leap across cliffs and rocks:

> I heard him say that, when he was shamanizing, he could fly over rocks. And often he would jump from one big rock to the next, for instance from Surar yaja to Soyny yaja (two cliffs that are about half a kilometer apart).[7]

In the course of a conversation with the Siberian shamans Sunchugasev and Kyzlasov, whose experiences we have described earlier, Diószegi asked what kind of things the soul of a shaman might encounter on its journey to the Land of the Dead. Sunchugasev replied:

> His soul is taken to the shaman ancestor, and there they show him a kettle full of boiling tar. There are people in it. There are some who are known to the shaman. A single rope is fastened across the kettle and they order him to walk over it. If he succeeds, he will live long. If he falls into the kettle, he still might become a Kam (shaman), but usually they do not survive.

Then the wife of Kyzlasov spoke up:

> That kettle is always there. Not only the shamans fall into it. They say that the soul of a sick person might also tumble into it. Some of the shamans cannot be persuaded to attempt passing over the kettle. This I know from certain people who told me that they were forced to pass around the edge of the kettle. They did it, and as they did not fall into the kettle, they became shamans.[8]

Here the shaman becomes a tightrope walker, not physically but in a psychic sense. Outer calm and composure reflect psychic equilibrium. On his journey to the Land of the Dead, the shaman must be equipped with steadfastness and concentration. To pass the tests imposed by the shaman ancestors, to walk the rope across that kettle of tar—a symbol of hell, of course—calls for complete meditative wakefulness, such as only true shamans possess.

PART FOUR

Religion and Science

The white people, he said, saw with their eyes a part of the world to which he was blind. On the other hand when they looked into the soul they could see very little. With the people of his race, it was the other way around. They perceived a great world within themselves which was a good world. Because of that, the white people were black within. But the black people inside themselves were white. [Göbel 1976, p. 36]

25

When the Anthropologists Arrive, The Gods Leave the Island[1]

Of all the hard facts of science, I know of none more solid and fundamental than the fact that if you inhibit thought (and persevere) you come at length to a region of consciousness below or behind thought, and different from ordinary thought in its nature and character—a consciousness of quasi-universal quality, and a realization of an altogether vaster self than that to which we are accustomed. And since the ordinary consciousness with which we are concerned in ordinary life is before all things founded on the little local self, and is in fact self-conscious in the little local sense, it follows that to pass out of that is to die to the ordinary self and the ordinary world.

It is to die in the ordinary sense, but in another sense it is to wake up and find that the "I," one's real, most intimate self, pervades the universe and all other beings—that the mountains and the sea and the stars are part of one's body and that one's soul is in touch with the souls of all creatures. . . .

So great, so splendid is this experience, that it may be said that all minor questions and doubts fall away in face of it. And certain it is that in thousands and thousands of cases the fact of its having come even once to a man has completely revolutionized his subsequent life and outlook on the world.[2]

I know of no more apt description of shamanic experience than the above passage from Edward Carpenter's *The Drama of Love and Death*. Indeed, the "little local self" must die. The everyday ego of the prospective shaman—his logical, causal and mechanical understanding of the world—must be demolished. Yet he does not really die; it is only that the ties bind-ing him to the mundane and temporal fall from him. He experiences existential unity—the *samadhi* of the Hindus, or what Western spiritualists and mystics would call enlightenment, illumination, *unio mystica*.

William James has written that "there is a continuum of cosmic consciousness against which our individuality builds but accidental fences, and into which our several minds plunge as into a mother sea or reservoir"[3] and in this context asked himself whether we could be trained to reach the upper limit of our energy since we were accustomed to use only a small part of our potential powers. James believed that ordinary human beings are only half awake, like hysterics with a greatly restricted range of perception. According to him, "There seems to be no doubt that we are each and all of us to some extent victims of habit neurosis."[4] And elsewhere he observed:

> I have no doubt whatever that most people live, whether physically, intellectually, or morally, in a very restricted circle of their potential being. They make use of a very small portion of their possible consciousness and of their souls' resources in general, much like a man who, out of his whole bodily organism, should get into a habit of using and moving only his little finger. . . . We all have reservoirs of life to draw upon, of which we do not dream.[5]

Similarly, Evelyn Underhill considers the way we perceive and experience the world a predominantly mental construct with little reference to what actually is, whereas mysticism to her constitutes a genuine union with reality.[6] C. J. Jung believed that our Western consciousness is by no means consciousness *per se* but is historically and geographically conditioned, and represents only a tiny aspect of total consciousness.

What then is the nature of this much criticized ordinary consciousness?

Plato compares our everyday consciousness to a vessel, the crew of which has mutinied and locked the captain and navigator below deck. As the ship sails on, no crew member wants to stay at the helm for any length of time, because they get either bored or too tired. Nor can the crew agree about the course, so the vessel cruises aimlessly to and fro. It drifts helplessly upon the waves, and only after the captain and navigator have been released and resumed their tasks can the ship make good speed toward its destination.

In this context, William James speaks of a "stream of consciousness and thoughts"; thinking never stops, there is a continuous flow of thoughts, one leading to the next, so that we do not ever become truly conscious of ourselves. All mental techniques aimed at withdrawing from the compulsive character of continuous thought and associations employ methods such as concentration, restricted or one-pointed attention, hypnoid focusing of consciousness, stilling thought processes, relaxation of physiological functions and standardization of the sensory field.

Vomiting, visits to the sweat lodge, smoke, fasting, prayer, and sacrifices are some of the methods of inner purification used by tribal people to bring about a loosening of our attachment to mental concepts and material possessions. With the shedding of the ego motivations that constitute our everyday world, a more comprehensive universal "I"—the higher Self— emerges which appears to be at one with the whole of nature. All spirituality aims at the surrender of the ego and the discovery of cosmic unity, of a transindividual cosmic self. Fasting, surrendering in prayer to higher powers, "making ourselves humble—lower than the smallest ant" as the Sioux medicine man Black Elk puts it, and giving up our precious possessions: These are some of the ways in which we can train to loosen our bonds and free ourselves from greed, lust, and egocentricity.

The "I" is composed of such external factors and produces the illusion of an orderly dualistic world. Prayers, offerings, rites, and ceremonies—by their focused concentration—open the way to unity with nature. They loosen our attachment to this illusory "I" and lead to a new way of experiencing the world.

Not wishing to enter into a complicated analysis of the nature of consciousness, we would simply like to say that in very general terms ordinary consciousness is composed of the emotional, cognitive, and motivational elements known to science and is dominated by causality, three-dimensional thought, and a linear sense of time. On closer examination, however, it turns out to be rather difficult to say exactly where normal consciousness ends and a state of altered consciousness begins, because the mental characteristics of a change in consciousness are already present during sleep, in dreams, day-dreams, inner dialogue, imagination, and creativity. For that reason we expect that in the light of further research work, the present dichotomy between "normal" and "altered" consciousness will give way to the idea of a whole spectrum and a multiplicity of discreet intermerging states of mind.[7]

Erika Bourguignon has shown that 90 percent of 488 societies—that is, 57 percent of all known societies—make use of institutionalized and culturally influenced forms of alternative states of consciousness.[8]

In very general terms, the following such uses could be listed:

1. Alternative states of consciousness play an important role in ceremonies and rituals that serve to maintain the traditional framework of a given culture.

2. They have a stabilizing effect in times of social crisis and in the course of acculturation, but can also produce new social institutions appropriate to the change in existing conditions.

3. They are an effective method of teaching and learning as tribal traditions are passed on during rites of passage and initiation.

4. They bring about an enhanced control of physical and psychic functions.

5. They may be employed to influence people or animals—either negatively in order to harm them, positively for the purpose of healing, or simply to create a productive and sacred atmosphere at rituals and séances.

6. They serve as a means of establishing contact with nonterrestrial, extransensory realms and entities.

7. They help to establish a constructive relationship with atmospheric and stellar forces, as well as with flora and fauna.

8. They play an important part in psychotherapy, self-discovery, and shamanic initiation.

9. They are a generally acknowledged prerequisite for the ability to transcend time and space and for acquiring information not normally accessible to us.[9]

Everywhere and at all times, cultures have striven to produce and train people of parapsychic ability so that they might effectively support the struggle for the survival of the tribe or community in question. At the same time, the search for psychic experiences of, or related to, the paranormal is one of the most ancient motivations of mankind and may in fact be considered an essential aim of man—a true "peak experience" in the sense Abraham Maslow uses this term.

Now that Freud has presented us with theories about the "sick half" of the psyche, Maslow demands that we should study healthy people instead of just those suffering from psychic or mental aberrations.[10] He describes the mode of perception of a sane and healthy human being as nonmanipulative, noninterfering, nonabstracting, and without expectations or demands. At the same time, such a person would display a great love for the world, seeing it objectively and without distortion, and be free from subjective projections.

For Maslow, a sane person is self-realized and capable of experiencing things in a wholly selfless way, but with perfect concentration and in total absorption, because he no longer has ego-generated, subjective expectations, or harbors selfish desires. Once our negative impulses—envy, fear, hatred, and neurosis—have gone, we are capable of arriving at the zenith of mystic experience. Maslow considers creativity to be a preparatory stage for this, because in truly creative activity we are completely in the present and therefore free from our conventional experience of time and space. Supreme creativity and "peak experience" are identical. In a truly creative state of mind we are capable of selflessly surrendering ourselves to the world without strategies or expectations.

The elimination of fear, defensiveness, and inhibition is a further prerequisite for the occurrence of this spontaneous psychic process. We have complete trust in ourselves. The mundane world and conscious ego control have faded away and, in Maslow's words, a kind of "Taoist receptivity" emerges. This totally spontaneous activity, in which the individual and the world merge, could be termed "realization of being." It is a mode of experiencing which occurs at the high points of their life to people with an extremely high degree of self-realization. This "peak experience" is the aim of Maslovian psychotherapy.

Maslow's Psychology of Being is therefore concerned with ultimate states, ultimate experiences, sexual climax, totality, pure bliss, ecstasy, states that are free from desire, motivation towards personal growth, and metamotivation—and also with negative states such as hopelessness, failure, regression, acute psychosis, abject depression, and moral degradation (nadir states) that can produce mystic insight and inspiration.

As a founder of Humanist—and, later, Transpersonal—psychology, Maslow has energetically and consistently opposed mechanistic methodology and science which, in his view, do not fully take into account that which is truly human, are ethnocentrically and atomistically oriented, based on abstract data rather than experiential findings, and do not concern themselves with such matters as the total psychic personality, subjective knowledge, self-realization, and mystic experience. Maslow strove to initiate a process of rehumanization and thereby diminish the growing claim of orthodox science to be the only true path of knowledge.

He takes the view that mechanistic and objectivistic methodology— being a world view dominated by obsessive ideas—does not understand that there is no way in which the observer can intentionally dissociate himself from the object of his observation. He is inevitably involved with it, because the observer is part of the observation, so that both subject and object need to be examined. We can see that in the field of consciousness research Maslow, almost from the outset, raised the question of the unity of the "I" and the world.[11]

He is of the opinion that what psychology calls "normal" is no more than a "psychopathology of the average," so undramatic and pervasive that generally we do not even notice it.[12] Without tragedies, near-death experiences, traumata, death/rebirth experiences and shocks we cannot escape from this generally accepted normality. Once again we encounter the theme of shamanic suffering—a suffering intense enough to kill.

A self-realized and growth-motivated person—as opposed to people who are caught in a stimulation/reaction mechanism—will more often have experiences bordering on the transpersonal, be more creative, spontaneous, autonomous, have richer emotions and be capable of genuine empathy with his fellow men. Over and above that, he will have a strong sense of "I," but, paradoxically, will be able to transcend this "I" more easily than other people and solve his problems in a meditative and contemplative manner. Compared to less developed people who live in a narrow world of Aristotelian definitions and categories, a self-realized and growth-motivated person is wholly oriented towards continuity and unity. His mode of perception is passive/receptive rather than active, because the more we forget about ourselves, the more we are able to perceive. Love for the world and for that which is perceivable is an important prerequisite for this.

Maslow distinguishes between "love of being" (undemanding) and "deficit love" (selfish). Love of being is nonpossessive and amounts to an aesthetic or mystical experience on the boundary of the transpersonal. Such "boundary" or "peak" experiences are similar to the way a shaman understands the world, who does not just perceive a given number of fragmentary aspects of being but, by virtue of approaching the world without labeling and categorizing, experiences it as incomparable and unique. There is no room for subjective interests in a peak experience. Time and space are forgotten and time is expanded as in ecstasy. It is a state marked by awe, modesty, and wonder.

Border experiences are related to death and dying, and during such experiences the world reveals itself as a Whole. Contradictions and dichotomies merge and opposites are seen as a product of fragmentary understanding. This experience is the central agent both in Maslow's psychotherapy and in the practice of shamanism. It has a therapeutic effect, because through it fear and fragmentation disappear, and there is a strong urge to repeat the experience—a kind of longing for ecstasy and unity. On the basis of these insights and the coming into being of a new psychology of consciousness, Maslow believes that psychology is in the process of reassessing its ideas about human capacity, human potential, and human aims, and that a new view of the possibilities open to man and of his destiny is beginning to emerge.[13]

Apart from a number of cultural features, there is little difference between shamanic peak experiences and mystical experiences in other cultures and religions. The shamanic view of the world can therefore be considered an integral part of a universal mystical tradition, which Aldous Huxley has called the *philosophia perennis*. An examination of religio-ethnological literature regrettably shows that no more than a few authors share this conclusion. Mircea Eliade is one of the few who have forged a link between shamanism, Buddhism, and Christian mysticism. In his opinion, "shamanism represents the most credible mystical experience of the religious world of primitives and, within this archaic world, fulfills the same role as does mysticism in the official faith of the great historical religions from Buddhism down to Christianity."[14]

Part of the difficulty of proving that shamanic vocation involves a mystical experience is due to the fact that tribal terminology only approximates the classical characteristics of the phenomenology of enlightenment. Moreover, all tribal cultures express psychic experiences within a framework of culturally conditioned metaphors or as personified energies in the form of gods, spirits, animals, and so on. In order to make it all understandable, the abstract life of the psyche is concretized and expressed as myth, so that in many cases only a pale glimmer of the original experience shines through this veil of mental constructs.

For that reason, the anthropologist who studies the world of the shaman is all too often faced by an impenetrable web of cosmological theories and cultural characteristics, which prevent him from understanding their psychic origin and background. This, we believe, is why we are unwilling to acknowledge the mystical inspiration of the shaman and to put him on a par with other religious mystics.

This is not to say that a medium, a seer, or a rainmaker—such as many shamans are—must of necessity have had an experience of cosmic unity. Only a relatively small number of shamans could justifiably be described as mystics. The remainder confine their practices to specific facets of the transpersonal realm such as prophecy, magic, or various forms of hypnotic and visionary psychotherapy.

Most authors would seem to agree that the classical characteristics of mystical experience are more or less as follows:

After a long period of disturbances, sickness, and a crisis, the higher Self awakens, and there is an experience of illumination, ecstasy, and of the Absolute. By the death of the subjective ego and the breakthrough to the transpersonal self, the individual feels purified and liberated, so that his former lifestyle appears inappropriate and banal to him. An expanded outlook—the realization of unity—brings about a sense of sacredness, of transcending time and space, and the absolute certainty that present, past, and future are artificial concepts. At the same time there is a feeling of being totally submerged in the moment and guided by a higher power, from which grows the conviction that a supersensory source of energy exists. After returning to everyday reality, a positive echo remains, so that life is lived more intensively and experienced more fully and directly. Simultaneously there is a turning away from a materialist outlook on life.[15]

Maslow has described this experience as follows: There is a feeling of effusive joy, triumph, awe, and amazement; a feeling of suddenly understanding the whole universe and of being united with it. The individual is filled with a sense of spiritual awakening, of transcendent compassion, and love. The fear of death dissolves, and there is a psychic rejuvenation and a strengthening of mental capacities. The individual wants to share his experience with others and help them to experience the same. A charismatic change of personality takes place, and this frequently is accompanied by the development of extrasensory capabilities.[16]

We have said that the shaman lives in a psychic universe in which, in addition to his ratio-analytical level of consciousness, he has access to a trancelike and holistic form of awareness. Anyone who tries to understand the shaman's experience of the world by the use of causal categories of space and time is doomed to failure. He will construct a picture of the shaman which is more a mirror image of himself. He is like someone who tries to record the "tones" of a painting on a tape recorder—all he captures on tape is the background noise of the recorder itself. What we are trying to say is that just as an audio recorder is not suitable for recording pictures, so the mechanistic and objectivistic methodology of shamanic research cannot lead to a correct understanding of the nature of a sorcerer.

When it comes to studying shamans, our findings are no more than what we have fed into the research itself, namely our own concepts and philosophies, our contemporary projections. Hundreds of theses on shamanism have been written, but their methodology has only explored the cultural skin of the shaman—his external appearance. The essence of altered states of consciousness and the inner world of the shaman are not touched upon.

Researchers may return laden with findings and records, but in reality they have only reinforced and confirmed themselves. They set out armed with rational thought and Euclidean concepts and value judgments, and returned home no wiser. The greater part of shamanic research so far is meaningful only in that it tells us something about *our own* world view and about *our* entanglement in *our* cultural values. A critical assessment of the literature on shamanism can help us analyze our own projections and ritualized expectations toward other cultures and develop a morphology of Western man's introspection.

The attempts of most researchers to understand inner experience are confined either to recording physiological changes that occur during an altered state of consciousness or to reproducing the narratives of people who have experienced such states. Apart from the fact that shamans have up to now not shown a great spirit of cooperation when it comes to taking physiological measurements or recording their psychic experiences, it must be said that such methods are, in any case, incapable of recreating the cathartic atmosphere of a ceremony or the feeling of sacredness that pervades an altered state of consciousness—which are the essential characteristics of healing or initiation.

Our scientific methods remain dissociated from actual life, whereas the shaman seizes life by its roots and experiences blazing reality. Words like "sacred" or "magical" ultimately can tell us nothing about other realms of consciousness. They are empty and without substance—mere shadows of a dimension closed to us. Religion is experience, a transformation of waking consciousness which can never be conveyed by words. The map is not the terrain. A painting is not real life, and our obsessively literate culture all too often forgets that rationality and language do not reflect life as it is lived.

The English nineteenth-century poet Alfred, Lord Tennyson said:

> I never had any revelations through anaesthetics, but a kind of waking trance—this for lack of a better word—I have frequently had, quite up from boyhood, when I have been all alone. This has come

upon me through repeating my own name to myself silently, till all at once, as it were out of the intensity of the consciousness of individuality, individuality itself seemed to dissolve and fade away into boundless being, and this not a confused state but the clearest, the surest of the surest, utterly beyond words—where death was an almost laughable impossibility—the loss of personality (if so it were) seeming no extinction, but the only true life. I am ashamed of my description. Have I not said the state is utterly beyond words?[17]

And Lame Deer says the same in his way:

You understand that there are certain things one should not talk about, things that must remain hidden. If all was told, supposing there lived a person who could tell all, there would be no mysteries left, and that would be very bad. Man cannot live without mystery. He has a great need of it.[18]

Shamans are said to be reluctant to talk about their experiences of altered states of consciousness. It is not that the shaman considers it sacrilegious to speak of such matters to strangers or the noninitiated, nor that he cannot remember what he experienced in his trance; the reason is much more likely that he simply cannot find the words to describe what he has seen. At best he will make use of descriptions handed down within his culture, but these in themselves are once again no more than categorizations of that which cannot be categorized. Because of our ingrained Western faith in the communicativeness of language, we take his words literally, assuming that they correspond exactly to processes of our external environment.

Bertrand Russell suspected that for that very reason we know so much about physics and so little about anything else.[19] Our linguistic repertoire is geared to a one-sided interpretation of Time, Space, and Causality and thus contains no terms to describe the paradox and acausal nature of the inner world. Even the findings of modern physics can barely be expressed in words because of the mechanistic/materialistic structure of our language. We may therefore ask with some justification whether we do not need a supplementary vocabulary that allows fresh associations and makes it possible to formulate and describe paradoxical thoughts and feelings. What we really need is a multivalent logic, multidimensional figures of speech, and ambiguous concepts capable of giving us a better idea of ambivalences. However, in attempting to realize such an undertaking we would be like creatures of a two-dimensional world dreaming of a three-dimensional universe.

Can the problem of providing an ethnological methodology for research into shamanism be solved at all then? Perhaps the researcher himself will have to become a shaman if he wants to have anything to say. We consider this the optimal solution, but not necessarily the most practical one. Science only knows the absolutely neutral approach of observation from the outside, but what we need is a total surrender to the process of shamanic consciousness. Yet there is, between those two extremes, a growing area of empathy and sensitivity. The researcher is becoming aware of the shamanic view of the world. The path of consciousness transformation is one of growing sympathy, of an increasing abandonment of rational dissociation. It is a path characterized by a natural continuum of intensified awareness from the ordinary state of mind to the highest state of altered consciousness.

The more directly researchers experience the various states of consciousness themselves, the better they ought to be able to describe them in rational terms. The yogin/scientist, the shaman/scientist—the man who embodies two worlds—is surely better qualified than anyone to explore the whole spectrum of consciousness, because he is capable of basing his descriptions on his own inner experience and so will know what he is talking about.

The introduction of a scientific researcher to the universe of the shaman could conceivably pass through the following stages:

1. Pure external observation and objective description of behavior
2. Empathic resonance with and sympathy for the shaman's way of life, coupled with an attempt to give a description based on personal participation
3. The ethnologist must seriously acknowledge the mental techniques and experiences of the shaman and should himself experiment with some of them. (Some researchers, such as V. Brown, Boyd, Cushing, David-Neel, Eaton, Katz, Kunze, J. R. Walker, and others, either have taken psychoactive drugs, fasted, and prayed or have gone in search of visions. In this way they have, to a certain extent, acquired an inner understanding of the shaman's way of life.)
4. The ethnologist becomes an apprentice of the shaman, thereby transcending his traditional role as a scientist, raising

his scientific curiosity to a new and higher level, and attempting to combine learning with active reflection. (By now, a number of Westerners have entered into or partially completed such an apprenticeship, as for instance Boshier, Códova-Rios, Derlon, Harner, and Prem Das.)

The most complete description of and the deepest insight into the life of the shaman will, of course, come from researchers who themselves enter into a surrender to altered states of consciousness. The more we manage to close the gap between the scientist and the shaman, the closer we come to a truly transpersonal and transcultural science.

Larry Peters, too, calls for such an experiential approach, but would like to go beyond mere participation and introduce into the scientific discussion the experiences and observations of the ethnographer as he follows and comes to understand the shaman's lifestyle.[20] Peters is one of the researchers who have entered the trance-state and have derived new methodological demands from their experience.

It may be said that Adolf Friedrich,[21] the well-known researcher into shamanism, favored a similar approach, although he did not carry out objective research but personally and passionately experienced a shamanic view of the world. He encountered great psychic problems when it came to talking or writing about his experiences in an academically acceptable way.

The anthropological genius F. H. Cushing was a relatively unknown protagonist of the new experiential approach. He lived for five years with the Zuni Indians in the southwestern United States and was made a Bow Priest and War Chief of the tribe. He even took the scalp of a hostile Apache warrior, went through various rites of initiation, and completely adapted himself to the lifestyle of these people. In an attempt to justify his "unserious" approach before the scientific community, he described it as a "reciprocal method," in accordance with which he would not merely collect the myths of the Zuni but, in exchange, describe to them the traditions and rituals of the Christian church or tell them sagas and fairy tales from our culture.

Cushing did not adopt the distant attitude of the academic ethnologist. His relationship with the Indians was completely natural and unencumbered. Free from theoretical prejudices, he did not behave toward his hosts like a scientist and did not keep his personal feelings, problems, and thoughts separate from his research work. His enthnographic descriptions are so vivid and exciting that they have been praised again and again as creations of genius and described as epoch-making, despite the fact they do not fit into the traditional framework of scientific descriptions and have been said to go too far. As a result of his personal involvement in the life of the Zuni, this *enfant terrible* of science later had to leave the Zuni Pueblo on the orders of the Washington Smithsonian Institute, because he had turned against leading American politicians hostile to the Indians.[22]

Robert van de Castle went even further. He visited the Cuna Indians of the San Blas Islands off the Panamanian coast in the company of a Western medium, who so impressed the local shamans by his powers of healing and clairvoyance that he and his companion were quickly accepted by the native Indian village people.[23] There can be no doubt that the bringing together of Western mediums and traditional shamans will form one of the most interesting chapters of future literature on shamanism.

Ethnology resists a strictly psychological analysis of shamanism—and rightly so, because our Western psychology undeniably has been ethnocentric from its very beginnings and has always refused to accord any kind of recognition to tribal psychologies and philosophies. In fact, it has been unwilling to pay them any attention. Transpersonal science, on the other hand, has come into being from a fusion of Asian philosophy and Western consciousness research, just as transpersonal anthropology also takes account of the wisdom and systems of knowledge of other cultures. It is this kind of transcultural science that can bridge the gap between traditional and modern societies; it may be a hermaphrodite, feeding on the energies of several ways of life, but it is giving stimulus to a new universal science of man. Soon transcultural science will overtake the kind of narrowminded research into shamanism, which considers the shaman as no more than an object and product of social circumstances.

Shirokogorov, who has written about many Siberian shamans, says about this kind of mechanistic research:

> I am certain that no European scholar would permit an ignorant outsider to come into his laboratory to poke a thick finger into delicate instruments, and to ask with an ironical smile questions concerning the influence of the scholar's sexual complex on his laboratory experiments. Only an extreme politeness and the recognition of the necessity of submitting to the overbearance of powerful representatives of "civilization" keep the shamans from sending off such investigators.[24]

The exact opposite of such an approach is represented by the work of Kai Donner, who visited the Siberian Samoyed around the beginning of this century. Being one of the few researchers able to overcome their objectivistic/materialistic research mentality, he emerges from his descriptions of a séance among the Samoyed of the Upper Ket as an extremely human and sympathetic explorer. He writes:

> The fire had slowly gone out and the age-old trees of the forest made contours against the starry heavens like large powerful shadows. The snow lay softly on the barren earth and nature in its unending loneliness seemed to lie in a half slumber. The men had told their old legends of dead heroes and the shamans had talked with the spirits of the heavens and with those of the underworld. I had forgotten all that made me a man of civilization; I was thinking neither of Christianity nor of other teachings but rather I was completely involved in childlike admiration of what I saw and heard.
>
> I suddenly felt like a child and, as in childhood, I imagined that every object had its spirit, that water and air were populated by mysterious invisible beings who, in inexplicable fashion, ruled the course of the world and the fate of men. In the untouched wilderness and its infinite silence, I was encompassed by the traditional mysticism and religious mysteries through which faith touches so many things.
>
> After several of these meetings, I naturally became inured and did not let myself be so completely captivated, but even today, because of what I have seen and heard, I have retained a deeper understanding of what and how these children of the wilderness feel and think. Their religion has become alive for me, and I think that such understanding and knowledge could be and is useful in many ways.[25]

Western psychology's idea of human capacity comes from a scientific tradition which had its beginnings in the materialistically oriented Age of Enlightenment and which, by either systematically rejecting the idea of alternative or higher states of consciousness or by pathologizing such states, has presented us with a restricted concept of an ego capable only of concerning itself with the vital necessities of existence. Yet all around this ego a vast number of psychic reserves lie fallow and remain blocked by a reductionist need for security posing in the guise of experimental and empirical science. In actual fact, however, our ideas about what is empirically and experimentally acceptable are conditioned by history. Things which today cannot be scientifically investigated—because of generally accepted social taboos or unfounded moral or epistemological value systems—will tomorrow by general consensus be regarded as perfectly acceptable areas of scientific endeavor.

The fear of romanticism and mysticism that academics experience in connection with the study of shamanism and magic is completely unwarranted. We are not calling for the abolition of empiricism, but rather would like to see it expanded and become more objective—indeed, more empiricist. Scientists believe that objectivity is brought about by narrowing the perceptive horizon, by removing all disruptive factors from the field of observation. It is obvious, however, that such an attitude excludes from study and observation whole areas of what it means to be a human being, such as the human potential for higher consciousness and all such "prescientific" notions as magic, mysticism, and alchemy, as well as all non-Western traditions of wisdom and knowledge.

For that reason, Mircea Eliade pleads for the rediscovery of the spiritual history of mankind. He writes:

> Western man will not be able to live indefinitely cut off from an important part of himself, a part that is made up of fragments of a spiritual history, the significance and message of which he is incapable of deciphering. Sooner or later the dialogue with the "others"—the representatives of traditional Asiatic or "primitive" cultures—will have to be conducted, no longer in the empirical and utilitarian language of today (which is only capable of describing social, economic, political, medical, etc. circumstances) but in a cultural language capable of expressing human realities and spiritual values. Such a dialogue is inevitable; it is prescribed in the book of historical destiny, and it would be tragically naive to imagine that it can be pursued indefinitely on the mental level at which it takes place today.[26]

What we have suppressed or condemned to unconsciousness ever more frequently triggers off an epistemological counteroffensive which in the foreseeable future will bring down many narrowminded edifices of theory. Then the prophecy of William James will have been fulfilled. He was of the opinion that the separation of scientific and religious facts will not necessarily last forever and that the strictly objective view of science may one day be considered as a useful kind of eccentricism rather than hold the ultimate triumphant position our present-day dissecting scientists so confidently accord to it.[27]

We are still unable to assess many facets of shamanic experience and power, because ethnology lacks a yardstick. In fact, we might say that it lacks the "eyes" for making such an assessment. We have no map that shows the exact location of indefinable, unknown, parapsychic phenomena. Science, moreover, being based on our normal state of consciousness, will probably prove inadequate for an examination of altered psychic dispositions. The scientific principles of a continuous flow of time and of a stream of consciousness are irreconcilable with both the idea of an emptied consciousness and with the irregular time intervals, the feeling of timelessness, or time neutrality experienced in states of altered consciousness.

We have only scratched the surface of the nature of the psyche—in fact, psychology has only just begun to be a science. We have yet to open the doors of our inner temple. We stand before them filled with expectation, because there are signs of a new era of the spirit, a rebirth of true science. As far as research into shamanism goes, we have only just taken the first steps toward a new approach that makes mere descriptions of events obsolete and accords proper recognition to the researcher's consciousness as a means of understanding—as a window upon the world.

Epilogue

To those who did not invent gunpowder nor the compass,
who neither harnessed steam nor electricity,
who explored neither the oceans nor the sky,
. . . but surrendered to the nature of things, deeply moved,
. . . truly the firstborn of this world,
To those who shall survive in shoots of grass!

—Aimé Césaire

Too Much Think about White Man, No More Can Find Dream

The majority of tribal cultures have either been exterminated or condemned to a miserable existence. The tellers of tales have died, and the tradition of myths is largely lost or has been replaced by Christian elements. The sacred has deteriorated into black magic, and the shamans, to make up for the loss of native knowledge, have adopted various Western cultural practices into their healing rituals. Many tribal cultures now consider their gods and ancestral spirits to be less important than the luxuries of our modern way of life, and the economic basis of the few surviving tribes has been completely, or at least greatly, undermined. Yet, despite all this, some tribes believe that it is necessary to revive their ancient culture and religion.

It may well be that among some of these peoples the birthrate is increasing; that there is a shaky recovery of a dubious economic wealth; and that shamanism is even reestablishing itself to a limited degree—giving rise to a modern kind of shaman, who knows more about fixing a car than he does of his own language and history and so acts as a mediator between cultures. But the call for a return to the good old days rings out over denuded forests, fenced prairies, tundras littered with drilling rigs, and lakes empty of fish. As a cultural basis, the world of the hunter and nomad has long since disappeared.

As an aspect of farming, hunting, and gathering cultures, shamanism may be dead, but its spiritual and biological potency has survived. Every year dozens of tribal groups perish as the last remaining areas of retreat are cleared along the Amazon, in Assam, in Indonesia and Micronesia. During the next few decades the tribal way of life will cease to exist for all but a very few exceptions. Our Western obsession with progress offers no room for such a way of life. Although various scientific arguments have been put forward in favor of the preservation of tribal communities, it is only in recent years that a few subcultural groups, living in a modern environment, have begun to long for a return to their tribal way of life. Too late! According to the calculations of realistic demographers, the remaining 6% of nonindustrial, nonhistorical or primitive peoples—it doesn't matter which inappropriate label we give them—will have disappeared from the face of our planet by the turn of the century.

In this hopeless situation, shamans, in particular, are pillars of resistance against continuously encroaching Western influences. As long as they do not allow themselves to be corrupted, the decline and destruction of their culture can be delayed, because they are the cornerstones of the cultural identity of their tribal communities. At the same time, however, the shaman is an intercultural messenger, who softens the harsh effects of acculturation by carefully and thoughtfully leading his people toward another way of life, as he tries to salvage their traditional beliefs for their new world. The shaman is often the first to introduce new ways of thought and new material goods. While he unreservedly disapproves of any contact with modern civilization and forbids others to have such contacts, he nevertheless takes a realistic view of his own impotence in the face of such a mighty foe. By studying and analyzing the other culture to his own advantage, he develops into a man with a foot in both camps and acts as a cultural shock absorber. During this process his attitude toward his own powers and healing practices necessarily undergoes a change, and this often gives rise to neoreligious methods of healing, religious syncretism, and revivalist cults.

Due to the struggle of "original" nations for liberation and emancipation, we have in recent years developed some appreciation for the positive aspects of tribal cultures. This development is given added impetus by the fact that the latest scientific insights are increasingly based on or related to the knowledge of so-called archaic societies. Modern psychology, too, is beginning to discover that what happens during shamanic initiation is also relevant to the health and self-realization of the individual. It has come to recognize that without pain and suffering, the psyche cannot make any transpersonal gains.

Were we, then, unable to see the reality of transpsychic structures because of our ignorance, blindness, backwardness, and false paradigms? It would seem so: As the power of the shaman wanes and his brain is dominated by the thought "Too much think about white man—no more can find dream,"[1] we are rediscovering methods of initiation, spiritual healing, mediumship, and paranormal communications buried by our civilization. We have for centuries fought a merciless battle against magic and mutilated it beyond all recognition. Now we are slowly becoming aware of the raging blindness of Western subjectivity and ethnocentricity, which forced everything that was culturally alien into the straitjacket of its "progressive" thinking.

Today the tide is turning. White people are combing Latin American villages, desolate North American Indian reservations, and remote Polynesian islands in their search for "shamanic initiation," because the mind of modern man knows no rest, whether it conjures up devilish faces or concocts noble and sublime ideals. We are witnessing the birth of a new mythos of the shaman. The former savage is seen as an immaculate spiritual guide and elevated to the level of a saint. Discrimination against and sterile admiration of the shaman have always gone hand in hand.

Nevertheless, what we are left with is the rejection of a complex transpersonal phenomenon and the destruction of original cultures. This destruction is reflected in the sadness of the Mazatec healer María Sabína—made world-famous by Western researchers—whose psychedelic mushroom ceremonies attracted the ethno-mycologist Gordon Wasson and, after him, numerous Americans and "drug apostles" in their search for "chemical enlightenment":

> Since then, when the strangers came to look for god, the sacred mushrooms (niños santos) have lost their power. They have lost their purity. They have been destroyed. Now and in the future they will be worthless. Nothing can be done about this. Before Wasson came I could feel the niños santos raise me up. Now I no longer feel anything. The power is gone.[2]

APPENDIX

Tribes and Their Locations

Ainu—Northern Japan (Hokkaido),
  Southern Sakhalin
Aivilik Eskimo—Canada
Altai—Central Asia (Altai Mountains)
Ammassalik Eskimo—East Coast of
  Greenland
Arunta—Central Australia
Avá-Chiripá and
  Avá-Nembirará—Paraguay

Badyaranké—Senegal
Barkinyi—Australia (New South Wales)
Batak—Indonesia (Northern Sumatra,
  Lake Toba)
Bella Coola—Canada (Northwest
  Coast)
Bhujel—Nepal
Bivar Tungus—(Northern Group of
  the Tungus), Northeast Siberia
Buryat—Siberia (around Lake Baikal)

Carib—Dutch Guiana (Surinam)
Caribou Eskimo—Canada (West bank
  of Hudson Bay)
Cahsia Pomo—California
Chemehueve—Southern California
Chumash—Southern California
Copper Eskimo—Canada (Northwest
  Territories and Victoria Island)
Cuna—San Blas Island off Panama

Dayak—Indonesia (Borneo)
Desana—(Subgroup of the Tukano),

Northeast Peru and Southeast
  Colombia)
Dolgan—Siberia (central Lena Basin)

Evenki—(Northern Group of the
  Tungus) Northeast Siberia
Ewe—Southern Togo and Southern
  Dahomey

Flathead—(also known as Salish) West
  Montana

Gitksan—Northwest Coast of Canada
Gold—(Southern Group of the
  Tungus) Northeast Siberia
Guajiro—Colombia

Haida—American Northwest Cost,
  Queen Charlotte Island, Canada
Hain/om—Southwest Africa
Hawaiian—South Pacific Hawaiian
  Islands

Iglulik Eskimo—Canadian Northwest
  Territories, Baffin Land

Kamayurá—Alto Xingú, Brazil
Kikuyu—Kenya
Kulin—Australia (Victoria, Coastal
  region)
Kurnai—Australia (Victoria, Coastal
  region)
Kwakiutl—Canada (Northwest Coast)

Lakh—Southeast Asia
Lapp—North Scandinavia
Luiseno—Southern California

Magar—West Nepal
Malisseet—Passamaquoddy—
Maine
Mandan—North Dakota
Manchurian—(Southern Group of the
Tungus) Northeast Siberia
Mentawai—Mentawai Islands, off the
West Coast of Sumatra

Rengma-Naga and
Sanstam-Naga—India (Assam)
Parang Negritos—Southeast Asia
Netsilik Eskimo—Canada (Northwest
Territories)
Nung—(Subgroup of the Thai)
Southeast Asia, South China

Ojibway—USA/Canada (north of the
Great Lakes)
Oruncha—see: Arunta
Ostyak—West Siberia (Lower and
central Ob)

Paviotso—Nevada
Penobscot—Maine
Point Hope Eskimo—Alaska, Bering
Strait
Polar Eskimo—Thule, Northwest
Greenland
Pukapuka—Polynesia

Rai—Northwest Australia

Sagay—Siberia (on the River Yes)
Salish (Thompson River)—Canada
(Northwest Coast)
Saora—India
Selk'nam—Patagonia
Semang—Central region of Malaysian
Peninsula
Seneca—(Subgroup of the Iroquois)
Northeast USA

Shortzy—Central Asia (Altai
Mountains)
Sima-Sima—Indonesia (Central
Ceram)
Sioux—Montana, North Dakota,
Minnesota
Soyot—Northeast Siberia
Sunuwar—Nepal

Takali—West Nepal
Theddora—Australia (New South
Wales)
Thompson—Canada (British
Columbia)
Tobelorese—Indonesia (Halmahera
Island)
Tlingit—Northwest Coast of Canada
Tofa—Siberia
Tsimsyan (Also:
Tsimshian)—Northwest Coast of
Canada
Tukano—Northeast Peru and
Southeast Colombia
Tungus—Northeast Siberia

Unambal—Northwest Australia
Ungarinyin—Northwest Australia
Utkuhikyaling Eskimo—Central
Eskimos, Canada (Northwest
Territories)

Wahaerama/Tanabaru—Indonesia
(Central Ceram)
Walapai—Arizona
Warramunga—Central Australia
(Northern Territory)
Washo—California (Pyramid Lake)
Winnebago—West bank of Lake
Michigan
Wiradjeri—Australia (New South
Wales)

Yakut—Northeast Siberia (Central
Lena Basin)
Yamana—Patagonia
Yebámasa—Amazonas

Yokut—Central California

Yualai—Australia (New South Wales)

Yugakir—Northeast Siberia

Yuki—Northern California

Yuma—Southern California

Zulu—South African (Natal)

Zuni—New Mexico

NOTES

Introduction
1. Vinson Brown 1974, p. 18.
2. Lame Deer, Erdoes 1980, p. 157.

1. A Geography of Death
1. Osis and Haraldsson 1977.
2. Gallagher 1982.
3. Ring 1981, p. 201.
4. Ibid., p. 198.
5. Ibid., p. 201.
6. Garfield 1977.
7. Moody 1978, p. 24ff.
8. Ring 1980.
9. Siegel 1981.

2. Life beyond Birth and Death
1. Rasmussen 1931, Vol. 8, p. 315.
2. Rasmussen 1930, Vol. 7, No. 2, p. 56ff.
3. Eliade 1978, p. 44.
4. Ibid.

3. The Reality of the Soul
1. Beaglehole 1938, p. 326.
2. Rasmussen 1931, Vol. 8, p. 501.
3. Tyler 1871.
4. Ibid., Vol. I, p. 453.
5. Rasmussen 1930, Vol. 7, No. 1, p. 60f.
6. Ibid., p. 96.
7. Nordenskiöld 1938.
8. Swanton 1908.
9. Warneck 1909.
10. Skeat 1900.
11. Boas 1884/85.
12. Münzel 1971.
13. Ibid.

14. Hulkrantz 1953.
15. Iokhel'son 1924.
16. Friedrich 1955.
17. Shirokogorov 1935a, p. 135.
18. Petri 1952.
19. Johnston 1979, p. 178.
20. Simmons 1971, p. 74f.
21. Schefold 1980.
22. Shirokogorov 1935a.
23. Fischer 1965.

4. Soul Journeys and Teachings about the Beyond
1. Rasmussen 1927, p. 386.
2. Green 1968.
3. Bourguignon 1973, 1977.
4. Dobkin de Rios 1977.
5. Harner 1980.
6. Halifax 1979.
7. Sheils 1978.
8. Donner 1954, p. 74f.
9. Neihardt 1974, p. 160f.
10. Ibid., p. 170f.
11. Ibid., p. 173.
12. Ibid., p. 173.
13. Ibid., p. 173f.
14. Kalweit 1983, quoting Green 1929.
15. Wallace 1970, p. 240ff.
16. Meighan and Riddell 1972.
17. Quasha 1975, p. 27f.
18. Lommel 1952; Petri 1954, 1952/53, 1962.

5. The Body/Spirit Connection: Ropes of Air and Invisible Threads
1. Eliade 1960.

2. Rose 1957.
3. Crookall 1970; Green 1968.
4. de Martino 1972.
5. David-Neel 1984, p. 33.
6. Friedrich 1955.
7. Handleman 1972, p. 90.
8. Rasmussen 1930, p. 93.
9. Furst 1967.
10. Coate 1966.
11. Petri 1954, p. 229ff.
12. Ibid., p. 248f.
13. Petri 1952, p. 282.
14. Ibid., p. 298.
15. Ibid.
16. Ibid.
17. Ibid., p. 302.
18. Evans 1927, p. 20.
19. Eliade 1960, p. 225.
20. Crookall 1970.

6. The Out-of-Body Experience (OBE)

1. Green 1968.
2. Tart 1967, 1968, 1974.
3. Garrett 1949, p. 26.

7. The "True Earth"

1. Gayton 1935.
2. Russell 1935, p. 49.
3. Handleman 1972.
4. Iokhel'son 1924.
5. Shirokogorov 1935a.
6. Holmberg 1964.
7. Nordenskiöld 1938.
8. Grube 1897.
9. Swanton 1905.
10. Röder 1948, p. 126f.
11. Iokhel'son 1924.
12. Nordenskiöld 1938, p. 297.
13. Fischer 1965, p. 173.
14. Skeat 1900, p. 50.
15. Ibid., p. 194.
16. Ibid., p. 22f.
17. Johnston 1979, p. 134ff.
18. Swanton 1905.
19. Röder 1948.

20. Blackburn 1975, p. 98.
21. Radin 1970, p. 69ff.
22. Ibid., p. 222.
23. Agapitow 1887, p. 316f.
24. Landes 1968, p. 189ff.
25. Ibid., p. 198f.
26. Beuchelt 1975a.
27. Watson-Franke 1975, p. 205.
28. Beaglehole 1938.
29. Forde 1931.
30. Shirokogorov 1935a, p. 125f.

8. Suffering Kills, Suffering Enlivens: Sickness and Self-Healing

1. Diószegi (1968), p. 58.
2. Ibid., p. 57.
3. Ibid., p. 279.
4. Diószegi 1959, p. 273ff.
5. Diószegi 1963b, p. 267ff.
6. Boas 1969, p. 41ff.
7. Ibid., p. 46ff.
8. Park 1934, p. 99.
9. Loeb 1929, p. 66ff.
10. Callaway 1884, p. 259ff.
11. Ibid., p. 185ff.
12. Good 1980.
13. Harvey 1980.
14. Sich 1980, p. 215.
15. Beuchelt 1975a, p. 146ff.
16. Lee 1981, p. 173ff.
17. Sharon 1978, p. 11.
18. Ibid., p. 12.
19. Sieroszewski 1902, p. 310.
20. Shternberg 1974, p. 476.
21. Sandschejew 1927, p. 977.
22. Harva 1938, p. 453.
23. Boshier 1974.
24. Watson-Franke 1975, p. 204.
25. Cho Hung-Youn 1982, p. 28f.

9. Rituals of Dismemberment and Bone Displays in the Underworld

1. Blacker 1975, p. 188f.

2. Röder 1948, p. 123.
3. Wagner-Robertz 1976, p. 536ff.
4. Thalbitzer 1908, p. 452ff.
5. Harner 1980.
6. Winnipeg 1979.
7. Murphy 1964, p. 58.
8. Spencer/Gillen 1899, p. 524.
9. Lommel 1959/1980.
10. Petri 1954, p. 248ff.
11. Elkin 1945, p. 102.
12. Coate 1966.
13. Elkin 1945, p. 112ff.
14. Ksenofontov, in: Friedrich/Buddruss 1955, p. 208ff.
15. Ibid., p. 211f.
16. Ibid., p. 132.
17. Popow, in: Lehtisalo (1937), p. 9f. Comp. Nachtigall 1952.
18. Friedrich (1955), p. 52.
19. Ksenofontov, in: Friedrich/Buddruss 1955.
20. Diószegi 1968, p. 61f.

10. Imaginary Friends, Partial Personalities, and Genuine Spirits of the Dead

1. Rasmussen 1930, Vol. 7, No. 1, p. 113.
2. Kunze 1982, p. 88.
3. In: LeShan 1966, p. 73.
4. Swedenborg 1837–1870, p. 68.
5. Slocum 1900.
6. Messner 1978, p. 168.
7. Stokes 1980, p. 14ff.
8. Garrett 1968, p. 17.
9. Rasmussen 1908, p. 147ff.
10. Spencer and Gillen 1904, p. 482f.
11. Christiansen 1953, p. 34.
12. Gillin 1956, p. 132ff.
13. Park 1934, p. 99.
14. Kelly 1936, p. 129.
15. Findeisen 1960, p. 197.
16. Lame Deer 1980.

11. Sacred Weddings, Spirit Marriages, and Dream Sexuality

1. Garrett 1968..
2. Elwin 1955.
3. Ibid., p. 153.
4. Ibid., p. 168.
5. Ibid., p. 138.
6. Ibid., p. 149.
7. Ibid., p. 139.
8. Eder 1958.
9. Spiro 1967.
10. Shternberg 1974, p. 74.
11. Ibid., p. 75ff.
12. Shternberg 1935, p. 246ff.
13. Ibid., p. 261ff.
14. Madsen 1955, p. 48ff.

12. The Song of Power: Joy, Joy, Joy!

1. Rasmussen 1931, Vol. 8, p. 321.
2. Rasmussen 1930, p. 118.
3. Cloutier 1980, p. 72ff.
4. Barbeau 1958, p. 51.
5. Bartolomé 1979.
6. Underhill 1969.
7. Rasmussen 1927, p. 34.
8. Diószegi 1968, p. 142ff.
9. Boas 1969, p. 50ff.
10. Ohnuki-Tierney 1973, p. 18f.
11. Capra 1975.

13. Sacred Drugs: Where the World Is Born

1. Estrada 1980, p. 72.
2. James 1969, p. 367.
3. Harner 1973a.
4. Langdon 1979.
5. Deltgen 1978.
6. Ibid., p. 69.
7. Andres-Bonn 1939.
8. Ibid.
9. Watson-Franke 1975, p. 201.
10. Ibid., p. 202.
11. Ibid., p. 200.

11. Ibid., p. 200.
12. Reichel-Dolmatoff 1971, 1975.
13. Reichel-Dolmatoff 1971, p. 174.
14. Ibid.
15. Reichel-Dolmatoff 1972, p. 101ff.
16. Ibid., p. 94.
17. Reichel-Dolmatoff 1978.
18. Reichel-Dolmatoff 1975, p. 76ff.
19. Reichel-Dolmatoff 1972, p. 11.
20. Huxley 1970.
21. Mandel 1978.
22. Myerhoff 1974.
23. Harman and Fadiman 1971.
24. Harner 1973c, p. 172; 1980, 1981.
25. Harner 1973c, p. 156.
26. Kensinger 1973.
27. James 1969, p. 368.
28. Slotkin 1979.
29. Estrada 1980, p. 61.
30. Ibid., p. 46.

14. Acquisition of Power by Inheritance, Transmission, and Change of Sex

1. Kelly 1936, p. 130.
2. Lame Deer, Erdoes 1980, p. 159.
3. Rasmussen 1930, Vol. 7, No. 1, p. 132.
4. Trigger 1978, p. 132.
5. Röder 1948, p. 72.
6. Shirokogorov 1935a.
7. Ibid., p. 346.
8. Comp. Krader 1975, 1978.
9. Gusinde 1931, Vol. 1.
10. Rainey, in Winnipeg Art Gallery 1979, p. 35.
11. Horse Capture 1980, p. 98.
12. Jones 1972.
13. Findeisen 1957, p. 140.
14. Bogoras 1907, p. 450ff.
15. Murphy 1964, p. 75.
16. Newcomb 1964.

15. The Rejection of Power

1. Diószegi 1968, p. 59.
2. Underhill 1969, p. 266.
3. Gusinde 1931, Vol. 2, p. 1398f.
4. Christiansen 1953, p. 30f.

16. The Loss of Power

1. Itkonen 1960, p. 27.
2. Rasmussen 1925, p. 127.
3. Howitt 1887, p. 408.
4. Steffansson 1913, p. 372ff.
5. Diószegi 1968, p. 58f.
6. Barbeau 1958, p. 54.
7. Rasmussen 1908, p. 305ff.
8. Itkonen 1960, p. 18.
9. Watson-Franke 1975, p. 204.
10. Curtis 1915, p. 80ff.
11. Kelly 1936, p. 130.
12. Warner 1958, p. 205ff.
13. Park 1930, p. 24f.
14. Prem Das 1978, p. 133.

17. In the Bowels of the Earth

1. Fournier 1976, p. 103.
2. Kroeber 1935, p. 188ff.
3. Lommel 1952, p. 41ff.
4. Howitt 1887, p. 408.
5. Barbeau 1958, p. 76ff.
6. Turney-High 1937, p. 35ff.

18. Experiences of Light and Balls of Fire

1. Friedrich/Buddruss 1955, p. 124ff.
2. Rasmussen 1952, p. 130.
3. Rasmussen 1932, Vol. 9, p. 28.
4. Rasmussen 1930, Vol. 7, No. 1, p. 112.
5. Rasmussen 1927.
6. Rasmussen 1930, Vol. 7, No. 1, p. 122f.
7. Rasmussen 1908.
8. Bunzell 1929–1930, p. 481f.
9. Reichel-Dolmatoff 1971, p. 126.
10. Reichel-Dolmatoff 1975, p. 77.
11. Lommel 1952, p. 41ff.
12. Neumann 1981, p. 33.
13. Fortune 1932, p. 295.
14. Rasmussen 1952, p. 131.
15. Speck 1919, p. 252.

17. Berndt 1946–1948, p. 45f.
18. Neal 1966; Schenk 1980.
19. Kelsey 1980; comp. Rodman 1979, p. 93.

19. Ascending the World Tree

1. Harva 1938, p. 486ff.
2. Hitchcock 1976, p. 175.
3. Oppitz 1981.
4. Howitt 1887, p. 408.
5. Diószegi 1968, p. 65f.
6. Friedrich/Buddruss 1955, p. 213.
7. Ibid., p. 156.

20. Portals to Heaven and the Underworld

1. Howitt 1904.
2. Petri 1952, p. 293.
3. Reichel-Dolmatoff 1975.
4. Popow 1963, p. 149ff.
5. Röder 1948, p. 124.
6. Blackburn 1975, p. 233f.

21. Rulers of Nature and Givers of Life

1. Katz 1981, p. 68.

22. Crystal Came Whirling, Crystal Came Raining

1. Cloutier 1980, p. 83f.
2. Lommel 1952, p. 41ff.
3. Petri 1952.
4. Waters 1963.
5. Reichel-Dolmatoff 1975, p. 90.
6. L. A. White 1930.
7. Kroeber 1925, p. 199.
8. Underhill 1946, p. 271.
9. Spencer/Gillen 1899, p. 526ff.
10. Cloutier 1980, p. 88f.

23. The Rhythm of Life

1. Spott 1971, p. 535ff.
2. Benedict 1934, p. 60f.
3. Ibid.

24. Walk in Balance, Walk in Beauty

1. Twigg 1973, p. 65.
2. Laski 1959, p. 128f.
3. Myerhoff 1976a, p. 8.
4. Comp. Myerhoff 1966.
5. Myerhoff 1976b, p. 100.
6. Myerhoff 1966, 1976b.
7. Diószegi 1963b, p. 347.
8. Diószegi 1968, p. 60.

25. When the Anthropologists Arrive, the Gods Leave the Island

1. Haitian proverb.
2. Carpenter 1912.
3. James 1912, p. 204.
4. James 1962, p. 222.
5. James 1890, p. 68.
6. Underhill 1928.
7. Comp. Musès/Young 1979; Ornstein 1972, 1973; Pelletier/Garfield 1976; Pelletier 1978; Tart 1969, 1975, 1977; Woods 1980; Zinberg 1977.
8. Bourguignon 1968a, 1968b, 1973, 1977.
9. Deikman 1966; Fischer 1978; Schwartz/Shapiro 1976; Silverman 1968; Walsh/Vaughan 1980; Welwood 1977.
10. Maslow 1971, 1973.
11. Maslow 1969, 1977.
12. Maslow 1973, p. 34.
13. Ibid., p. 189.
14. Eliade 1951, p. 96.
15. Laski 1959; James 1902.
16. Maslow 1964.
17. Quote from James 1907, p. 360.
18. Lame Deer 1980, p. 173.
19. Russell 1935.
20. Peters 1981.
21. Friedrich 1955.
22. Kalweit 1983.
23. Van de Castle 1974, p. 281.

24. Shirokogorov 1935, p. 375.
25. Donner 1954, p. 69.
26. Eliade 1965, p. 14f.
27. James 1907, p. 454.

Epilogue

1. Lommel 1952, p. 40.
2. Estrada 1980, p. 139.

BIBLIOGRAPHY

Aberle, David F.: "'Artic Hysteria' and Latah in Mongolia," *Transactions of the New York Academy of Sciences*, 14, No. 7 (1952), pp. 291–297.

Agapitow, N. N., and Changalow, M. N.: "Das Schamanenthum unter den Burjäten," *Globus*, No. 52 (1887), pp. 286–288, 299–301, 316–318.

Albers, Patricia, and Parker Seymour: "The Plains Vision Experience: A Study of Power and Privilege," *Southwestern Journal of Anthropology*, No. 27 (1971), pp. 203–233.

Allen, Nicholas: "Shamanism among the Thulung Rai," in: Hitchcock/Jones 1975 (a).

Amiotte, A.: "Eagles Fly Over," *Parabola*, 1, No. 3 (1976), pp. 28–41.

Andres-Bonn, Friedrich: "Die Himmelsreise der caraibischen Medizinmänner," *Zeitschrift für Ethnologie*, No. 70 (1939), pp. 331–343.

Andrews, Lynn V.: *Medicine Woman*, San Francisco 1981.

Arbman, Ernst: *Ecstasy or Religious Trance*, Uppsala 1963–1970, 3 Vols.

Arndt, Paul: "Zur Religion der Dongo auf Sumbawa," *Anthropos*, No. 47 (1952).

Bäckman, Louise, and Åke Hultkrantz: "Studies in Lapp Shamanism." *Stockholm Studies in Comparative Religion*, No. 16. Stockholm 1978.

Barbeau, Marius: "Medicine Men of the North Pacific Coast," *National Museum of Canada, Bulletin* 152 (Anthropological Series No. 42), Ottawa 1958.

Bardens, Dennis: "Profile–Adrian Boshier," *Parapsychology Review*, 5, No. 4 (1974), pp. 4–5.

Bartolomé, Miguel A.: "Shamanism among the Avé-Chiripá," in: Browman/ Schwarz 1979.

Basilov, V. N.: "Shamanism in Central Asia," in: Bharati 1976 (b).

———. "Vestiges of Transvestism in Central-Asian Shamanism," in: Diószegi/ Hoppal 1978.

Baumann, Hermann: *Das doppelte Geschlecht*, Berlin 1955.

Beaglehole, Ernest and Pearl: "Ethnology of Pukapuka," *Bernice P. Bishop Museum, Bulletin*, No. 150, Honolulu 1938.

Beattie, John, and Middleton John: *Spirit Mediumship and Society in Africa*, London 1969.

Beck, Pegg V., and Walters A. L.: *The Sacred*, Navajo Community College, Tsaile, Arizona, Albuquerque 1977.

Beck, Robert J.: "Some Proto-Psychotherapeutic Elements in the Practice of the Shaman." *History of Religions*, 6, No. 1 (1966), pp. 303–327.

Benedict, Ruth: "The Vision in Plains Culture," *American Anthropologist*, No. 24 (1922), pp. 1–23.

_____. "The Concept of the Guardian Spirit in North America," *Memoirs of the American Anthropological Association*, No. 29, Menasha, Wisc., 1923.

_____. "Anthropology and the Abnormal," *Journal of General Psychology*, No. 10 (1934), pp. 59–79.

Benitez, Fernando: *In the Magic Land of Peyote*, Austin 1975.

Bentov, Itzhak: *Stalking the Wild Pendulum*, London 1977.

Berglie, Per-Arne: "On the Question of Tibetan Shamanism," in M. Braun and Per Kraerne (Ed.): *"Tibetan Studies*, Völkerkundemuseum Zürich, 1978.

Bergman, Robert L.: "A School for Medicine Men," *American Journal of Psychiatry*, 130, No. 6 (1973), pp. 663–666.

_____. "Learning from Indian Medicine," Vortrag beim Winter Meeting der Oregon Psychiatric Association, Portland, Jan. 27–29, 1977.

Berndt, Catherine H.: "The Role of Native Doctors in Aboriginal Australia," in: Kiev 1964.

Berndt, R. M.: "Wuradjeri Magic and 'Clever Men'," *Oceania*, No. 17 (1946–47), pp. 327–365 and No. 18 (1947–48), pp. 60–86.

Berrin, Kathleen, (Ed.): *Art of the Huichol Indians*, San Francisco 1978.

Beuchelt, Eno: "Zur Status-Persönlichkeit koreanischer Schamanen," *Sociologus*, 25, No. 2 (1975) (a), pp. 139–154.

_____. "Die Rückrufung der Ahnen auf Cheju do (Südkorea). Ein Ritual zur psychischen Stabilisierung," *Anthropos*, No. 70 (1975) (b), pp. 145–179.

Bharati, Agehananda, (Ed.): *The Realm of the Extra-Human, Ideas and Actions*, The Hague 1976 (a).

_____. (Ed.): *The Realm of the Extra-Human, Agents and Audiences*, The Hague 1976 (b).

Blackburn, Thomas C.: *December's Child. A Book of Chumash Oral Narratives*, Berkeley 1975.

Blacker, Carmen: *The Catalpa Bow. A Study of Shamanistic Practices in Japan*, London 1975.

Blumensohn, Jules: "The Fast among North American Indians," *American Anthropologist*, No. 35 (1933), pp. 451–469.

Boas, Franz: "The Central Eskimo," *6th Annual Report of the Bureau of Ethnology*, 1884–1885, pp. 399–669, Washington, D.C., 1888.

_____. *The Social Organisation and the Secret Societies of the Kwakiutl Indians*, Washington 1897.

_____. "The Eskimo of Baffin Land and Hudson Bay," *American Museum of Natural History, Bulletin*, No. 15 (1901).

_____. *The Religion of the Kwakiutl Indians*, Part Two, New York 1930.

Bogoras, Waldemar: "The Chuckchee," The Jesup North Pacific Expedition, 1904 to 1909, Vol. 7, No. 2. *Memoir of the American Museum of Natural History*, Leiden.

_____. *Einstein und die Religion. Eine Anwendung der Relativitätstheorie auf die Erforschung religiöser Phänomene*, Moscow 1923 (in Russian).

_____. "Ideas of Space and Time in the Conception of Primitive Religion," *American Anthropologist*, No. 27 (1925), pp. 205–266.

_____ "The Shamanistic Call and the Period of Initiation in Northern Asia and Northern America," *Proceedings of the 23rd International Congress of Americanists*, pp. 441–444, New York 1930.

_____. "Schilderung zweier schamanischer Séancen der Küsten-Tschuktschen (Nordsibirien)," *Abhandlungen und Aufsätze aus dem Institut für Menschen-und Menschheitskunde*, Augsburg 1956.

Bohm, David: *Wholeness and the Implicate Order*, London 1981.

Bonin, Werner F.: "Der Geist der Medizin und das nicht-aristotelische Denken," *Curare*, 1, No. 2 (1978), pp. 107–124.

Boshier, Adrian K.: "What makes a Witchdoctor?," *Scientific South Africa*, No. 2 (1965), pp. 317–320.

_____. "Madame Witchdoctor," *Perspective*, No. 3 (1966), pp. 15–17.

_____. "African Apprenticeship," *Parapsychology Review*, 5, No. 4 (1974), pp. 1–3 and 25–27.

_____. "ESP amongst African Priest Diviners," *Odyssey*, No. 1/3 (Sep./Oct. 1977).

Bourguignon, Erika: *A Cross-Cultural Study of Dissociational States*, Ohio State University Research Foundation, Columbus 1968 (a).

_____. "World Distribution and Patterns of Possession States," in: Prince 1968 (b).

_____. *Religion, Altered States of Consciousness, and Social Change*, Columbus 1973.

_____. "Altered States of Consciousness, Myths, and Rituals," in: Du Toit 1977.

Bourke, John G.: "The Medicine-Men of the Apache," *9th Annual Report of the Bureau of Ethnology*, pp. 443–603. Washington, D.C., 1892.

Bouteiller, M.: *Chamanisme et guérison magique*, Paris 1950.

Boyd, Doug: *Rolling Thunder. Erfahrungen mit einem Schamanen der neuen Indianer-bewegung*, Munich 1978.

Boyer, L. B.: "Further Remarks Concerning Shamans and Shamanism," Israel Annals of Psychiatry and Related Disciplines, No. 2 (1964), pp. 235–257.

Bozzano, Ernesto: *Übersinnliche Erscheinungen bei Naturvölkern*, Freiburg 1975.

Browman, David L., and Schwarz, Ronald A. (Ed.): *Spirits, Shamans, and Stars. Perspectives from South America*, The Hague 1979.

Brown, Joseph Epes: "The Wisdom of the Contrary. A. Conversation with Joseph Epes Brown," *Parabola*, 4, No. 1 (1979), pp. 54–65.

Brown, Vinson: *Voices of Earth and Sky. Vision Search of the Native Americans*, Happy Camp, Calif. 1974.

Bryant, A. T.: *Zulu Medicine and Medicine-Men*, Cape Town 1966.

Butler, K. J.: "My Uncle Went to the Moon," *Artscanada*, No. 184–187 (Dec. 1973/Jan. 1974), pp. 154–158.

Byrd, Richard: *Alone*, New York 1938.

Callaway, Canon H.: *The Religious System of the Amazula*, Publications of the Folk-Lore Society, No. 15, London 1884.

_____. "The Religion of the Amazulu of South Africa as Told by Themselves," in: Kroeber/Waterman 1965.

Campbell, Joseph: *Der Heros in tausend Gestalten*, Frankfurt 1978.

BIBLIOGRAPHY

Campbell, Ronald L., and Staniford, Philip S.: "Transpersonal Anthropology," *Phoenix. New Directions in the Study of Man*, 2, No. 1 (1978), pp. 28–40.
_____. "The Nature of Transpersonal Anthropology," *Phoenix. Journal for Transpersonal Anthropology*, 5, No. 1 (1981), pp. 119–132.

Capps, W. H., (Ed.): *Seeing with a Native Eye*, New York 1976.

Capra, Fritjof: *Das Tao der Physik*, Berne, Munich, Vienna 1984.

Carneiro, Robert L.: "The Amahuaca and the Spirit World," *Ethnology*, No. 3 (1964), pp. 6–11.

Carpenter, Edward: *The Drama of Love and Death*, New York 1912.

Carroll, Lewis: *Alice im Spiegelland*, Munich 1981.

Casanowicz, I. M.: "Shamanism of the Natives of Siberia," *Annual Report of Regents*, 1924, pp. 415–434. Washington, D.C., 1924.

Catlin, George: *Die Indianer Nordamerikas*, 1851.

Chadwick, Nora K.: "Shamanism among the Tatars of Central Asia." *The Journal of the Royal Anthropological Institute of Great Britain and Ireland*, No. 66 (1936), pp. 75–112.

Chagnon, N. A., et al.: "Yanamamö Hallucinogens: Anthropological, Botanical and Chemical Findings," *Current Anthropology*, 7, No. 1 (1971), pp. 3–32.

Chamberlain, A. F.: "Kootenay 'Medicine-Men'," *Journal of American Folk-Lore*, No. 14 (1960), pp. 95–99.

Chessner, B.: "The Anthropomorphic Personal Guardian Spirit in Aboriginal South America," *Journal for Latin American Lore*, 1, No. 2 (1975), pp. 107–126.

Chew, Geoffry F.: "'Bootstrap': A Scientific Idea?" *Science*, 161 (23 May 1968), pp. 762–765.

Christiansen, Reidar Th.: "Ectasy and Arctic Religion," *Studia Septentrionalia*, No. 4 (1953), pp. 19–92.

Closs, Alois: "Die Ekstase des Schamanen," *Ethnos*, 34, No. 1–4 (1969), pp. 70–89.

Cloutier, David: *Spirit Spirit*, Providence, 1980.

Coate, H. H. J.: "The Rai and the Third Eye. North-West Australian Beliefs," *Oceania*, No. 37 (1966/67), pp. 93–123.

Coe, Michael D.: "Shamanism in the Bunun Tribe, Central Formosa," *Ethnos*, 20, No. 4 (1955), pp. 181–198.

Corlett, William T.: *The Medicine-Man of the American Indian and his Cultural Background*, Springfield 1935.

Crashing Thunder: "The Teachings of my Father," in: Jesse D. Jennings and E. A. Hoebel (Ed.): *Readings in Anthropology*, New York 1955.

Crookall, Robert: *Out-of-the-Body Experiences*, New York 1970.

Csikszentmihalyi, Mihaly: "Play and Intrinsic Rewards," *Journal of Humanistic Psychology*, 15, No. 3 (1975), pp. 41–63.
_____. "The Flow Experience," in: Daniel Goleman and Richard J. Davidson (Ed.): *Consciousness, Brain, States of Awareness, and Mysticism*, New York 1979.

Curtis, E. S.: *The North American Indian*, Vol. 10, Cambridge 1915.

David-Neel, Alexandra: *Heilige und Hexer*, Leipzig 1931.
———. *Magic and Mystery in Tibet*, London 1984, Unwin paperback.
Deikman, A. J.: "Deautomatization and the Mystical Experience," *Psychiatry*, No. 29 (1966), 329–338.
Deltgen, Florian: "Culture, Drug and Personality," *Ethnomedizin*, 5, No. 1/2 (1978).
Derlon, Pierre: *Unter Hexern und Zauberern. Die geheimen Traditionen der Zigeuner*, Basle 1976.
Devereux, George: "Mohave Soul Concepts," *American Anthropologist*, No. 39 (1937), pp. 417–422.
Diamond, Stanley: "A Revolutionary Discipline," in: Walter Goldschmidt (Ed.): *Exploring the Ways of Mankind*, New York 1960.
———. "Anthropology in Question," in: Hymes 1969 (a).
———. (Ed.): *Primitive Views of the World*, New York 1969 (b).
———. *Kritik der Zivilisation*, Frankfurt 1976.
Diószegi, Vilmos: "Die Überreste des Schamanismus in der ungarischen Volkskultur," *Acta Ethnographica*, No. 7 (1958), pp. 97–134.
———. "Der Werdegang zum Schamanen bei den nordöstlichen Sojoten," *Acta Ethnographica*, No. 8 (1959), 269–291.
———. "Die Typen und interethnischen Beziehungen der Schamanentrommel bei den Selkupen (Osjak-Samojeden)," *Acta Ethnographica*, No. 9 (1960), pp. 159–179.
———. "Problems of Mongolian Shamanism," *Acta Ethnographica*, No. 10 (1961), pp. 195–206.
———. "Tuva Shamanism: Intraethnic Differences and Interethnic Analogies," *Acta Ethnographica*, No. 11 (1962), pp. 143–190.
———. (Ed.): *Glaubenswelt und Folklore der sibirischen Völker*, Budapest 1963 (a).
———. "Zum Problem der ethnischen Homogenität des tofischen (karagassischen) Schamanismus," in: Diószegi 1963 (a).
———. "Denkmäler der samojedischen Kultur im Schamanismus der ostsajanischen Völker," *Acta Ethnographica*, 12, No. 1–2 (1963) (c), pp. 139–178.
———. *Tracing Shamans in Siberia*, Oosterhout 1968.
———. and Hoppál, M. (Ed.): *Shamanism in Siberia*, Budapest 1978.
Dixon, Roland B.: "Some Shamans of Northern California," *Journal of American Folk-Lore*, No. 17 (1904), pp. 23–27.
———. "Some Aspects of the American Shaman," *Journal of American Folk-Lore*, No. 21 (1908), pp. 1–13.
Dobkin de Rios, Marlene: *Visionary Vine. Psychedelic Healing in the Peruvian Amazon*, San Francisco 1972.
———. "Plant Hallucinogens, Out-of-Body Experiences and New World Monumental Earthworks," in: Du Toit 1977.
Donner, Kai: *Among the Samojeds in Siberia*, New Haven 1954.
Dorsey, J. Owen: "A Study of Siouan Cultse," *11th Annual Report of the Bureau of Ethnology*, 1889–1890, pp. 361–549. Washington, D.C., 1894.

Downs, James: *The Two Worlds of the Washo*, New York 1966.

Drury, Nevill: *The Path of the Chameleon*, St. Helier, Jersey, 1973.

_____. *The Shaman and the Magician*, London 1982.

Duerr, H. P. (Ed.): Der Wissenschaftler und das Irrationale, Bd. 1, Frankfurt am Main, 1981.

Dusenberry, Verne: "Visions among the Pend d'Oreille Indians," *Ethnos*, 24 No. 1–2 (1959), pp. 52–57.

_____. "The Significance of the Sacred Pipes to the Gros Ventre of Montana," *Ethnos*, 26 No. 1–2 (1961), pp. 12–29.

Du Toit, Brian M. (Ed.): *Drugs, Rituals and Altered States of Consciousness*, Rotterdam 1977.

Eaton, Evelyn: "Towards Initiation," *Parabola*, 1, No. 1 (1976), pp. 42–53.

_____. *I Send A Voice*, Wheaton, Ill., 1978.

Eder, Matthias; "Schamanismus in Japan," *Paideuma*, 4/7 (1958), pp. 367–380.

Edsman, Carl-Martin, (Ed.): *Studies in Shamanism*, Stockholm 1967.

Eger, Susan, and Collings, Peter R.: "Huichol Woman's Art," in: Abrams 1978.

Ehrenberg, G.B.: "Homosexualität und Transvestition im Schamanismus," *Anthropos*, No. 115 (1970), pp. 189–228.

Einstein, Albert: *Mein Weltbild*, Frankfurt 1977.

Eliade, Mircea: "Einführende Betrachtung über den Schamanismus," *Paideuma*, No. 5 (1951), pp. 87–97.

_____. *Schamanismus und archaische Ekstasetechnik*, Zürich 1957 (a).

_____. *Das Heilige und das Profane*, Hamburg 1957 (b).

_____. *Yoga. Unsterblichkeit und Freiheit*, Zürich 1960 (a).

_____. "Spiritual Thread, Sūtrātman, Catena Aurea," *Paideuma*, 7, No. 4/6 (1960) (b), pp. 225–234.

_____. "Recent Works on Shamanism. A Review Article," *History of Religions*, 1, No. 1 (1961) (a), pp. 152–186.

_____. *Mythen, Träume und Mysterien*, Salzburg 1961 (b).

_____. *The Two and the One*, New York 1965.

_____. *Kosmos und Geschichte*, Munich 1966.

_____. *Australian Religions. An Introduction*, London 1973.

_____. *Das Okkulte und die moderne Welt*, Salzburg 1978.

Elkin, A.P.: "Notes on the Psychic Life of the Australian Aborigines," *Mankind*, 2, No. 3 (1937), p. 50.

_____. *The Australian Aborigines*, London 1938.

_____. *Aboriginal Men of High Degree*, Sydney 1945.

Elwin, Verrier: *The Religion of an Indian Tribe*, Oxford 1955.

Emsheimer, E.: "Schamanentrommel und Trommelbaum," *Ethnos*, No. 11 (1946), pp. 166–181.

_____. "Zur Ideologie der lappischen Zaubertrommel," *Ethnos*, No. 9 (1944), pp. 141 to 169.

Enderwitz, Ulrich: *Schamanismus und Psychoanalyse*, Wiesbaden 1977.

Estrada, Alvaro: *Maria Sabina. Botin der beiligen Pilze*, Munich 1980.

BIBLIOGRAPHY

Evans, Ivan: *Papers of the Ethnology and Archaeology of the Malay Peninsula*, Cambridge 1927, p. 20.

Evans-Pritchard, E.E.: *Theorien über primitive Religion*, Frankfurt 1968.

Fabrega, Horacio, and Silver, Daniel: "Some Social and Psychological Properties of Zinacanteco Shamans," *Behavioral Science*, 15, No. 6 (1970), pp. 471–486.

Fairchild, William P.: "Shamanism in Japan," *Folklore Studies*, No. 21 (1962), pp. 1–122.

Findeisen, Hans: "Schamanentum im tungusischen Kinderspiel," *Zeitschrift für Ethnologie*, 78, No. 2 (1953), pp. 307–308.

_____. "Besessene als Priester," *Kosmos*, No. 3 (1954), pp. 148–154.

_____. *Das Tier als Gott, Dämon und Ahne*, Stuttgart 1956 (a).

_____. "Okkulte Begebnisse im schamanischen Raum," *Abhandlungen aus dem Institut für Menschen- und Menschheitskunde*, Augsburg 1956 (b).

_____. "Sowjetwissenschaftliche Thesen über das Schamanentum," *Abhandlungen und Aufsätze aus dem Institut für Menschen-und Menschheitskunde*, No. 30, Augsburg 1956 (c).

_____. *Schamanentum*, Stuttgart 1957 (a).

_____. "Die 'Schamanenkrankheit' als Initiation," *Abhandlungen aus dem Institut für Menschen- und Menschheitskunde*, Augsburg 1957 (b).

_____. "Das Schamanentum als spiritistische Religion," *Ethnos*, 25, No. 3–4 (1960), pp. 192–213.

Fischer, Hans: *Studien über Seelenvorstellungen in Ozeanien*, Munich 1965.

Fischer, Roland: "Hallucinations Can Reveal Creative Imagination," *Fields within Fields*, No. 11 (1974), pp. 29–33.

_____. "Cartography of Conscious States: Integration of East and West," in: Sugerman/Tarter 1978.

_____. "State-Bound Knowledge: 'I Can't Remember What I Said Last Night, But It Must Have Been Good'," in: Woods 1980.

Fock, Niels: "Waiwai — Religion and Society of an Amazonian Tribe," *National Museets Skrifter Ethnografisk Raekke*, 8, Copenhagen 1963.

Forde, C. Daryll: *Ethnography of the Yuma Indiana*, Berkeley 1931.

Fornander, Abraham, and Thrum, Thomas G.: *Fornander Collection of Hawaiian Antiquities and Folk-Lore*, Honolulu 1919.

Fortune, Reo F.: *Sorcerers of Dobu*, London 1932.

Fournier, Alain: "A Preliminary Report on the Puimbo and the Ngiami: The Sunuwar Shamans of Sabra," in: Hitchcock/Jones 1976.

Frazer, G. J.: *Man, God and Immortality*, London 1927.

Friedrich, Adolf: "Das Bewußtsein eines Naturvolkes. Von Haushalt und Ursprung des Lebens," *Paideuma*, 6, H. 2 (1955): pp. 47–53."

Friedrich, Adolf, and Buddruss, Georg (Ed. and Transl.): *Schamanengeschichten aus Sibirien* (by Ksenofontov, 1930), Munich 1955.

Freuchen, Peter: *Book of the Eskimo*, Greenwich, Conn., 1961.

Furst, Peter T.,: "Huichol Conceptions of the Soul," *Folklore Amerikas*, 27, No. 2 (1967), pp. 39–106.

_____. *Flesh of the Gods. The Ritual Use of Hallucinogens*, New York 1972.
_____. *Hallucinogens and Culture*, San Francisco 1976.
_____. "The Roots and Continuities of Shamanism," in: A. Trueblood Brotzky, R. Daneswich and N. Johnson: *Stones, Bones and Skin: Ritual and Shamanic Art*, Toronto 1977 (a).
_____. "'High-States' in Culture-Historical Perspective," in: Zinberg 1977 (b).
Gabbard, Glen O., Twemlow, S.W., and Jones, F.C.: "Do 'Near Death Experiences' Occur Only Near Death?," *The Journal of Nervous and Mental Disease*, 169, No. 6 (1981), pp. 374–377.
Gallagher, Hugh G.: *Etok: A Story of Eskimo Power*, New York 1974.
_____. "Over Easy: A Cultural Anthropoligist's Near-Death Experience," *Anabiosis: The Journal for Near-Death Studies*, 2, No. 2 (1982), pp. 140–149.
Garfield, Charles A.: "Ego Functioning, Fear of Death, and Altered States of Consciousness," in: C. A. Garfield (Ed.): *Rediscovery of the Body*, New York 1977.
Garrett, Eileen J.: *Adventures in the Supernormal*, New York 1968 (1949).
Gayton, A. H.: "The Orpheus Myth in North America," *Journal of American Folklore*, No. 48, (1935), pp. 263–293.
Geertz, Chifford: *The Religion of Java*, Glencoe, Ill., 1960.
Gillin, John: "The Making of a Witchdoctor," *Psychiatry*, 19, No. 2 (1956), pp. 131 to 136.
Gillham, Charles E.: *Medicine Men of Hooper Bay*, London 1955.
Göbel, Thomas: *Erde, die die Seele trägt*, Stuttgart 1976.
Goleman, Daniel: "Perspectives on Psychology, Reality and the Study of Consciousness," *The Journal of Transpersonal Psychology*, 6, No. 1 (1974), pp. 73–85.
_____. and Davidson Richard J. (Ed.): *Consciousness: Brain, States of Awareness and Mysticism*, New York 1979.
Good, C. M., Kimani, V., and Lawry, J. M.: "Gũkunũra mũndũ: The Initiation of a Kikuyu Medicine Man," *Anthropos*, 75, No. 1/2 (1980), pp. 87–116.
Green, Celia: *Out-of-the-Body Experience*, New York 1968.
Greschat, Hans-Jürgen: *Mana und Tap. Die Religion der Maori auf Neuseeland*, Berlin 1980.
Grey, George: "The Two Sorcerers," in: Lessa/Vogt 1979.
Grof, Stanislav: *Realms of the Human Unconscious. Observations from LSD Research*, New York 1976.
_____. "Modern Consciousness Research and the Quest for a New Paradigm." *Re-Vision*, 2, No. 1 (1979) 41–52.
_____. "Die Erfahrung des Todes. Beobachten und Einsichten aus der psychedelischen Forschung," *Integrative Therapie*, No. 2/3 (1980), pp. 257–280.
_____. and Joan Halifax: *The Human Encounter with Death*, New York 1977.
_____. and Christina: *Beyond Death. The Gates of Consciousness*, London 1980.
Grosso, Michael: "Plato and Out-of-the Body Experiences," *Journal of the American Society for Psychical Research*, 69, No. 1 (1975), pp. 61–74.

Grube, Wilhelm: "Das Schamanentum bei den Golden," *Globus*, No. 71 (1897), pp. 89–93.

Gruber, Elmar: *Tranceformation. Schamanismus und die Auflösung der Ordnung*, Basle 1982.

Gusinde, Martin: *Die Feuerlandindianer*, Vienna 1931–1974, 3 Vols.: "Der Medizinmann bei den südamerikanischen Indianern," Sonderdruck aus den *Mitteilungen der Anthropologischen Gesellschaft in Wien*, No. 62, Vienna 1932.

Gussow, Zachary: "A Preliminary Report of Kayak-Angst among the Eskimo of West Greenland: A Study in Sensory Deprivation," *International Journal of Social Psychiatry*, No. 9 (1963), pp. 18–26.

Haas, Jochen U.: *Schamanentum und Psychiatrie*, Dissertation, Freiburg i.Br. 1976.

Haile, Berard: "A Note on the Navaho Visionary," *American Anthropologist*, No. 42 (1940), p. 359.

Hajdú, P.: "Von der Klassifikation der samojedischen Schamanen," in: Diószegi 1963.

Halifax, Joan: *Die andere Wirklichkeit der Schamanen, Erfahrungsberichte von Magiern, Medizinmännern und Visionären, Berne, Munich, Vienna* 1981.

_____. "The Sacred Way of the Wounded Healer," *Laughing Man*, 2, No. 4 (1981), pp. 9–12.

_____. *Shaman, The Wounded Healer*, London 1982.

Hallowell, A. Irving: "The Passing of the Midewiwin in the Lake Winnipeg Region," *American Anthropologist*, No. 38 (1936), pp. 32–51.

_____. "Ontologie, Verhalten und Weltbild der Ojibwa," in: Tedlock 1975.

Handelman, Don: "The Development of a Washo Shaman," *Ethnology*, No. 6 (1967) (a), pp. 444–464.

_____. "Transcultural Shamanic Healing: A Washo Example," *Ethnos*, No. 1–4 (1967) (b), pp. 149–166.

_____. "Shamanizing on an Empty Stomach," Review of Julian Silverman: *Shamans and Acute Schizophrenia*, *American Anthropologist*, No. 70 (1968), pp. 353–356.

_____. "Aspects of the Moral Compact of a Washo Shaman," *Anthropological Quarterly*, 45, No. 2 (April 1972), pp. 84–101.

Hargous, Sabine: *Beschwörer der Seelen. Das magische Universum der südamerikanischen Indianer*, Basle 1976.

Harmon, Willis W.: "The New Copernican Revolution," *The Journal of Transpersonal Psychology*, 1, No. 2 (Autumn 1969), pp. 21–30.

Harner, Michael J.: "Jîvaro Souls," in: John Middleton (Ed.): *Gods and Rituals*, London 1967.

_____. (Ed.): *Hallucinogens and Shamanism*, Oxford 1973 (a).

_____. "The Sound of Rushing Water," (b), in: Harner 1973 (a).

_____. "Common Themes in South American Indian Yagé Experience," (c),in: Harner 1973 (a).

_____. "The Jivaro. People of the Sacred Waterfalls," New York 1973 (d).

——. *The Way of the Shaman*, San Francisco 1980.

——. "The Way of the Shaman," Interview in: *Laughing Man*, 2, No. 4 (1981), pp. 24–29.

Harva, U. (= U. Holmberg): "Die religiösen Vorstellungen der altaischen Völker," *Folklore Fellows Communications*, No. 52, p. 125, Helsinki 1938.

Harvey, Youngsook Kim: *Six Korean Women: The Socialisation of Shamans*, St. Paul 1979.

——. "Possession Sickness and Women Shamans in Korea," in: Nancy A. Falk and Rita M. Gross (Ed.): *Unspoken Worlds. Woman's Religious Lives in Non-Western Cultures*, San Francisco 1980.

Heissig, Walter: "Schamanen und Geisterbeschwörer in Küriye-Banner," *Folklore Studies*, No. 3 (1944), pp. 39–72.

Hermanns, Matthias: *Die religiös-magische Weltanschauung der Primitivstämme Indiens*, Wieswbaden 1964–1973, 3 Vols.

——. *Das National-Epos der Tibeter. Gling König Ge Sar*, Regensburg 1965.

——. "Medizinmann, Zauberer, Schamane, Künstler in der Welt der frühen Jäger," *Anthropos*, 61, No. 3/4 (1966), pp. 883–889.

——. *Schamanen — Pseudoschamanen, Erlöser und Heilbringer*, Wiesbaden 1970, 3 Vols.

Hitchcock, John T.: "Nepalese Shamanism and the Classic Inner Asian Tradition," in: *History of Religions*, 7, No. 2 (1967), pp. 149–158.

——. "Aspects of Bhujel Shamanism," in: Hitchcock/Jones 1976.

——. and Jones, Rex L.: *Spirit Possession in the Nepal Himalayas*, Warminster 1976.

Hoffman, Helmut: *Symbolik der tibetischen Religionen und des Schamanismus*, Stuttgart 1967.

——. "Erscheinungsformen des tibetischen Schamanismus," in: Zutt 1972.

Hoffman, Walter James: "The Mide'wiwin or 'Grand Medicine Society' of the Ojibwa," *7th Report of the Bureau of Ethnology*, pp. 143–300. Washington, D.C., 1891.

——. "Schamanentum bei den Ojibwa und Menomini," *Globus*, No. 61 (1892), pp. 92–95.

Holm, Gustav: "Ethnological Sketch of the Angmagsalik Eskimo," in: William Thalbitzer (Ed.): *The Ammasalik Eskimo*, Copenhagen 1914.

Holmberg, Uno: "Die Religion der Tschermissen," *FCC Communications*, 61, Helsinki 1962.

——. "Finno-Ugric, Siberian," Vol. 1 in: C. J. A. MacCulloch (Ed.): *The Mythology of all Races*, New York 1964.

Holtved, Erik: "Eskimo Shamanism," in: Edsman 1967.

Honko, Lauri: "Role-taking of the Shaman," *Temenos*, No. 4 (1969), pp. 25–55.

Horse Capture, George (Ed.): *The Seven Visions of Bull Lodge*, Ann Arbor, Michigan, 1980.

Howitt, Alfred W.: "On Australian Medicine Men or Doctors and Wizards of Some Australian Tribes," *The Journal of the Anthropological Institute of Great Britain and Ireland*, No. 16 (1887), pp. 23–59.

_____. *The Native Tribes of South-East Australia*, London 1904.

_____. "Australian Medicine Men and Magic," in: Thomas 1909.

Huffman, Phyllis: "The Incredible World of Thought," *Many Smokes*, 14, No. 1 (1980). pp. 24–26.

Hultkrantz, Åke: *Conceptions of the Soul Amoing North American Indians*, Stockholm 1953.

_____. "Die Religion der Lappen," in: I. Paulson, A. Hultkrantz and K. Jettmar (Ed.): *Die Religionen Nordasiens und der amerikanischen Arktis*, Vol. 3, in: C. M. Schröder (Ed.): *Die Religionen der Menschheit*,Stuttgart 1962.

_____. "The Contribution of the Study of North American Indian Religions to the History of Religions," in: Capps 1976.

_____. "Ecological and Phenomenological Aspects of Shamanism," in: Diószegi/Hoppál 1978.

_____. *The Religion of the American Indians*, Berkeley 1979 (1967).

_____. "Ritual und Geheimnis: Über die Kunst der Medizinmänner, oder: Was der Herr Professor verschwieg," in: Duerr 1981.

Humphrey, B.: "Paranormal Occurrences Among Preliterate Peoples," *Journal of Parapsychology*, No. 8 (1944), pp. 214–229.

Hung-Youn, Cho: *Koreanischer Schamanismus*, Hamburgisches Museum für Völkerkunde, Hamburg 1982.

Huxley, Aldous: *Die Pforten der Wahrnehmung. Himmel und Hölle*, Munich 1970.

_____. "Visionary Experience," in: White 1972.

_____. *Moksha. Writings on Psychedelics and the Visionary Experience* (1931–1963), edited by Michael Horowitz and Cynthia Palmer, New York 1977.

Hymes, Dell (Ed.): *Reinventing Anthropology*, New York 1969.

Iokhel'son, Vladimir: "Religion and Myths of the Koryak. The Jesup North Pacific Expedition," 1905–1908, No. 6. 1. *Memoir of the Museum of Natural History*, Leiden.

_____. "The Yukaghir and the Yukaghirized Tungus. The Jesup North Pacific Expedition," No. 9, 2. *Memoir of the Museum of Natural History*, Leiden 1926.

Itkonen, T. I.: "Der 'Zweikampf' der lappischen Zauberer (Noai'di) um eine Wildrentierherde," *Journal de la Société Finno-Ougrienne*, No. 62 (1960), pp. 27–76.

James, William: *The Principles of Psychology*, New York 1890, 2 Vols.

_____. *Die religiöse Erfahrung in ihrer Mannigfaltigkeit*, Leipzig 1907.

_____. *Memoires and Studies*, New York 1912.

_____. "The Energies of Man," in: Ralph B. Perry (Ed.): *Essays on Faith and Morals*, New York 1962.

_____. "Subjective Effects of Nitrous Oxide," in: Tart 1969.

Jarring, Gunnar: "A Note on Shamanism in Eastern Turkestan," *Ethnos*, 26, No. 1–2 (1961), pp. 1–4.

Jettmar, Karl: "Schamanismus in Nord- und Zentalasien," in: Zutt 1972.

Joergensen, Ole: *Sjael göer dig smuk*, Århus 1981.

Johnson, Frederick: "Notes on Micmac Shamanism," *Primitive Man*, 16, No. 3–4 (1943), pp. 53–80.

Johnston, Basil: *Und Manitu erschuf die Welt. Mythen und Visionen der Ojibwa*, Cologne 1979.

Johnston, Thomas F.: "Auditory Driving, Hallucinogens, and Music-Color Synesthesia in Tsonga Ritual," in: Du Toit 1977.

Joki, A. J.: "Notes on Selkup Shamanism," in: Diószegi/Hoppál 1978.

Jones, David Earle: *Sanapia: Comanche Medicine Woman*, New York 1972.

⸺. "Face the Ghost," *Phoenix. New Directions in the Study of Man*, 4, No. 1 and 2 (1980), pp. 53–57.

Jones, Rex L.: "Shamanism in South Asia: A Preliminary Survey," *History of Religions*, 7, No. 4 (1968), pp. 330–347.

Jules-Rosette, B.: "The Conversion Experience," *Africa*, No. 7 (1976), pp. 132–164.

⸺. "The Veil of Objectivity: Prophecy, Divination, and Social Inquiry," *American Anthropologist*, No. 80 (1978), pp. 549–570.

Jung, C. G.: *Erinnerungen, Träume, Gedanken*, edited by A. Jaffé, Zürich 1961.

Kalweit, Holger: "Alles ist eins," *Esotera*, No. 5 (1981), pp. 402–409.

⸺. "Transpersonal Anthropology and the Comparison of Cultures," *Phoenix Journal of Transpersonal Anthropology*, 5, No. 2 (1981), pp. 97–105.

⸺. "Die Entfesselung des Bewußtseins," *Psychologie heute*, No. 7 (1982), pp. 54–60.

⸺. "Das Paradox ist unser Barometer für Erleuchtung," *Psychologie heute*, No. 8 (1982), pp. 46–53.

⸺. "Der Trickster. Ein Nachwort zu 'Castaneda'," *Curare*, No. 6 (1983), pp. 91–92.

⸺. "Gewiß, es gehört immer zum Wesen der Anthropologie, die Dinge von außen zu betrachten," *Curare*, No. 7 (1983), pp. 203–208.

⸺. (Ed.): *Frank Hamilton Cushing. Ein weißer Indianer. Mein Leben mit den Zuni*, Olten 1983.

⸺. "Formen transpersonaler Psychotherapie bei nicht-westlichen Kulturen," *Integrative Therapie*, (1984).

Karajalainen, K. F.: "Die Religionen der Jugra-Völker," *FF Communications*, No. 63, Helsinki 1927.

Katz, Fred, and Dobkin de Rios, Marlene: "Hallucinogenic Music: An Analysis of the Role of Whistling in Peruvian Ayahuasca Healing Sessions," *Journal of American Folklore*, No. 84 (1971), pp. 320–327.

Katz, Richard: "Education for Transcendence: Lessons from the !Kung Zhu/twasi," *The Journal of Transpersonal Psychology*, 5, No. 2 (1973), pp. 136–155.

⸺. "Education as Transformation: Becoming a Healer Among the !Kung and Fijians," *Harvard Educational Review*, 51, No. 1 (1981), pp. 57–78.

⸺. *Boiling Energy: Community Healing Among the Kalahari !Kung*, Cambridge, Mass. 1982.

Kelly, Isabel T.: "Chemehuevi Shamanism," in: *Essays in Anthropology*, Presented to A. L. Kroeber, Berkeley 1936.

_____ "Southern Paiute Shamanism," *Anthropological Record*, 2, No. 4 (1939).

Kelsey, Theodore: "Flying 'Gods' of Hawaii," in: *Full Moon: A Report from the Islands*, 1, No. 3 and 4 (1980),1.

Kensinger, Kenneth M.: "Banisteriopsis Usage among the Peruvian Cashinahua," in: Harner 1973 (a).

Keutzer, C.: "Whatever Turns You On: Triggers to Transcendent Experiences," *Journal of Humanistic Psychology*, 18 No. 3 (1978), pp. 77–80.

Kiesewetter, Karl: Geschichte des neueren Okkultismus, mit einem Anhang von Ludwig Kuhlenbeck: "Der Okkultismus der nordamerikanischen Indianer," Leipzig 1909.

Kiev, Ari, (Ed.): *Magic, Faith, and Healing*, New York 1964.

Kihm, Walter: *Zur Symbolik im Schamanismus*, Dissertation, Freiburg i. Br. 1974.

Kikuchi, William K.: "The Fireball in Hawaiian Folklore," *Full Moon: A Report from the Islands*, 1, No. 1 (1980), pp. 6–11.

Kim, K.: "Psychoanalytic Consideration of Korean Shamanism," *Journal of the Korean Neuropsychiatric Association*, 11, No. 2 (1972), pp. 121–129.

Knoll-Greiling, Ursula: "Die sozial-psychologische Funktion der Schamanen," *Beiträge zur Gesellungs- und Völkerwissenschaft*, Berlin 1950.

_____ "Berufung und Berufungserlebnis bei den Schamanen," *Tribus. Jahrbuch des Linden-Museums Stuttgart*, No. 2/3, (1952/1953), pp. 227–238.

Knudtson, Peter H.: "Flora, Shaman of the Wintu," *Natural History*, 84, No. 5 (1975), pp. 12–13, 16–17.

Köpping, Klaus-Peter: "Bewußtseinszustände und Stufen der Wirklichkeit," in: *Kölner Zeitschrift für Soziologie und Sozialpsychologie*, 24, No. 4 (1972), pp. 821–835.

Kohl, Johann Georg: *Kitschi-Gami oder Erzählungen vom Oberen See*, Bremen 1859, Vol. II.

Krader, Lawrence: "The Shamanistic Tradition of the Buryats (Siberia)," *Anthropos*, No. 70 (1975), pp. 105–144.

"_____ "Shamanism: Theory and History in Buryat Society," Diószegi/ Hoppál 1978.

Kramer, Fritz: *Verkehrte Welten. Zur Ethnographie des 19. Jahrhunderts*, Frankfurt 1977.

Kremsmayer, Heimo: "Schamanismsus und Seelenvorstellungen im alten China," *Archiv für Völkerkunde*, No. 9 (1954), pp. 66–78.

Kreutzer, Caroline S.: "Physics and Consciousness," *Journal of Humanistic Psychology*, 22, No. 2 (1982), pp. 74–90.

Kroeber, A. L.: "The Eskimo of Smith Sound," *Bulletin of the American Museum of Natural History*, No. 12 (1899).

_____ *The Religions of the Indians of California*, Berkeley 1906.

_____ "Walapai Ethnography," *Memoirs of the American Anthropological Association*, No. 42 (1935).

_____ and Watermann, T. T. (Ed.): *Source Book in Anthropology*, New York 1965.

Kroeber, Theodora: *Ishi in Two Worlds*, Berkeley 1961.

Kunze, Gerhard: *Ihr baut die Windmühlen — den Wind rufen wir. Alternative Technik und Stammestradition*, Munich 1982.

La Barre, Weston: *The Ghost Dance*, New York 1972.

_____. Anthropological Perspectives on Hallucination and Hallucinogens," in: R. K. Siegel and L. J. West (Ed.): *Hallucinations*, New York 1975.

Lafleur, Laurence J.: "On the Midé of the Ojibway," *American Anthropologist*, No. 42 (1940), pp. 706–708.

Lamb, F. Bruce: *Der weiße Indio vom Amazonas*, Berne, Munich, Vienna, 1982.

Lame Deer/John Fire and Erdoes, Richard: *Lame Deer, Sioux Medicine Man*, London 1980, Quartet Paperback.

Landes, Ruth: *Ojibwa Religion and the Midéwiwin*, London 1968.

Langdon, E. Jean: "Yagé Among the Siona: Cultural Patterns in Visions," in: Browman/Schwarz 1979.

Lankenau, H. von: "Die Schamanen und das Schamanenwesen," *Globus*, No. 22 (1872), pp. 278–283.

Lantis, Margaret: "The Social Culture of the Nunivak Eskimo," *Transactions of the American Philosophical Society*, 35, Part 3 (1946).

_____. "The Religion of the Eskimo," in: V. T. A. Ferm (Ed.): *Forgotten Religions*, New York 1950.

Larsen, Stephen: *The Shaman's Doorway*, New York 1976.

Laski, Marghanita: *Ectasy: A Study of Some Secular and Religious Experiences*, London 1961.

Lauf, Detlef-Ingo: *Symbole. Verschiedenheit und Einheit in östlicher und westlicher Kiltur*, Frankfurt 1976.

Laufer, Berthold: "Origin of the Word Shaman," *American Anthropologist*, No. 19 (1917), pp. 361–371.

Layard, J. W.: "Shamanism. An Analysis Based on Comparison with the Flying Tricksters of Malekula," *Journal of the Royal Anthropological Institute*, No. 60 (1930), pp. 525–550.

Lechner-Knecht, Sigrid: *Reise ins Zwischenreich: Gegegnungen mit Wundertätern und Zauberpriestern*, Freiburg i.Br. 1978.

Lee, Jung Young: *Korean Shamanistic Rituals*, The Hague 1981.

Lee, R. B., and DeVore, I. (Ed.): *Kalahari Hunter-Gatherers. Studies of the !Kung San and Their Neighbors*, Cambridge, Mass., 1976.

Lehtisalo, T.: "Der Tod und die Wiedergeburt des künftigen Schamanen," *Journal de la Société Finno-Ougrienne*, No. 48 (1937), pp. 1–34.

LeShan, Lawrence: *The Medium, the Mystic, and the Physicist*, London 1966.

_____. "Physicists and Mystics: Similarities in World View," *The Journal of Transpersonal Psychology*, 1, No. 2 (1969), pp. 1–20.

Lessa, William A., and Vogt, Evon Z. (Ed.): *Reader in Comparative Religion*, New York 1979.

Lévi-Strauss, Claude: "Die moderne Krise der Anthropologie," *Unesco Kurier*, 2, No. 11 (Nov. 1961), pp. 1–15.

_____. *Das wilde Denken*, Frankfurt 1968.

_____. *Strukturale Anthropologie*, Frankfurt 1972.

———. "Medizinmänner und Psychoanalyse (1956)," *Integrative Therapie*, 5, No. 4 (1979), pp. 297–302.

———. *Mythos und Bedeutung*, Frankfurt 1980.

Lewis, I. M.: *Ecstatic Religion*, Harmondsworth 1971.

Lex, Barbara W.: "Altered States of Consciousness in Northern Iroquoian Ritual," in: Bharati 1976 (b).

Loaiza, Hector: *Wañu Pura. Le chemin des Sorciers des Andes*, Paris 1976.

Loeb, E. M.: "The Shaman of Niue," *American Anthropologist*, No. 26 (1924), pp. 394–402.

———. "Shaman and Seer," *American Anthropologist*, No. 31 (1929), pp. 60–84.

Lommel, Andreas: "Traum und Bild bei den Primitiven in Nordwest-Australien," *Psyche*, 5, No. 3 (1951), pp. 187–209.

———. *Die Unambal. Ein Stamm in Nordwest-Australien*, Monographien zur Völkerkunde, No. 11, Hamburgisches Museum für Völkerkunde, Hamburg 1952.

———. "Shamanism, the Beginnings of Art," (17 reviews of Lommel's book), *Current Anthropology*, 11, No. 1 (1970), pp. 39–48.

———. *Shamanism in Australia. Commemorative Publication for T. G. H. Strehlow*, Adelaide 1980.

———. *Schamanen und Medizinmänner. Magie und Mystik früher Kulturen*, Munich 1980 (1965).

Lone Dog, Louise: *Strange Journey. The Vision Life of a Psychic Indian Woman*, Healdsburg, Calif., 1964.

Long Lance and Buffalo Child: *Long Lance. The Autobiography of a Blackfoot Indian Chief*, London 1976 (1928).

Lowie, Robert H.: "Beiträge zur Völkerkunde Nordamerikas," *Mitteilungen aus dem Museum für Völkerkunde, Hamburg*, No. 23 (1951).

———. *The Crow Indians*, New York 1924.

———. *Indians of the Plains*, New York 1963.

———. "The Vision Quest Among the North American Indians," (a), in: Lessa/Vogt 1979.

———. "Shamans and Priests Among the Plains Indians," (b), in: Lessa/Vogt 1979.

Lublinsky, Ida: "Der Medizinmann bei den Naturvölkern Südamerikas," *Zeitschrift für Ethnologie*, No. 52 (1921), pp. 234–263.

Lvova, E. L.: "On the Shamanism of the Chulym Turks," in: Diószegi/Hoppál 1978.

Macdonald, A. W.: "Preliminary Notes on some jhākri of the Muglan," in: Hitchcock/Jones 1976.

MacIntosh, A.: "Beliefs about Out-of-the-Body Experiences Among the Elma, Gulf Kamea and Rigo Peoples of Papua New Guinea," *Journal of the American Society for Psychical Research*, No. 50 (1980), pp. 460–478.

Maddox, John Lee: *The Medicine Man*, New York 1923.

Madsen, William: "Shamanism in Mexico," *Southwestern Journal of Anthropology*, No. 11 (1955), pp. 48–57.

Mails, Thomas E.: *Sundancing at Rosebud and Pine Ridge*, Sioux Falls 1978.

_____. *Fools Crow*, New York 1979.

Mandel, Arnold J.: "The Neurochemistry of Religious Insight and Ectasy," in: Berrin 1978.

Manker, Ernst: *Die lappische Zaubertrommel*, Stockholm 1938.

Martino, Ernst de: *Magic, Primitive and Modern*, Sydney 1972.

Maslow, Abraham H.: *Religions, Values, and Peak-Experiences*, New York 1964.

_____. "Theory Z," *The Journal of Transpersonal Psychology*, 1, No. 2 (1969), pp. 31–48.

_____. *The Farther Reaches of Human Nature*, New York 1971.

_____. *Psychologie des Seins*, Munich 1973 (1968).

_____. Die Psychologie der Wissenschaft, Munich 1977 (1966).

Maxwell, W. W.: "Shamanism in Perak," *Journal of the Straits Branch of the Royal Asiatic Society*, (Dec. 1883). No. 222–232.

McBride, L. R.: *The Kahuna, Versatile Mystics of Old Hawaii*, Hilo, Hawaii.

McIlwraith, T. F.: *The Bella Coola Indians*, Toronto 1948.

Meier, P. Joseph: "Die Zauberei bei den Küstenbewohnern der Gazelle-Halbinsel, Neupommern, Südsee," *Anthropos*, No. 8 (1913), pp. 1–11, 285–305, 688–713.

Meighan, Clement W., and Ridell, Francis A.: *The Maru Cult of the Pomo Indians: A California Ghost Dance Survival*, Southwest Museum, Los Angeles 1972.

Melville, Leinani: *Children of the Rainbow*. Wheaton, Ill., 1969.

Mercier, Mario: *Chamanisme et Chamans*, Paris 1977.

Messerschmidt, Donald A.: "Ethnographic Observations of Gurung Shamanism in Lamjung District," in: Hitchcock/Jones 1976.

Messner, Reinhold: *Grenzbereich Todeszone*, Cologne 1978.

Métraux, Alfred: "Le shamanisme araucan," *Revista del Instituto de Antropologia de la Universidad nacional de Tucamán*, 2, No. 10 (1942), pp. 309–362.

_____. "Le chamanisme chez les Indiens de L'Amérique du Sud tropicale," *Acta Americana*, No. 2 (1944), pp. 197–219, 320–341.

Michael, Henry N. (Ed.): *Studies in Siberian Shamanism*, Toronto 1963.

Mikhailowskii, V. M.: "Shamanism in Siberia and European Russia," *The Journal of the Anthropological Institute of Great Britain and Ireland*, No. 24 (1895), pp. 62–100, 126–158.

Miles, Douglas: "Shamanism and the Conversion of Ngadji Dayaks,"*Oceania*, No. 37 (1966/67), pp. 1–12.

Miyakawa, H. and Kollatz, A.: "Zur Ur- und Vorgeschichte des Schamanismus," *Zeitschrift für Ethnologie*, No. 91 (1966), pp. 161–193.

Mollenhauer, Gaby: "Schamanismus bei den Eskimos," *Saeculum*, No. 28 (1877), pp. 235–240.

Monmouth, Geoffrey von: *Das Leben des Zauberers Merlin*, Amsterdam.

Moody, Raymond A.: *Leben nach dem Tod*, Reinbek 1975.

_____. *Reflections on Life after Life*, London 1978.

BIBLIOGRAPHY

Moray, Ann: "The Celtic Heritage in Ireland," *Horizon*, 7, No 2 (1965), pp. 33–39.

Morrill, Sibley S.: *The Kahunas*, Boston, Mass. 1969.

Morris, H. S.: "Shamanism Among the Oya Melanau," in: Maurice Freedman (Ed.): *Social Organization. Essays Presented to Raymond Firth*, London 1967.

Motzki, Harald: *Schamanismus als Problem religionswissenschaftlicher Terminologie: Ein Untersuchung*, Cologne 1977.

Mühlmann, Wilhelm E.: *Rassen, Ethnien, Kulturen*, Neuwied and Berlin 1964.

Müller, Werner: *Weltbild und Kult der Kwakiutl-Indianer*, Wiesbaden 1955.

_____. *Glauben und Denken der Sioux*, Berlin 1970.

_____. *Indianische Welterfahrung*, Stuttgart 1976 (a).

_____. *Geliebte Erde. Naturfrömmigkeit und Naturhaß im indianischen und europäischen Nordamerika*, Bonn 1976 (b).

Münzel, Mark: *Medizinmannwesen und Geistervorstellungen bei den Kamayurá (Alto Xingú — Brasilien,)* Wiesbaden 1971.

Muldoon, Sylvan J.: *Die Aussendung des Astralkörpers*, Freiburg 1973.

Munn, Henry: "The Mushrooms of Language," in: Harner 1973.

Murdock, George Peter: "Tenino Shamanism," *Ethnology*, No. 4 (1965), pp. 165–171.

Murphy, Jane M.: "Psychotherapeutic Aspects of Shamanism on St. Lawrence Island, Alaska," in: Kiev 1964.

Musès, Charles, and Young, Arthur M. (Ed.): *Consciousness and Reality*, New York 1972.

Mutwa, Credo: *My People. Writings of a Zulu Witchdoctor*, New York 1971.

Myerhoff, Barbara G.: "The Doctor as Culture Hero: The Shaman of Rincon," *Anthropological Quarterly*, No. 39 (1966), pp. 60–72.

_____. *Peyote Hunt*, Ithaca, N.Y., 1974.

_____. "Balancing between Worlds: The Shaman's Calling," *Parabola*, 1, No. 2 (1976) (a), pp. 6–13.

_____. "Shamanic Equilibrium: Balance and Meditation in Known and Unknown Worlds," in: Wayland D. Hand (Ed.): *American Folk Medicine: A Symposium*, Berkeley 1976 (b).

_____. "Peyote and the Mystic Vision," in: Berrin 1978.

Nachtigall, Horst: "Die kulturhistorische Wurzel der Schamanenskelettierung," *Zeitschrift für Ethnologie*, No. 77 (1952), pp. 188–197.

_____. "Schamanismus bei den Paez-Indianern," *Zeitschrift für Ethnologie*, No. 78 (1953), pp. 210–223.

_____. "The Cultural-Historical Origin of Shamanism," in: Bharati 1976 (b).

Nadel, S. F.: "A Study of Shamanism in the Nuba Mountains," in: Lessa/ Vogt 1979.

Naranjo, Claudio: "The Healing Journey, New York 1973.

Naranjo, Plutarco: "Hallucinogenic Plant Use and Related Indigenous Belief Systems in the Ecuadorian Amazon," *Journal of Ethnopharmacology*, 1, No. 2 (1979), pp. 121–145.

Neal, James H.: *Ju-Ju in my Life*, London 1966.

Neihardt, John: *Black Elk Speaks*, London 1974, Abacus Paperback.

Neher, Andrew: "A Physiological Explanation of Unusual Behavior in Ceremonies Involving Drums," *Human Biology*, 34, No. 2 (1962), pp. 151–160.

Neumann, Wolfgang: *Der Mensch und sein Doppelgänger*, Wiesbaden 1981.

Neverman, Hans, Worms, Ernest A., and Petri, Helmut: *Die Religionen der Südsee und Australiens*, Vol. 5,2 Stuttgart 1968, in: *Die Religionen der Menschheit*, edited by C.. M. Schröder.

Newcomb, Franc Johnson: *Hosteen Klah. Navaho Medicine Man and Sand Painter*, Norman 1964.

Nioradze, G.: *Der Schamanismus bei den sibirischen Völkern*, Stuttgart 1925.

Nordenskiöld, Erland: A *Historical and Ethnological Survey of the Cuna Indians*, Comparative Ethnographical Studies, No. 10, Gothenburg 1938.

Nordland, Odd: "Shamanism as an Experiencing of 'the Unreal'," in: Edsman 1967.

Noyes, J. Russell: "Dying and Mystical Consciousness," *Journal of Thanatology*, No. 1 (1971), pp. 25–41.

———. "The Experience of Dying," *Psychiatry*, No. 35 (Mai 1972), pp. 174–184.

———. and Kletti, R.: "Depersonalization in the Face of Life-Threatening Danger: A Description," *Psychiatry*, No. 39 (1976), pp. 19–27.

———. and Kletti, R.: "Depersonalisation in Response to Life-Threatening Danger," *Comprehensive Psychiatry*, 18, No. 4 (1977), pp. 375–384.

Österreich, T. K.: *Possession, Demonical and Other, among Primitive Races in Antiquity, the Middle Ages, and Modern Times*, New York 1966.

Ohlmarks, Åke: *Studien zum Problem des Schamanismus*, Copenhagen 1939.

Ohnuki-Tierney, Emiko: "The Shamanism of the Ainu of the Northwest Coast of Southern Sakhalin," *Ethnology*, No. 12 (1973), pp. 15–29.

———. "Shamanism and World View: The Case of the Ainu of the Northwest Coast of Southern Sakhalin," in: Bharati 1976.

Olsen, Dale A.: "Music-Induced Altered States of Consciousness among Warac Shamans," *Journal of Latin American Lore*, 1, No. 1 (1975), pp. 19–33.

Oppitz, Michael: *Schamanen im blinden Land*, Frankfurt 1981.

Ornstein, Robert (Ed.): *The Nature of Human Consciousness*, San Francisco 1973.

———. *Die Psychologie des Bewußtseins*, Cologne 1974.

Osis, Karlis, and Haraldsson, Erlendur: *At the Hour of Death*, New York 1977.

Oswalt, R. L.: *Kashya Texts*, University of California Publications in Linguistics, No. 36, Los Angeles 1964.

Pahnke, Walter N., and Richards William A.: "Implications of LSD and Experimental Mysticism." *The Journal of Transpersonal Psychology*, 1, No. 2 (1969), pp. 69–102.

Paper, Jordan: "From Shaman to Mystic in Ojibwa Religion," *Studies in Religion*, 9, No. 2 (1980), pp. 185–199.

Park, Willard: *Shamanism in Western North America*, Evanston/Chicago 1938.

_____. "Paviotso Shamanism," *American Anthropologist*, No. 36 (1934), pp. 98–113.

Parker, Arthur C.: "Secret Medicine Societies of the Seneca," *American Anthropologist*, No. 11 (1909), pp. 161–185.

Partanen, Jorma: "A Description of Buriat Shamanism," *Journal de la Société Finno-Ougrienne*, No. 51 (1941/42), pp. 7–34.

Paulson, Ivar: "Zur Phänomenologie des Schamanismus," *Zeitschrift für Religions-und Geistesgeschichte*, 16, No. 2 (1964), pp. 121–141.

_____. "Der Schamanismus in Nordasien (Sibirien)," *Paideuma*, No. 11 (1965), pp. 91–104.

Pelletier, Kenneth R.: *Toward a Science of Consciousness*, New York 1978.

Pelletier, Kenneth, and Garfield Charles: *Consciousness East and West*, New York 1976.

Peters, Larry G.: "Psychotherapy in Tamang Shamanism," *Ethos*, No. 6 (1978), pp. 63–91.

_____. "An Experiential Study of Nepalese Shamanism," *The Journal of Transpersonal Psychology*, 13, No. 1 (1981) (a), pp. 1–26.

_____. *Ectasy and Healing in Nepal*, Los Angeles 1981 (b).

Petitt, George A.: "The Vision Quest and the Guardian Spirit," in: J. D. Jennings and E. A. Hoebel (Ed.): *Readings in Anthropology*, New York 1955.

Petri, Helmut: "Der Australische Medizinmann," *Annali Lateranensi*, No. 16 (1952), pp. 159–317, and No. 17 (1953), pp. 157–227.

_____. *Sterbende Welt in Nordwest-Australien*, Brunswick 1954.

_____. "Australische 'Medizinmänner' am Rande der technischen Zivilisation," *Die Umschau in Wissenschaft und Technik*, No. 62 (1962), pp. 171–174.

Pilsudski, Bronislav: "Der Schamanismus bei den Ainu-Stämmen von Sachalin," *Globus*, No. 95 (1909), pp. 72–78.

Popow, Andrei A.: "Wie Sereptie D'aruoskin zum Schamanen erwählt wurde," in: Diószegi 1963.

Potapow, L. P.: "Die Schamanentrommel bei den altaischen Völkerschaften," in: Diószegi 1963.

_____. "Certain Aspects of the Study of Siberian Shamanism," in: Bharati 1976 (b).

Powers, W. K.: *Yuwipi. Vision and Experience in Ogalala Ritual*, Lincoln 1982.

Prem Das: "Initiation by a Huichol Shaman," in: Berrin 1978.

Primbram, Karl H.: "What the Fuss Is All About," *Re-Vision*, 1, No. 3/4 (1978), pp. 14–18.

Prince, Raymond, (Ed.): *Trance and Possession States*, Montreal 1968.

_____. (Ed.): "Shamans and Endorphins," *Ethos*, 10, No. 4 (1982).

Pukui, Mary Kawena, Haertig, E. W., and Coe, C. A.: *Nānā I Ke Kumu*, Vol. II, Honolulu 1979.

Quasha, George: "Aufzeichnung einer Rede von Essie Parrish, gehalten am 14. März 1972," *Alcheringa*, No. 1 (1975), pp. 27–19.

Radin, Paul: *The Road of Life and Death*, New York 1945.

_____. *The Autobiography of a Winnebago Indian*, New York 1963.

_____. *The Winnebago Tribe*, Lincoln 1970 (1923).

Radloff, Wilhelm: *Aus Sibirien. Lose Blätter aus dem Tagebuch eines reisenden Linguisten*, Leipzig 1983, Vol. 1–2.

Rahmann, Rudolf: "Shamanistic and Related Phenomena in Northern and Middle India," *Anthropos*, No. 54 (1959), pp. 681–760.

Rasmussen, Knud: *Neue Menschen. Ein Jahr bei den Nachbarn des Nordpols*, Berne 1907.

_____. *The People of the Polar North. A Record*, edited by G. Herring, London 1908.

_____. *Across Arctic America. Narrative of the Fifth Thule Expedition*, New York 1927; in German as: *Die große Schlittenreise*, Essen 1946.

_____. *Rasmussens Thulefahrt: Zwei Jahre im Schlitten durch unerforschtes Eskimoland*, edited by F. Sieburg, Frankfurt 1926.

_____. *Intellectual Culture of the Hudson Bay Eskimos. Report of the Fifth Thule Expedition*, 1921–1924, Vol. VII, Copenhagen 1930.

_____. *Intellectual Culture of the Iglulik Eskimos. Report of the Fifth Thule Expedition*, 1921–1924, Vol. VII, 1, Copenhagen 1930.

_____. *Observations on the Intellectual Culture of the Caribou Eskimos. Report of the Fifth Thule Expedition*, 1921–1924, Vol. VII, 2, Copenhagen 1930.

_____. *The Netsilik Eskimos: Social Life and Spiritual Culture. Report of the Fifth Thule Expedition*, 1921–1924, Vol. VIII, Copenhagen 1931.

_____. *Intellectual Culture of the Copper Eskimos. Report of the Fifth Thule Expedition*, 1921–1924, Vol. IX, Copenhagen 1932.

_____. *The Alaskan Eskimos. As described in the posthumous Notes of Dr. Knud Rasmussen*, edited by H. Ostermann, *Report of the Fifth Thule Expedition*, 1921–1924, Vol. X, 3, Copenhagen 1952.

Ravizza, Kenneth: "Peak Experiences in Sport," *Journal of Humanistic Psychology*, 17, No. 4 (1977), pp. 35–40.

Reichard, Gladys A.: *Navajo Medicine Man. Sandpaintings*, New York 1977 (1939).

Reichel-Dolmatoff, Gerado: *Amazonian Cosmos. The Sexual and Religious Symbolism of the Tukano Indians*, Chicago 1971.

_____. "The Cultural Context of an Aboriginal Hallucinogen: Banisteriopsis Caapi," in: Furst 1972.

_____. *The Shaman and the Jaguar. A Study of Narcotic Drugs among the Indians of Colombia*, Philadelphia 1975.

_____. *Beyond the Milky Way. Hallucinatory Imagery of the Tukano Indians*, Los Angeles 1978.

Ridington, Robin: *Swan People: A Study of the Dunne-za Prophet Dance*, National Museum of Canada, Ottawa 1978.

Riester, J.: "Medizinmänner und Zauberer der Chiquitano-Indians," *Zeitschrift für Ethnologie*, 96, No. 2 (1971), pp. 250–265.

Ring, Kenneth: *Life at Death*, New York 1980.

_____. "Precognitive and Prophetic Visions in Near-Death Experiences," *Anabiosis: The Journal of Near-Death*, 2, No. 1 (1982), pp. 47–74.

_____ and Franklin, Stephen: "Do Suicide Survivors Report Near Death Experiences?," *Omega*, 12, No. 3 (1981), pp. 191–208.

Rodman, Julius S.: *The Kahuna Sorcerers of Hawaii, Past and Present*, Hicksville, N.Y., 1979.

Röder, J.: *Alahatala: Die Religionen der Inlandstämme Mittelcerams*, Bamberg 1948.

Rogers, S.: *The Shaman*, Springfield, Ill., 1982.

Rose, Ronald: *Living Magic*, London 1957.

Roux, Jean Paul: "Le chaman gengiskanide," *Anthropos*, No. 54 (1959), pp. 401–432.

Russell, Bertrand: *Religion and Science*, London 1935.

Russell, Frank: "The Pima Indians," *26th Annual Report of the Bureau of American Ethnology*, 1904–1905, Washington, D.C., 1908.

Sagant, Philippe: "Becoming a Limu Priest: Ethnographic Notes," in: Hitchcock/Jones 1976.

Sandner, Donald F.: "Navaho Indian Medicine and Medicine Men," in: David S. Sobel (Ed.): *Ways of Health*, New York and London 1979.

Sandschejew, Garma: "Weltranschauung und Schamanismus der Alaren-Burjäten:" *Anthropos*, No. 22 (1927), pp. 576–613, 933–955; No. 23 (1928), pp. 538–560, 967–986.

Sargant, William: *Battle for the Mind*, London 1957.

_____. *The Mind Possessed*, London 1973.

Schefold, Reimar: *Spielzeug für die Seelen. Kunst und Kultur der Mentawai-Inseln (Indonesia)*, Museum Rietberg, Zürich 1980.

Schenk, Amelie: "JuJu, tödlicher Zauber in Afrika," *Esotera* 31, No. 8 (1980), pp. 713–721.

Schlosser, Katesa: *Zauberei im Zululand. Manuskripte des Blitz-Zauberers Laduma Madela*, Kiel 1972.

Schrödinger, Erwin: *Geist und Materie*, Brunswick 1959.

_____. *Was ist Leben?*, Berne 1946.

Schultes, R. E. and Hofman, A.: *Pflanzen der Götter*, Berne 1980.

Schumacher, E. F., *Rat für die Ratlosen*, Hamburg 1979.

Schuster, Meinhard: "Die Schamanen und ihr Ritual," in: B. Freudenfeld (Ed.): *Völkerkunde*, Munich 1960.

Schwartz, Gary E. and Shapiro, David (Ed.): *Consciousness and Self-Regulation*, New York 1976.

Seaver, James E.: *Niederschrift der Lebensgeschichte der Mary Jemison, welche im Alter von knapp 15 Jahren 1758 von Indianern entführt wurde und fortan mit ihnen lebte bis zu ihrem Tod im Jahre 1833 im Seneca Reservat bei Buffalo*, New York 1979.

Secunda, Brant: "The Dance of the Deer," *The Laughing Man*, 2, No. 4 (1981), pp. 22–23.

Shah, Idries: *The Magic Monastary*, New York 1972.

Sharon, Douglas: "A Peruvian Curandero's Séance: Power and Balance," in: *Bharati* 1976 (b).

_____. *Wizards of the Four Winds*, New York 1978.

Sheils, Dean: "A Cross-Cultural Study of Beliefs in Out-of-the-Body Experiences, Waking and Sleeping," *Journal of the Society for Psychical Research*, No. 49 (1978), pp. 697–741.

Sheldrake, Rupert: "A New Science of Life," *New Scientist*, No. 90 (1981), pp. 766–768.

Shirokogoroff, S. M.: "General Theory of Shamanism among the Tungus," *Journal of the North-China Branch of the Royal Asiatic Society*, No. 54 (1923), pp. 246–249.

——. *Psychomental Complex of the Tungus*, London 1935 (a).

——. "Versuch einer Erforschung der Grundlagen des Schamanismus bei den Tungusen," *Baessler Archiv*, No. 18 (1935) (b), No. 41–96.

Shonle, Ruth: "Peyote, the Giver of Visions," *American Anthropologist*, No. 27 (1925), pp. 53–75.

Shternberg, L. J.: "Die Auserwählung im sibirischen Schamanismus," *Zeitschrift für Missionskunde und Religionswissenschaft*, No. 50 (1935), pp. 229–252, 261–274.

——. "Shamanism and Religious Election," in: Stephen P. Dunn and Ethel Dunn (Ed.): *Introduction to Soviet Ethnology*, Vol. 1, Berkeley 1974.

Sich, Dorothea: "Ein Beitrag zur Volksmedizin und zum Schamanismus in Korea," *Curare*, No. 4 (1980), pp. 209–216.

Siegel, Ronald: "Der Blick ins Jenseits," *Psychologie heute*, No. 4 (1981), pp. 23–33.

Sieroszewski, W.: "Du chamanisme d'après les croyances des Yakoutes," *Revue de L'Histoire des Religions*, No. 46 (1902), pp. 204–235, 299–338.

Siiger, Halfdan: "Shamanistic Ecstasy and Supernatural Beings. A Study Based on Field-Work among the Kalash Kafirs of Chitral," in Edsman 1967.

Siikala, Anna-Leena: *The Rite Technique of the Siberian Shaman*, FF Communications, No. 220, Helsinki 1978.

Silver, D. B.: *Zinacanteco Shamanism*, Dissertation, Cambridge, Mass., 1966.

Silvermann, Julian: "A Paradigm for the Study of Altered States of Consciousness," *The British Journal of Psychiatry*, 144, No. 512 (1968), pp. 1201–1218.

Simmons, Leo W.: *Sun Chief, The Autobiography of a Hopi Indian*, New Haven and London 1976.

Sinha, Surajit: "Training of a Bhumij Medicine-Man," *Man in India*, No. 38 (1958), pp. 111–128.

Siskin, E.: *The Impact of the Peyote Cult upon Shamanism among the Washo Indians*, Dissertation, Yale University 1941.

Skeat, Walter William: *Malay Magic*, London 1900.

Slocum, Joshua: *Sailing Alone Around the World*, New York 1900.

Slotkin, J. S.: *The Peyote Religion*, Glencoe, Ill. 1956.

——. "The Peyote Way" in: Lessa/Vogt 1979.

Speck, Frank G.: "Penobscot Shamanism," *Memoirs of the American Anthropological Association*, 6, No. 4. Menasha, Wisc., 1919.

Spencer, Baldwin, and Gillen, F. J.: *The Native Tribes of Central Australia*, London 1899 (1969).

——. *The Northern Tribes of Central Australia*, London 1904 (1969).

Spencer, Dorothy M.: "The Recruitment of Shamans among the Mundas," *History of Religions*, 10, No. 1 (1970), pp. 1–31.

Spencer, Robert F.: *The North Alaskan Eskimo. A Study in Ecology and Society*, New York 1976.

Spier, Leslie: *Yuman Tribes of the Gila River*, New York 1978 (1933).

Spindler, George and Louise: *Dreamers without Power. The Menomini Indians*, New York 1971.

Spiro, Melford E.: *Burmese Supernaturalism*, Englewood Cliffs, N.J., 1967.

Spott, Robert and Kroeber, A. L.: "Yurok Shamanism," in: R. F. Heizer and M. A. Whipple (Ed.): *The California Indians*, Berkeley 1971.

Standing Bear, Luther: *Land of the Spotted Eagle*, Lincoln 1978 (1933).

Stabelein, William: "Mahākāla the Neo-Shaman: Master of the Ritual," in: Hitchcock/Jones 1976.

St. Clair, David: *Pagans, Priests, and Prophets*, Englewood Cliffs, N.J., 1976.

Steiger, Brad: *Medicine Power*, New York 1974.

———. *Medicine Talk*, New York 1975.

Sterly, Joachim: "*Heilige Männer*" *und Medzinmänner in Melanesien*, Dissertation, Cologne 1965.

Stiglmayr, Engelbert: "Schamanismus der Negritos Südostasiens," *Wiener Völkerkundliche Mitteilungen*, 2 No. 2 (1954), pp. 156–164; 3, No. 1 (1955), pp. 14–20; 4, No. 2 (1956), pp. 135–147.

———. "Schamanismus in Australien," *Wiener Völkerkundliche Mitteilungen*, 5, No. 2 (1957), pp. 161–190.

———. "Schamanismus, eine spiritistische Religion," *Ethnos*, 27, No. 1–4 (1962), pp. 40–48.

Stimson, J. Frank: "Tuamotuan Religion," *Bernice P. Bishop Museum, Bulletin*, No. 103. Honolulu 1933.

Steward, Kilton: *Pygmies and Dream Giants*, New York 1954.

Stokes, Doris, and Dearsley, Linda: *Voices in my Ear — The Autobiography of a Medium*, London 1980.

Sturtevant, William C.: "A Seminole Medicine Maker," in: J. B. Casagrande (Ed.): *In the Company of Man*, New York 1960.

Sugerman, A. Arthur, and Tarter, R.E., (Ed.): *Expanding Dimensions of Consciousness*, New York 1978.

Swanton, John R.: "Contribution to the Ethnology of the Haida. The Jesup North Pacific Expedition, 1905–1909," Vol. 5, No. 1, *Memoir of the American Museum of Natural History*, Leiden.

———. "Social Condition, Beliefs, and Linguistic Relationship of the Tlingit Indians," *26th Annual Report of the Bureau of American Ethnology, 1904–1905*, Washington, D.C., 1908.

Swedenborg, Emanuel: *Arcana Coelestia*, 1837–1870.

Tart, Charles T.: "A Second Psychophysiological Study of Out-of-the-Body Experience in a Gifted Subject," *International Journal of Parapsychology*, No. 9 (1967), pp. 251–258.

———. "A Psychophysiological Study of Out-of-the Body Experiences in a Selected Subject," *Journal of the American Society for Psychical Research*, No. 62 (1968), pp. 3–27.

———. (Ed.): *Altered States of Consciousness*, New York 1969.: "States of Consciousness and State-Specific Sciences," in: R. Ornstein (Ed.): *The Nature of Human Consciousness*, San Francisco 1973.

———. "Out-of-the-Body Experiences," in: E. D. Mitchell: *Psychic Exploration*, edited by John White, New York 1974.

———. *States of Consciousness*, New York 1975 (a).

———. "Some Assumptions of Orthodox, Western Psychology," in: C. T. Tart (Ed.): *Transpersonal Psychologies*, London 1975 (b).

———. "Putting the Pieces Together: A Conceptual Framework for Understanding Discrete States of Consciousness," in: N. E. Zinberg (Ed.): *Alternate States of Consciousness*, New York 1977.

Taube, Erika and Manfred: *Schamanen und Rhapsoden. Die geistige Kultur der alten Mongolei*, Leipzig 1983.

Tedlock, Dennis and Barbara: *Über den Rand des tiefen Canyons. Lehren indianischer Schamanen*, Cologne 1975.

Teit, James: "The Shuswap. The Jesup North Pacific Expedition, 1900–1908" Vol. 2, No. 7, *Memoir of the American Museum of Natural History*, Leiden.

Thalbitzer, William: "The Heathen Priests of East Greenland (Angakut)," *Proceedings of the 16th International Congress of Americanists*, Vienna 1908.

———. "Les Magiciens esquimaux, leurs conceptions du monde, de l'âme et de la vie," *Journal de la Société des Américanists*, Paris, No. 22 (1930).

———. "Shamans of the East Greenland Eskimo," in: A. L. Kroeber and T. T. Watermann (Ed.): *Source Book of Anthropology*, New York 1965.

Thiel, P. Jos: "Schamanismus im alten China," *Sinologica*, 10, No. 2/3 (1968), pp. 149–204.

Thomas, William I., (Ed.): *Source Book of Social Origins*, Chicago 1909.

———. "The Relation of the Medicine Man to the Professional Occupations," in: Thomas 1909.

Toben, Bob: *Space-Time and Beyond*, New York 1975.

Todd, D. M.: "Herbalists, Diviners and Shamans in Dimam," *Paideuma*, No. 23 (1977), pp. 189–204.

Tocker, Elisabeth: "An Ethnography of the Huron Indians, 1615–1649," *Bureau of American Ethnology, Bulletin*, No. 190. Washington, D.C., 1964.

Torrey, E. Fuller: *The Mind Game. Witchdoctors and Psychiatrists*, New York 1972.

Trigger, Bruce G., (Ed.): *Handbook of North American Indians, Northeast*, 15. General Editor W. C. Sturtevant, Smithsonian Institution, Washington, D.C., 1978.

Trueblood Brotzky, Anne, Daneswich, R., and Johnson, N. (Ed.): *Stones, Bones and Skin: Ritual and Shamanic Art*, Artscanada, The Society of Art Publications, Toronto 1977.

Turney-High, H. H.: "The Flathead Indians of Montana," *Memoirs of the American Anthropological Association*, No. 48. (1937).

BIBLIOGRAPHY

Twigg, Ena, and Brod R. H.: *Ena Twigg: Medium*, New York 1972.
Tyler, Edward: *Primitive Culture*, London 1958 (1871).
Underhill, Evelyn: *Mystik*, Munich 1928.
Underhill, Ruth M.: *Red Man's Religion*, Chicago and London 1965.
———. *Papago Indian Religion*, New York 1969.
———. *Singing for Power*, Berkeley and Los Angeles 1976 (1938).
Unzeitig, Detlef: "Sibirischer Schamanismus," *Saeculum*, No. 28 (1977), pp. 226–234.
Van de Castle, Robert L.: "Anthropology and Psychic Research," in: E. D. Mitchell: *Psychic Exploration*, edited by John White, New York 1974.
Wagner-Robertz, Dagmar: "Schamanismus bei den Hain//om in Südwestafrika," *Anthropos*, No. 71 (1976), pp. 533–554.
Walker, Evan Harries: "The Nature of Consciousness," *Mathematical Biosciences*, No. 7 (1970), pp. 138–178.
Walker, James R.: *Lakota Belief and Ritual*, edited by R. J. DeMallie and E. A. Jahner, Lincoln and London 1980.
Walker, Sheila S.: *Ceremonial Spirit Possession in Africa and Afro-America*, Leiden 1972.
Wallace, Anthony F. C.: *The Death and Rebirth of the Seneca*, New York 1970.
Walsh, Roger N., and Vaughan, Francis, (Ed.): *Beyond Ego. Transpersonal Dimensions in Psychology*, Los Angeles 1980.
Warneck, J.: *Die Religion der Batak*, Göttingen 1909.
Warner, W. Lloyd: *A Black Civilization*, New York 1958 (1937).
Wassén, S. Henry: "Was Espingo (Ispincu) of Psychotropic and Intoxicating Importance for the Shamans in Peru?," in: Bharati 1976 (b).
Wassiljewitsch, G. M.: "Erwerbung der Schamanenfähigkeiten bei den Evenken (Tungusen)," in: Diószegi 1963 (a).
Wasson, R. Gordon: *The Wondrous Mushroom. Mycolatry in Mesoamerica*, New York 1980.
Waters, Frank: *Book of the Hopi*, New York 1963.
———. *Pumpkin Seed Point. Being within the Hopi*, Chicago 1969.
Watson, Lyall: *Die Grenzbereiche des Lebens*, Frankfurt 1974.
———. *Gifts of Unknown Things*, Seven Oaks 1976.
———. *Lightning Bird. The Story of One Man's Journey into Africa's Unknown Past*, London 1982.
Watson-Franke, Maria-Barbara: "Guajiro-Schamanen (Kolumbien und Venezuela)," *Anthropos*, No. 70 (1975), pp. 194–207.
Wavell, Stewart, Butt, Audrey, and Epton, Nina: *Trances*, New York 1967.
Webb, Theodor T.: "The Making of Marrngit," *Oceania*, No. 6 (1936), pp. 336–341.
Weber, Renée: "The Enfolding-Unfolding Universe: A Conversation with David Bohm," *Re-Vision*, 1, No. 3/4 (1978), pp. 24–51.
Weinstein, S. I.: "Die Schamanentrommel der Tuwa und die Zeremonie ihrer 'Belebung'," in: Diószegi 1963.
Weizsäcker, Carl Friedrich von: *Die Einheit der Natur*, Munich 1971.

Welwood, J.: "Meditation and the Unconscious: A New Perspective," *The Journal of Transpersonal Psychology*, 9, No. 1 (1977), pp. 1–26.

White, Leslie A.: "A Comparative Study of Keresan Medicine Societies," *Proceedings of the 23rd International Congress of Americanists*, New York 1930.

White, John (Ed.): *The Highest State of Consciousness*, New York 1972.

——. and Krippner, Stanley, (Ed.): *Future Science*, New York 1977.

Wilbert, Johannes "Gaukler-Schamanen der Warao," in: R. Hartmann and Udo Oberem (Ed.): *Amerikanistische Studien. Festschrift für Hermann Trimborn*, (a), St. Augustin 1979, Vol. II.

——. "Magico-Religious Use of Tobacco among South American Indians," (b), in: Browman/Schwarz 1979.

Winkelman, Michael: "Magic and Parapsychology," *Phoenix Journal of Transpersonal Anthropology*, 4, No. 1–2 (1980), pp. 7–15.

Winkler, Walter F.: "Spirit Possession in Far Western Nepal," in: Hitchcock/Jones 1976.

The Winnipeg Art Gallery: *The Coming and Going of the Shaman. Eskimo Shamanism and Art*, edited by Jean Blodgett, Curator of Eskimo Art, 1978.

Winstedt, R. O.: *The Malay Magician Being Shaman, Saiva and Sufi*, London 1961.

Wolf, F. A.: *Taking the Quantum Leap*, New York 1981.

Woods, Richard (Ed.): *Understanding Mysticism*, New York 1980.

Wuthnow, Robert: "Peak Experiences. Some Empirical Tests," *Journal of Humanistic Psychology*, 18, No. 3 (1978), pp. 59–75.

Zerries, Otto: *Medizinmannwesen und Geisterglaube der Waika-Indianer des oberen Orinoco*, (Ethnologica N.F. 2), Cologne 1960.

——. "Die Vorstellung vom Zweiten Ich und die Rolle der Harpye in der Kultur der Naturvölker Südamerikas," *Anthropos*, No. 57 (1962), pp. 889–914.

——. *Waika*, Munich 1964.

——. "Die Bedeutung des Federschmuckes des südamerikanischen Schamanen und dessen Beziehung zur Vogelwelt," *Paideuma*, No. 23 (1977), pp. 277–324.

Zimmerly, David: "On Being an Ascetic: Personal Document of a Sioux Medicine Man," *Pine Ridge Research Bulletin*, No. 10 (1969), pp. 46–71.

Zinberg, Norman E. (Ed.): *Alternate States of Consciousness*, New York 1977.

Zutt, Jürg: *Ergriffenheit und Besessenheit*, Berne 1972.

INDEX